Modern Graphic Design with AI

By d. Neal Hettinger

Foreword to **Modern Graphic Design with AI**

I should begin by stating that I always felt writing this type of foreword was in my future. All universes would intersect somewhere in the multiverse of possibilities, with AI inevitably overlapping the artist's workspace. The second the first consumer-level computer hit the market, AI became inevitable. And here we are, in the third act of the first movie in what's sure to be a very long series. Welcome to Modern Graphic Design with AI, where our old friend, artificial intelligence, is no longer the new kid on the block. It's done hiding behind generative fills and digital healing brushes. In this act, AI takes center stage—whether as villain, hero, or antihero, that has yet to be determined, but it's undeniably here.

Reviewing the script shows that AI has subtly shaped our world, disguising itself as many of the "magical" tools we now take for granted, from Photoshop's trusty generative fills to the digital healing brush introduced a decade ago. These early tools—members of AI's extended family tree—gave artists superpowers never granted. Sure, AI might seem like it appeared out of nowhere. Still, the reality is that it's been quietly tweaking, adjusting, and accelerating our artistic workflows since we first cleaned up old family photos in digital software decades ago.

Now, let's talk about one of the most thrilling aspects of AI in design: its ability to take a single piece of original artwork and transform it into an endless array of unique styles and designs. Imagine creating one drawing and having AI help you explore dozens of new versions, from grungy to glamorous, without lifting a pen. It's like you're on an episode of Pimp My Art, and AI is the capable host, transforming your art. Suddenly, that single sketch isn't just one idea—a series, a whole collection of variations that open doors to concepts you hadn't even considered. I've taken paintings I completed in college and generated endless variations, adjusting colors, emphasizing specific themes, and developing countless design ideas.

Not everyone, of course, is sold on AI. Technological upgrades have always stirred a mix of excitement and panic. Many of us remember when computers first entered kindergarten classrooms—some feared computers would replace instructors (they haven't, even now). Word processors, too, sparked anxiety that we'd lose the ability to write altogether. Then came online learning, initially thought to be a short-lived experiment but now a staple of higher learning. And who could forget the controversies surrounding self-driving cars and the ubiquitous smartphone? Every time, there were concerns that these innovations could end the human story as we knew it. Yet here we are, coexisting just fine (mostly), and you'd be hard-pressed to pry these technologies from our hands today. I dare you to try taking Adobe Illustrator from any working graphic designer. We've forgotten its antihero backstory. AI's story in design is similar; it's just another chapter in our long saga of cautiously embracing or adapting to progress.

If you're worried that AI will replace the artist, remember it's just another tool, albeit a flashy one. The genie's out of the bottle, and frankly, it's not turning around. AI is here to stay, not to replace the brush but to give us new shades and colors we didn't know existed. This isn't about trading creativity for shortcuts; it's about finding fresh ways to partner with tech to accelerate our ideas and artistry even further.

This book is about that third act I mentioned. It introduces the processes and opportunities, showing you how AI can enhance, not hinder, the artistic process. It's likely just the first of many books on this evolving topic. So, dive in, and let's see where this adventure with AI takes us— because one thing's for sure: the design world will never be quite the same. But we're all used to change, and like every other industry shift, we'll adapt and, most likely, adopt AI-generated design.

Christian Bradley has been an administrator of digital art-based degree programs for over twenty years, serving as a Chair, Director, Dean, Institutional Director, and Instructor. He is currently the Director of Academic and Instructional Development, helping instructors craft better class materials and improve online curricula. Most importantly to this book, he has over 45 years of experience creating video game art, textures for virtual environments, paintings, concept sketches, and artwork for collectible toys.

Foreword to **Modern Graphic Design with AI**

"Creativity is seen as one of the final bastions of the human mind" (Lee & Cho, 2020). The intersection of creativity and technology has long been a driving force in the arts, and nowhere is this more evident than in the world of graphic design. As a new era of possibilities unfolds, the integration of Artificial Intelligence (AI) into the design process presents an exciting opportunity to redefine how visual communication is approached.

In some spaces, discussing ways in which AI can be used as a resource to enhance both productivity as well as output can be fraught. It is certainly sparking conversations about appropriateness, applicability, and ethics in myriad classrooms and workspaces. At times, the viewpoints held can be tinged with media-fueled escapist fear. George points out, "Critics (and fantasists) love to conjure a sci-fi future where machine overlords and sentient software threaten the existence of humankind. But it's important to remember the good that breakthrough tools such as AI can bring" (2024).

Far from diminishing creativity, AI can be a powerful tool that enhances it, helping designers—from novices to seasoned professionals—uncover fresh ideas and streamline their workflows without sacrificing artistic expression. As the Dean of Arts, English, and Humanities, at Oklahoma City Community College, I have seen how technology can enrich the creative process in many areas. As Clarke posits, "Emerging applications right now are more prosaic including moodboards for design consulting, storyboards for films, and mock-ups for interior design. . ." (2022). Here, the framework of utilizing AI to assist in the process of creation becomes a new fusion of mind and machine.

In the context of graphic design, AI offers a unique opportunity to break down barriers, allowing designers to focus on what truly matters: their vision. For beginners, AI tools provide an accessible entry point, making the complexities of design more approachable while still fostering originality. For more experienced designers, AI can serve as a partner, offering new ways to explore, experiment, and innovate in ways that were once unimaginable.

This book serves as a guide and an invitation to embrace the potential of AI as a collaborative asset—one that not only supports but amplifies the design process. Whether you're just beginning to experiment with design or have years of experience, I believe you will find both practical strategies and a sense of possibility for how AI can unlock new dimensions in your creative practice.

Dr. Jennifer Woolston, Dean of Arts, English, and Humanities at Oklahoma City Community College.

References

Clarke, L. (2022). When AI can make art—what does it mean for creativity? The Observer, https://www.theguardian.com/technology/2022/nov/12/when-ai-can-make-art-what-does-it-mean-for-creativity-dall-e-midjourney

George, S. C. (2024). The Good, the Bad, and the AI. Discover, 45(6), 12.

Lee, Y., & Cho, S. (2020). Design of Semantic-Based Colorization of Graphical User Interface Through Conditional Generative Adversarial Nets. International Journal of Human-Computer Interaction, 36(8), 699–708. https://doi.org/10.1080/10447318.2019.1680921

 About the Author

Neal Hettinger's academic background includes a Master of Arts degree in Mass Communications and a Bachelor of Arts degree in Graphic Arts, with a minor in English. His intention was to teach after graduation, but a professor gave some insightful advice: "Acquire experience—then teach."

His expertise grew by working at design firms and advertising agencies in Los Angeles, Nashville, Oklahoma City, and Birmingham. Neal's client list has included Nissan Motors, Universal Studios, Paramount Pictures, and Pioneer Electronics. With a background in martial arts, Neal has also designed for the UFC, Adidas, and Century Martial Arts. Publications such as The New York Times have quoted him, and he has written articles for various print magazines including Layers, as well as numerous online journals and websites. His own firm specializes in graphic design marketing, visual websites, UX software, and UI workflow platforms.

Professor Hettinger began his teaching career as an adjunct at Oklahoma City's Community College, where he received the Outstanding Adjunct Professor award. He has also been a professor at the Oklahoma State University Institute of Technology.

Neal found it a challenge to find a graphic design book that was beneficial to students, professionals, and marketers in a way that would be understandable and remembered. Based on his experience and knowledge, Neal has written Modern Graphic Design with AI to explain the creative process of visual design. It connects the software, including artificial intelligence generators, to design solutions.

 Acknowledgments

In my fun career, numerous individuals have played a crucial role in my creative development. I would like to express my gratitude to Paul Hebron for his insightful advice, Mark Witten, who pushed me to appreciate the art in graphic design, Nigel Sherry, the creative mastermind behind Lead Pencil, and Todd Bane, an art director who was not afraid to point out errors in his boss's designs. Jack Werner taught me to look at humor in life and said, "Life may be bleak now, but remember, it is always darkest before the storm." By seeing the art in graphic design, too many students to name have made teaching rewarding. Thank you to Christian Bradley and Jennifer Woolston who took the time to give me ideas for this book and write the Forewards on the potential they see in AI. This book would not have been possible without the involvement and support of my wife, Sheryl, the love of my life.

Contents

The study of graphic design

Learning Objectives

The reader will be able to draw thumbnails by the end of this chapter. They will be able to describe the design's objective. The student will be able to express the terms used in graphic design publishing.

Professional terminology

File: The digital collection of data stored by name and extension.

Font: A collection of characters with a specific face and size.

Freelancer: A self-employed graphic designer who works for several clients.

Greeking: Placeholder text.

Leading: Visual space from the bottom of a line of type to the top of another line but it is measured from baseline to baseline.

Sales: Presenting a service or product for purchase to a potential customer.

Symbol: A non-alphabetic mark that represents an object, words, or idea.

Symmetrical: The traditional layout approach centering and balancing all elements with space.

Template Print: A vector file showing paper or card stock trim, fold, and cutouts.

Verbiage: Encompasses all content, ranging from 'headlines' to 'call to action'.

Voice: How the communication is expressed through point of view or tone.

IMAGE 1-1
Graphic Designer at keyboards
AI Practicum} One image was generated with the online artificial intelligence software Adobe Firefly. Verbiage for the prompt: cartoon of crazy artists at computer keyboards in a store, an abstract edit; light painting.

Not long ago, one might visit a mall and access a music store that offered instruments for sale. They instruments are devised to engage with a technologically advanced electric keyboard and uncover far more than mere piano sounds. This device included controls that could activate and commence a drum solo. A trumpet would belt out high brassy notes by activating an auxiliary button, while a guitar would strum via an additional switch. This individual has the capability to execute their own keyboard compositions alongside these pieces. This individual was a musician!

Personal computers transformed the previously obscure processes of graphical layout production. This technique enabled anyone capable of typing to access a page template and modify certain content. They were visual designers.

Today, every technology is being affected by artificial intelligence. In the visual messaging arena, people can create graphic designs by prompting artificial generation of layouts. Anyone can be a graphic artist!

As silly as the second and third conclusions may seem, many people believe that is all that is needed to create a visually attractive design that successfully communicates a message. Just as a musician must understand timing, emphasis, contrast, rhythm, and how people listen, a graphic designer must understand those components and how and why people look at a layout.

The problem with the new technology is that it is good enough to look professional to an uneducated eye or ear. Technology is a tool and a means to a final design but just because someone can push a button, it does not mean they are musicians or commercial artists. Composing effective and successful music and graphic designs is a complicated process. Once a person finds out what is involved with laying out elements to attract an audience, the enormous undertaking may be frightening.

This book aims to simplify graphic design, but like any profession, it's not as simple as pressing a button. It will instruct the novice graphic designer or marketer in the many avenues for creating excellent solutions. Artificial intelligence generators will be show how to use prompts and which AI tools to use for different solutions. This book is not an AI software classroom learning step by step manual. When utilizing AI tools such as Adobe Firefly, there are numerous attempts to arrive at a solution that are not shown as well as using previous prompts that build upon ideas. For instance, Image 3-6 had prompts to build a fairy like file storage with eerie lighting. The prompt experiments for these attempts would fill a page. They were left out to keep the focus on the fundamentals of AI tool usage that the reader could quickly plug in and get results.

Professional graphic designers may possess the skills to design, although they could lack an understanding of the efficacy of the techniques, styles, or color palettes they employ. This book provides answers regarding the elements that constitute eye-catching design.

The professional designer-artist

IMAGE 1-2
Everyone has ideas, some are better ideas than others.
AI Practicum} Artificial intelligence images created with Adobe Firefly using the prompt: complicated mind thinking about many design ideas concept; creative and inspiration concepts.

In the beginning of graphic design, the talented people who figured out where and why to place elements in a layout were known as commercial artists. They were usually people who had been trained as fine artists and had the ability to draw or create lithographs for newspapers and magazine advertisements. Since commercial artists were creating designs for payment, they were looked down on by pure artists. The visual aspects of graphic design did not relate to fine art as far as true artists were concerned. When someone looks at these old designs, they can see why fine artists drew this conclusion since the ads and newspaper layouts were composed mostly of text and an illustration of the product, packaging, or a person.

The details of typography include structure, weight, proportions, and form but did not include color since the paper was printed with black ink. Grey tones were indicated with lines and later dots interspersed with space. The beauty of the hand drawn typefaces and customization for product labels and packaging was lost on the general public — but they did respond to the messages.

3

Technology developed a system that printed photography in publications. This advancement opened up the field of commercial art to people who were not talented artists. When technology continued on to printing color, it allowed marketing to grab the shoppers' attention and opened up the commercial artist profession to starving fine artists who would draw and paint their images and form content with inventive typefaces. Fine artists recognized and appreciated that these designs had the same elements and characteristics as art and soon referred to the creators as graphic artists.

Everything from image to type that appeared on magazine covers or advertisements could be created by graphic artists. They were artistically talented and visually oriented. Typefaces had forms as if they were images.

IMAGE 1-3

Adobe stock image of a Norman Rockwell dedication stamp. The oil painting first appeared on the cover of The Saturday Evening Post magazine.

Graphic artists understood the elements of fine art, the methods of printing, and how people see and read designs. They could draw, paint, sculpture, photograph, and compose this art to be printed. They were thought of as a graphic designers who could create those images with type on any medium.

A graphic designer would also be a student of creative methods who placed images, type, and color, in a coherent and visually attractive fashion on a wide variety of mediums. They managed the provided elements of a layout since they did not have the dexterity to create freehand images. There were graphic designers who were categorized as production artists and focused on taking the approved concept and setting it up as a mechanical for the printer.

The hierarchy of communication design changed with the introduction of computers. The software allowed creative talents to pursue a graphic design career even if they could not manually create an image. The opportunities seemed endless.

In the past, the terms commercial artist, graphic artist, and graphic designer were defined based on different abilities but today the terms are used interchangeably. In this textbook, these terms are used as one who is trained and educated with the knowledge of how to create successful visual messages.

IMAGE 1-4
The first concept of learning.
AI Practicum} Artificial intelligence images created with Adobe Firefly using the prompt: smiling child artist with paint on face and hands facing a wall in an old schoolhouse; view is from across the room. Settings: widescreen; art; dramatic reference; painting effect; warm tone with dramatic light.

The journey begins

The first concept in learning graphic design is to focus on the goal of the design. It is telling a story graphically — the design is a narrative about a product, service, or event. The key questions a story answers are known as the six W's which are Who, What, Why, When, Where and How.

A graphic artist's approach to every project is how to relate the design to the target market. The goal is to use all the graphic designer's available tools and elements to attract and convey the message to the reader. In many of the digital solutions today, the goal appears to have been lost or was not known by the graphic designer.

The second concept of learning is how to get to the solution in steps, not leaps. Students of design that go too far will get lost. The gap in design education is relying on the technological advances that have improved graphic design while not allowing the right side the brain to be creative and allow for happy accidents. An explanation of the fundamental processes of effective graphic design will provide any would be graphic artist the basics for using their creativity to solve the design problem.

Graphic design has evolved with technology. Quill pens replaced sharpened reeds in the Middle Ages, allowing calligraphy and drawing control. The printing press which allowed for mass communication instead of spreading information via depictions or word of mouth, created a need for professional graphic artists. Computers made design production less stressful for graphic designers and now artificial intelligence is simplifying creating images and content. There are many more technological inventions but the reason for these innovations was communication. Graphic design is also meant to accomplish communication. Visually, layouts should connect the message to the audience.

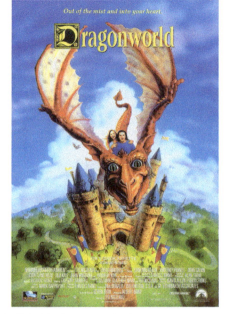

IMAGE 1-5

Graphic Designer: Neal Hettinger

Art Director: Nigel Sherry

This movie poster's narrative is aimed at a specific audience.

About this book

Before graphic designers learn how NOT to create bad designs, they must first acquire the skills to generate effective visual solutions. This information in this book provides a concise and easy-to-follow explanation of the rules, guidelines, methods, and history of design. The goal is to build valuable graphic designers.

The content of this book includes solutions that demonstrate a comprehension of how the viewer perceives the design. It starts at the beginning of graphic design, but it does not teach the software. There are plenty of books on how to operate software design programs. Students learn the software; they learn the guidelines but are not really taught or shown how to apply the knowledge to a project. This book does explain which software would deliver the most favorable result.

Each chapter covers critical concepts in graphic design today. Professional graphic designers have their own language. It is English but the terms are design oriented. As an example, space is a vast expanse in normal conversations but to the graphic artist, space is limited, and its use is the secret to professional design. There is a vocabulary segment in each chapter that all. A total of 200 design terms will be covered with short definitions. In an interview, the use of professional jargon shows the education and understanding of an applicant to the interviewer.

Communication for job interviews

One weakness in graphic design is the lack of writing skills. Professionals communicate with clients by more than texting. Some chapters will present the opportunity to write essays which improve an artist's communication abilities by getting experience in forming sentences with the correct terminology. Many of these essays are questions the applicant will be asked by interviewers. An example would be which AI generative program do they use for customization of type for a headline. Another question is which typographers do they follow and why. The applicant will be asked how they follow color trends, or which past design style do they think is coming back into vogue. If the interviewers do not ask these questions, the applicant can volunteer the information in the conversation to impress the interviewer.

IMAGE 1-6

The first concept of learning.

AI Practicum} Firefly prompt: old schoolhouse setting happy kid being painting by numbers with watercolor on textured paper. Photoshop created outlines of student and added numbers.

Design terminology

Working with clients to explain a graphic solution, designers will need to express an understanding of the client's goals and how the solution is based on achieving those goals. Their ability to use professional graphic design terms to a layman can be the difference between approval or starting the process over.

Portfolio samples

The graphic designer's portfolio is probably the most judged component of a job application. Usually, it is on a website, and it has to speak for itself. This textbook includes practical design assignments in order to build the user's portfolio.

Each chapter contains practicums that describe the process of creating images utilizing specialized tools and generative artificial intelligence. This approach enables design students to see the process, so minimizing the futility of attempting to determine the appropriate method for producing a visual solution.

Self quizzes

If a learner merely skims the book, they will not retain a substantial amount of the knowledge required for the graphic design industry. Progress quizzes are provided midway through the book and at its conclusion.

IMAGE 1-7
There are many doors to learning.

During the industrial revolution in 1800s, products were produced in mass quantities and the manufacturers needed to sell them. Hence, graphic artists evolved. One example was ivory soap which focused on the package design and advertising concepts to be memorable. It took over the marketplace. Later that century, the Art Nouveau style developed by artists such as Toulouse Lautrec and Aubrey Beardsley became the first major style in graphic design. It lifted the perception of the profession from an arts and crafts trade to a legitimate art. Classically trained artists soon studied commercial art in schools to became graphic artists.

Due to technology, graphic design has moved from a learned trade to an education-based profession. However, the requirements to creating a successful design have not changed — only the tools have changed.

The inquiries enable the evaluation of a learner's capabilities. Professionals possess the ability to assess their competency level.

IMAGE 1-8
AI Practicum} The online artificial intelligence program Adobe Express settings: Text, Font Bebas Regular, 230; Outline #3C8FF0 with 16 Thickness. Effects: Wood; Shape 18 with #FFE184; Photoshop Divide blending mode, saturation +40, High Pass 100, Unsharp 40.

The eight steps of the design process

The design process consists of a specific course of action: The process involves reviewing the project brief, researching the competition, strategize the approaches, creating thumbnails and layout options, thoroughly examining potential solutions, presenting the results, making revisions, and finally creating the mechanical design. While these steps are not infallible, skipping or rearranging the sequence would not effectively foster creativity. Many times, the graphic designer will have to repeat stages and understand how the eight turned sideways is the infinity sign. Sometimes the revisions will seem to go on forever.

The conceptualization process begins with the initial discussion of a project with a prospective client. The graphic designer must be prepared to seek out and constantly record information. They must receive a written brief that includes the company's contact details, deliverable timelines, and a budget. It is wise to annotate in the margins any questions regarding the project. Consider the following inquiries for the creative meeting:

A. Who constitutes the target audience?

B. What is the project's scope, including its objectives?

C. When are the anticipated payments for the project?

D. How will the project's success be evaluated?

E. Where will the solutions be executed and published?

F. Why did they decide to go with this medium for the design?

Although it might be challenging, once the project begins, understanding these answers will make the design approach easier.

The term "job creep" refers to a project's modifications and revisions by the client. This is a common issue that impacts the budget and timeline. The mutually established specifics of the project will maintain the client's focus on the end goal.

Beginner designers will sometimes start with thumbnails to sketch out ideas but usually start on the computer with ideas that have popped into their heads that visually do not solve the problem. This is not a very good process for creating compelling design solutions.

Professional graphic designers use a method that includes defining the problem, research strategy, thumbnails, comprehensives, and presentation. Establishing a routine approach will benefit the graphic artist by saving time, developing ideas, and creating a comprehensive solution. The process begins with defining the design objective by using phrases and descriptions. This step will guide the exploration, provide focus, and be beneficial when evaluating the solutions. If a designer is concerned, they will forget a brilliant idea, they should take a moment to jot down thoughts or sketch the concepts without building computer files.

The second step is to conduct research of the product, competition, and similar design situations. While this can help a designer formulate ideas, it usually exposes the designer to the latest styles and techniques that they probably would not think about. Research has two levels. Primary Research is the collecting of information by the designer that does not already exist such as sketching or photographing good design ideas. Secondary Research is when the graphic artist creates their own library of design references such as ads, magazine covers, color samples, dramatic images, and retouching techniques.

IMAGE 1-9

#3 in styles with illustrator

AI Practicum} Artificial intelligence contextual task bar prompts: #3 in a pop art style; #3 in a cartoon style; #3 in an art deco style.

The third step in the process is to develop a strategy of type choices, color palettes, images, and decide how many comps are going to be needed to creatively explore the project. Some designers collect these ideas in collage form and place on a "crazy wall" or "mood board." The strategy may include defining the brand position in the marketplace to achieve the goal of the design solutions.

This notation and sketch process should be accomplished quickly so the designer can move to next step of exploring ideas by generating simple sketches of ideas. The thumbnail step is crucial since it allows a designer to easily adjust the visual hierarchy and contrast before a lot of time has been wasted with the software.

To be distinctive, a logo must be meticulously designed. Developing a collection of outstanding logos for reference is an important task for aspiring graphic artists.

Where designers struggle

Typography, hue, and spacing. These design elements are the adversaries of graphic designers. Artists have access to millions of fonts; however inexperienced designers tend to use only those preloaded in the software. It is important to note that the individuals who chose the software font options were likely developers or programmers. They exhibit creativity, yet in a manner distinct from that of a graphic designer.

The color palette is created by replicating the primary, secondary, and tertiary hues from the color wheel, with only a limited number of shades and tints. It seldom pertains to the intended market. Graphic designers may once again opt for these colors in their solutions rather than developing their own libraries for selection during the creative process.

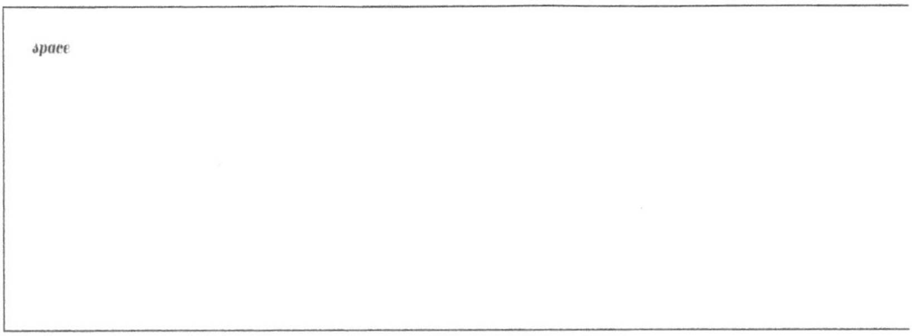

space

IMAGE 1-10

Space allows type to be smaller since there is not the competition to stand out as there is when all the type and images fill the space.

The concept of space is challenging. The monitor's display cannot accurately represent the physical size of the finished project. Designs on the screen can be significantly larger, enabling the graphic artist to pack the page with disproportionately large letter sizes and large shapes. The most effective technique in design is creating contrast which requires the presence of space. It is essential to allow room to assist the reader in comprehending a message.

The novice is restricting their solutions by utilizing the fonts and colors that are included in the software. A design's success or failure is reliant upon the presence of space. It will impress a client and appeal to individuals who are unaware of the reason for their attraction to a design.

These three critical areas of graphic design, typography, color, and space need to be mastered by graphic designers to be able to present a professional solution to the client and more importantly, communicate the message to the prospective target market.

Freelancer

The term freelancer contains intriguing medieval origins and literary connections. Sir Walter Scott popularized it in his 1820 novel Ivanhoe. In the novel, the phrase refers to a medieval mercenary, literally a "free lance," who used a spear-like weapon called a lance and offered his services to any paying employer. The term combines "free," signifying independence, and "lance." Unbound by loyalty or obligations to any lord, the story's mercenary knight was ready to fight for the highest bidder.

IMAGE 1-11

AI Practicum} In AI image generator Adobe Firefly prompt: 3D character wearing face mask in gold leaf silk armor looking at viewer, fantasy medieval

Currently, the term describes freelance professionals across various sectors who serve multiple clients instead of working for a single company. By the 20th century, the term freelancer had grown popular in disciplines such as journalism, art, and technology. It is unsurprising that fine artists held a negative perception of graphic designers, who consistently sought freelance opportunities to sell their creative skills to persuade viewers. They sold their creative souls for financial gain.

IMAGE 1-12

An abstract illustration showing that outside the comfort circle are unknown creative solutions for graphic designers.

The comfort circle

Graphic artists will encounter the phrase "Think outside the box" during client presentations, signifying the client's disinterest in the design and lack of direction. Because it gives them a sense of security, they might feel more comfortable with the design concept they have seen elsewhere. It is possible that the designer presented an innovative concept that will be noticeable and draw interest. Conversely, the concept may be not be engaging and trite. The basic idea is that we live in, drive in vehicles, and work within confined spaces. To create a distinctive and innovative design, we must step outside our comfort zones and challenge ourselves to discover the most effective layout for our clients.

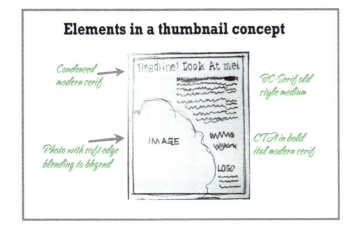

IMAGE 1-13
Layout of thumbnail marked up.

Publishing design terms

Designers and clients use many terms that refer to the degree of completion on design ideas. At times clients and professional graphic designers will have their own definitions so it is advisable that to clarify the terms in a briefing.

Each level of design from thumbnails to mechanical has more details pushed into the concept. As you can see thumbnails have the fewest elements which allows you to explore and quickly put down your ideas. You will find that as you go to the next stages sometimes the thumbnail looks much better since it is loose and creative but, as you fill in the comp, you lose the energy and space of your concept.

Thumbnails

Thumbnails are small hand sketches of concepts that might stimulate the brain to operate outside of its comfort zone and experiment with a variety of creative approaches. In the margins around the outside of the thumbnails, notes on color, lighting, and style can be jotted down. The explorations should contain: The headline roughed in; Image sketched in place; Indicate the call to action with lines; body content with lines; And ruff in the logo placement with contact info.

Basic Thumbnail Elements

The primary function of thumbnails is to allow the graphic designer to quickly and effortlessly arrange the elements. Images should be loosely sketched in place. A headline should be blocked in with notes in the margin to indicate the typeface. Lines or uniform squiggles will be used to denote a text block. Draw a border to indicate the trim and to appraise the usage of space. The logo must be positioned either in text form or as a rough representation of its shape.

IMAGE 1-14

Graphic Designer: Neal Hettinger

Thumbnails with final billboard.

Ruffs also known as Layouts

Loose digital layouts of several different design options full-size, with 'greek' text and images in place that can be shown to the art director or brainstorming team. They can be used to check off that all the elements from the brief have been included. Designers tend to like space and will forget elements and sacrifice the message for the visual flow.

The layouts are computer concepts ,usually 1/2 to full size, that have the actual font choice for headlines and loosely place images or sketches with "greeking" for placement text for body content. Graphic artists show these ideas to the art director and use them to work out the details to narrow down the direction.

Comprehensives also called Comps

Fairly tight full-sized digital layouts of several different design options, with actual text and images in place that is shown to the art director and possibly the client. Once again, the graphic designer should check off to see that all the elements have been included.

Mockups

If the project is packaging or has a cut-out shape, then a three-dimensional replica of the design should be presented to the client to convey the design. Many times, after assembling all the components to create the 3D model, the graphic artist will find flaws in the design. It is better to spend time creating a mockup than to see the mistakes on the press.

Mechanical

Camera-ready art was once the term used to describe completed artwork. With the advent of digital final mechanicals, this term has become obsolete. To ensure that every piece is high-resolution and positioned accurately, the print-ready file is examined. It is necessary to inspect the repaired photos in the proper color mode and resolution. Crops, bleeds, registration marks, and a color bar are all part of the mechanical. If possible, provide a corrected color printout for the pressman to match. Typically, the mechanical file is transferred to the print company or emailed in a PDF format.

Dummy

If the design is folded, 3D, or has a die-cut, a final printout of the design, also referred to as a dummy or folding dummy, should be sent to the printer. Use a similar paper stock for the prototype to ensure that the printer is aware of the folding configuration of the flat mechanical.

Proof

Before printing begins, the printer normally requests final approval from the graphic designer on the press ready file. It can be given as a PDF, a digital sample, or a physical proof from the press run.

Technical terms of graphic design

Greeking

Greeking is placeholder text for layouts which is usually represented by the Latin "Lorem ipsum dolor sit amet." This allows the art Director and copywriter to see what has been planned for text.

Image Area

The image area is the area inside the trim, where the text should go. No text should cross this margin since it could be in danger of being cut off in post press trimming.

Trim

The edges of the design where the printer will trim off any excess stock.

Bleed

The bleed is the color or image that extends past the document edge and gets trimmed during post press. This is what allows the piece to have no white border. Usually, the bleed is an eighth of an inch all around.

Elements

All the components that make up a graphic design.

Heading

Always write out the headline in block letters. It is the hook to read the ad. Either chose typefaces that represent the message, create an artistic headline that is eye-catching, or match the font to clever or humorous wording.

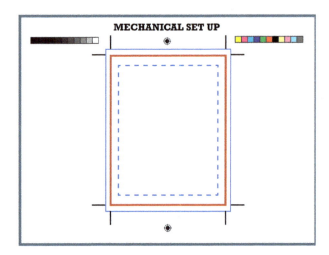

IMAGE 1-15

Example of basic layout terms used by graphic designers.

Titles in companies and firms

These following roles and titles will vary depending on the size and focus of the agency, but they all contribute to the overall creative process in graphic design. Employees may function as a combination of responsibilities in smaller markets or companies.

Junior graphic designer

This position normally focuses on creating basic projects and building the elements for a design to assist a senior designer. This an entry level position that can manage file backups and create visuals. Junior graphic designers should receive guidance, mentorship, and supervision from senior designers.

Graphic designer

This is the workhorse position in a company or firm. They are expected to know all facets of various design projects for print, web, and social media. This designer will compose design solutions under some supervision from the art director with creative direction supplied from the creative director.

Senior graphic designer

Besides being responsible for large campaigns, they will also team up with the copywriter and lead a creative team. They will mentor less experienced designers and attend meetings on the creative direction with the A.D. and C.D.

Art Director

Referred to as the A.D. their duties include managing the designers, retouching artists, and photographers in their group as well as directing them in the production of the design concepts, presentations, revisions, and mechanicals. The A.D. focuses primarily on the visual aspects of a project. They oversee the execution of visual elements, such as photography, typography, layout, and color schemes, ensuring that the look and feel of the project align with the creative brief. Their role is more hands-on when it comes to working with designers and ensuring the artistic quality of the work. They report to the creative director.

Creative Director

The C.D. position is responsible for the direction of creative solutions in a company or for a marketing campaign. They have a number of art directors and teams under their management. If they are in-house, they work with the head of sales and marketing to keep the focus on the brand. If they work for an agency or firm, they work with the account executive and client to manufacture the best solutions. Their role includes guiding both the visual and conceptual components, working on the tone, messaging, and storytelling aspects. They set the overall vision for the brand or project and ensure that all creative elements work together cohesively.

Demonstration – Thumbnail use

An electrician in New England wanted a colorful eye-catching logo. There was a lighthouse near his office that he wanted as part of the design. After going over my notes from the client, meeting I doodle with a number of sketches. These thumbnails indicated type and placement in relation to a lighthouse illustration.

1. These fast sketches are few of the many thumbnails drawn to explore the logo direction.

IMAGE 1-16

2. The concepts were based on the thumbnails. Then the comprehensive layouts were narrowed down. I did not want to overwhelm the client. The final logo design included input from the client.

HighPointe Electric Ocean City

IMAGE 1-17

The fundamentals of composition

Learning Objective

The learner will be able to name famous designers and their styles. They will be able to clarify the need for graphic design. The user will be able to show emphasis through cropping.

Professional Terminology

Asymmetrical:	Visually balanced layout of elements that are not mirrored vertically or horizontally.
Balance:	Where the visual weight of a layout's elements is harmonious.
Chiaroscuro:	An effect of light and shadow to create dimension on an image.
Composition:	The placement and structure of graphic elements into a cohesive design.
Contrast:	Visually different elements that attract a person's attention.
Critique:	An evaluation with positive and negative feedback.
Design:	The creative composition of elements to create a message.
Focal point:	The distinct area of a composition that attracts a reader.
Golden ratio:	The basic relationship of elements to create a sense of balance in a design.
Grid:	A structural system in a layout.
Hierarchy:	Elements are ranked by importance.
Narrative:	A created story or message.
Objective design:	A plan utilizing the results of research and testing to layout a project.
Rule of thirds:	Used to create structure in a layout with intersections that draw attention.

IMAGE 2-1

Example of grocery aisle to show how people are surrounded by messages Adobe stock photo.

The need for graphic design

The Industrial Revolution in the early 1800's created the need for graphic design. At that time the US economy transformed from producing goods by hand to using machines and suddenly the large cities were glutted with goods. Manufacturers realized they needed to sell mass quantities to the public. They needed to communicate in a better way than standing on a street corner hawking their wares. They needed advertising and flyers to mass communicate availability and push the potential customers into the stores to buy their products. Once the consumer was in the store, the manufacturers needed packaging and signage that continued to sell the consumer on their product's benefits.

200 years later, marketing has spread to virtually all mediums. Products, services, information, news or anything that a person might potentially pay to use, is promoted. If it is being visually marketed, it needs a graphic designer. Marketing has become such a part of life that only a few messages are actually seen or remembered.

Shoppers are exposed to over 4000 ads a day[1], which includes print advertisements, signage, vehicle wraps, billboards, magazines, social media and exploring the internet. For branding, potential buyers are shown over 5000 logos a day[2] such as on garments, signage, hats, banners, shopping bags, and labels. Social media alone spent over $173 billion for advertising in 2022.[3]

Considering the budgets for marketing, it is obvious there is a need for educated visual communicators which is why graphic design is a growing field. A career students of graphic design should study print and the internet, but not exclude motion graphic design used in streaming news, sports events, and presentations.

As a disclaimer, not everything that is a visual communication needs to be designed by a graphic artist. If it is a manual, warning label, a law label, size label, or other forms of information, someone who has a basic understanding of layout could create it.

Inspiration

Even though looking at modern design and technical practices is advantageous, graphic designers look at past styles and solutions in different cultures to get ideas. Before starting thumbnails, graphic artists should research other visually creative industries. For structure, shape, textures, and form study architectural design, automotive design, and entertainment design. For color, research interior design, fashion, paints, Pantone color forecasts, are always good resources.

IMAGE 2-2

Creative ideas are magical — let them flow!

AI Practicum} Artificial Intelligence image generator Firefly prompts: graphic designer with ideas, and numerous approaches to light bulbs. Composed with image manipulation software Photoshop using contextual bar to select subject and to add backgrounds.

Every successful and highly regarded graphic designer has their own philosophy and approach to creating visual solutions. After a meeting with a client or account executive they may thumb through research or a personal library collection of interesting design approaches. They may brainstorm with a group of fellow designers, or they may walk away and not think about the problem for a few days—letting their subconscious flow around ideas. Their methods help them organize their thoughts, explore creative solutions, and refine their concepts before the tackling the message.

Graphic designers have a number of tools available from using their own hands to assemble the design to using computer software. Every project deals with attracting viewers and communicating a message.

IMAGE 2-3

Graphic Designer: Neal Hettinger

While it would be nice to take credit for the blocks in the typeface, when viewed in outline, the structure presented itself creating a happy accident.

Sometimes an unplanned development occurs when a graphic designer is going for a certain solution that is visually fascinating. The software program will unintentionally create something with fonts, images, or color that the artist recognizes as a "happy accident," and will expand on it to solve the problem. That is the fun part of design — enjoying and capitalizing on the unplanned.

Inspiration is not planned. Perhaps, the most difficult part of design is recognizing when to make use of an unexpected development and when to trash it.

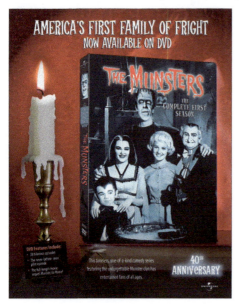

IMAGE 2-4

Graphic Designer: Neal Hettinger

Art Director: Nigel Sherry

Advertisement with photographic setting that creates a narrative.

Many graphic artists approach design as creating a visual narrative about the product or service so that it is memorable to an observer. This technique usually involves images, but typefaces can also communicate a time or place. Colors will establish a setting, and the content starts a message.

The basics of compelling compositions

Artists will use the same basic design rules and guidelines when laying out a vitamin bottle label and when they layout a billboard. These are the elements of composition. When used at the correct scale, design components must work together. Some designers grapple with coming up with a good idea. Other commercial artists have many ideas, but they are unable to know which, if any, are great solutions. Understanding and comprehending these ingredients will allow a graphic designer to know good from bad, plain for overused, and finished as opposed to needing more finesse.

Composition is the form and structure resulting from the arrangement of graphic elements in relation to one another that creates a visually cohesive communique. Graphic artists assemble type, color, texture, shapes, lines, images, and depth into a spatial arrangement. They need to gain the attention of the viewer. The number of ways to approach this goal is nearly endless. They start with research and narrow down their options. Everyone has ideas but not all ideas are good. It is difficult to critique their solutions. One way is to check off the main goals of the design. It needs to have a focal point that will lead the reader through a hierarchy of elements that set up a visual flow from the most important part of the message to the least important.

A guide to creating quality design is referred to as CARP which is an acronym for Contrast, Alignment, Repetition, and Proximity. CARP assists graphic designers in successfully arranging all the elements.

IMAGE 2-5

Graphic Designer: Neal Hettinger | Art Director: Nigel Sherry

An example of contrast where a large image of a vehicle is cropped to get the attention of someone waiting for the bus.

Contrast

Contrast is considered to be the most important technique in design. To attract viewers, the layout cannot treat all the features the same—it needs a focal point. This can be accomplished through the scale, color, and space. When contemplating a layout, it should have large, medium and small attributes to draw in the observer. To create contrast, scale should be applied to all the elements with one item overwhelming all the other elements.

To lead the eye of the viewer, contrast can be used to devise a visual hierarchy. Readers want to look over a message quickly. The layout will show what is most important—catching the attention of a prospect—then lead them through relevant information to a memorable brand or company logo. Visual hierarchy points to what comes next and indicates what is not important through size and color such as a copyright.

Contrast creates visual interest and focus to attract a viewer to a layout. Use different colors, shapes and images on the page to create contrast. Match items exactly or make them unique from one another.

Viewers are attracted by designs which have appealing contrast. Look at a tile floor with its equal spacing, textures, and sizes. How long will anyone look at the floor when all they see is tile, the same texture and color. They quickly move on to look at the rest of the house and spot an attractive rug. No creative designer wants their layout to be dismissed so readily.

There is no design skill that is more effective than how a commercial artist creates contrast. Graphic designers achieve contrast through scale. Large, medium, and small apply to image, type and space. Light, medium, and dark apply to all the elements in a layout and the space surrounding those elements. If everything is the same size, color, and texture the designer should be creating tile floors and not visual communications.

There are four major color contrasts. Color placement should be carefully considered. Dark/light is the relative contrast between values of color. Bright/dull is the relative contrast between intensities of colors. Warm/cool is the relative contrast between temperatures of colors. Large/small is the relative proportion of one color to another, with one usually dominant. Black and yellow are the two most contrasting colors.

Alignment

The strength of alignment in a design is frequently overlooked. Aligning the items to produce a sense of order and cohesion will improve the composition. A basic rule is to only use two types of alignment in the layout. Otherwise, the design will not appear structured or organized.

The basic alignments:

1. Centered is where images and type are centered with each other.
2. Left aligned is where the content is aligned along their left sides.
3. Right aligned is where the elements line up by their right sides.
4. Justified type adjusts the kerning and tracking to create even left and right edges.
5. Top aligned is where the top of the images line up
6. Bottom aligned which is where the bottom of each image aligns with the bottom of the other images.

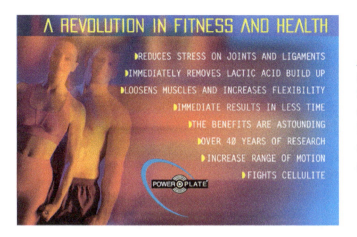

IMAGE 2-6

Graphic Designer: Neal Hettinger

Art Director: Nigel Sherry

Direct mail postcard demonstrates type aligned right.

Beginning designers will center the content which functioned for the first hundred years of graphic design but is safe and if it has space, creates no problems for the reader. More than five lines of content become difficult to read when centered. A person will struggle to follow the content and find the beginning of the next line. When they become frustrated, they will move one to another page.

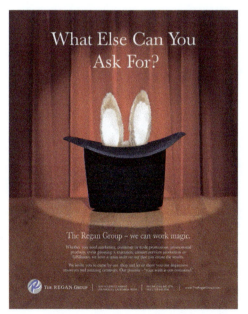

IMAGE 2-7

Graphic Designer: Nigel Sherry

Art Director: Neal Hettinger

Example of an alignment that is centered. Notice the bottom line consists of many elements that as a group are centered to provide a base for the layout.

Flush left is easier to read since it allows the eye to quickly find the next line of type. Images can be balanced with the body content flush left.

IMAGE 2-8

Graphic Designer: Neal Hettinger
**Example of flush left type on
website landing page.**

Justified type is spaced to align the left and right sides of a block of content. This alignment can be problematic as a result of the spacing between words and characters. The typeface cannot be large and the leading needs to aid in the readability. Gaps between the words can create an open spaces across a number of lines called rivers. Hyphenation will help but try to keep it to a minimum.

IMAGE 2-9

Graphic Designer: Nigel Sherry
Art Director: Neal Hettinger
**Example of a brochure with
justified type.**

Repetition

Viewers look for reoccurring shapes and images that tie a layout together. Repetition in multiple page projects such as magazines, newsletters, annual reports, and catalogs creates a sense of unity and familiarity. Utilizing similar elements builds consistency throughout the design. Hues, textures, and shapes are the obvious components but consistent alignment and choices in typefaces are equally important. Using more than three fonts will make the design busy and difficult to read. The frequency of a visual element's repetition builds on the probability of its retention in the observer's memory.

IMAGE 2-10

Graphic Designer: Neal Hettinger | Art Director: Nigel Sherry

The banner's repetitive background patten was inspired by the image. The green squares repeated the shape created by the fingers.

Brand identity creates a recognizable visual identification for shoppers. Implementing the same design features across various platforms or products such as websites, brochures, or social media posts reinforces a brand's identity. Repeating the way logos are shown with the same colors and typography builds a strong brand recognition.

IMAGE 2-11

Graphic Designer: Neal Hettinger
Art Director: Nigel Sherry

Example showing how a massive amount of type can be placed in groups to allow for space.

Proximity

When related elements are placed in close proximity to one another, they indicate a connection or relationship. By arranging the parts of a layout in sections, the designer utilizes the principle of Proximity to assist in producing order and a visual hierarchy. This allows the reader to skim past content that legally must be on a layout but is not important to the message.

A well-planned composition makes the content easier to navigate and produces an engaging message for the viewer. This approach allows the graphic designer to highlight the most important elements to get attention.

Balance

The reader does not want to work at figuring out a message. The design must be engaging. There are a number of ways to achieve this, but they all start with Balance. Our eyes are drawn to balanced layouts whether it's with design elements or space. The structure helps us quickly figure out the message and decide if we want to read more.

IMAGE 2-12

Graphic Designer: Nigel Sherry
Art Director: Neal Hettinger

Example of a symmetrical layout.

Role of the Midline

An imaginary vertical or horizontal line exists in the center of every piece of paper or side of a package that splits the page into two equal halves. As the graphic elements are positioned on a computer screen, the designer analyzes how each component interacts with that midline in terms of balance and visual flow and decides between two types of balance.

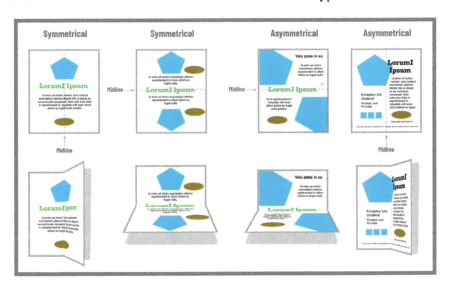

IMAGE 2-13

Midline and fundamental composition layout. Note the midline sets the center.

Symmetrical layouts are equally balanced on both sides of the axis with the elements a reflection of each other. This placement of the pieces in bilateral symmetry can easily create a structured and stable layout for the eye to follow. Posters and logo designs tend to have symmetrical arrangements.

This traditional balance places large images centered on the midline as well as the headline. The typeface can be letter spaced as capitals and there may be an additional decorative, script, or symbol fonts. In the symmetrical composition, the body content and individual lines of type are arranged with similar weight on either side of the midline. In general, balance achieved through symmetry presents a sense of stability with an easy flow of the elements from one form to the next.

IMAGE 2-14
Graphic Designer: Neal Hettinger
The asymmetrical layout creates tension (so does the large spider).

Asymmetrically balanced layouts can create more dynamic visuals and grab the potential consumer's attention. It takes time and trial and error to offset the elements away from the midline. A large image on the left can be offset with type, multiple small images, or just negative space.

In an asymmetrical composition, the parts of the composition are arranged to counterbalance each other's visual weight without mirroring opposite visual weight and positioning. To achieve a balanced asymmetrical composition, designers must consider the position and visual weight (size, texture, color, value) of each graphic element in relation to the other components. It takes time to arrange and rearrange the layout to make sure the contrasting counterbalancing pieces are correctly placed in the composition and have a visual flow.

Just like in life, most people prefer balance. They may be centered, or they may be a "fly by the seat of their pants" type person. Designers define the target market to know how the layout should balance.

The asymmetrical revolution can be traced back to the 1920s. The Bauhaus school in Germany experimented with layouts based on off-center axis. The designers used tension through the dynamic use of space. This style preferred flush right rag left body copy and headline. This caused tension since most of their readers preferred to read left to right. Bauhaus designers did not like ornamental graphics, decorative type, or even most serif typefaces. They preferred the modern sans serif type for their clean, uncomplicated lines. The Bauhaus' designs lead what is known today as Swiss design which also favors sans serif typefaces and dynamic space. Swiss design made popular use of lowercase headings and lines in a number of weights to create distinctive looks in color or in black and white.

Today, many designers prefer to integrate both styles by arrangement of the elements depending on visual hierarchy and the message. Mixing the styles takes experience and a thorough understanding of when not to use these styles. The designer must establish the function of the design before deciding the form. Bauhaus and Swiss design utilizes space so if the project does not have room for a lot of space, then another solution would better fit the design.

A balanced composition can be broken down into three levels. First, there is symmetrical and asymmetrical layouts. Imagine folding a piece of paper in half—vertical or horizontal. If the design elements mirror each other, then it is a symmetrical design. If they do not, it's asymmetrical. Whether in print or on the internet, each static single format has a midline. Evenly dispersing visual weight on both sides of the vertical axis is essential for achieving balance. Symmetry can be dull or effectively guide the reader through a visual hierarchy. Asymmetry can attract attention and emphasize a message, or it may appear so disordered that we disregard it entirely.

IMAGE 2-15
Graphic Designer: Neal Hettinger
Example of a laying out mixing centered elements with off centered elements.

Secondly, balance can be gridded out with some blocks holding large elements and clusters of elements . The blocks can hold more than one or two smaller elements The layout can look haphazard but with each piece specifically placed to visually counterbalance another piece, it can become harmonious with work and experimentation. Space takes up volume and should be considered when stabilizing the elements.

The third level is the argument on content versus imagery — which is the best approach for the design. Is the typeface the largest element or is the image the largest piece. What catches the reader's attention first? Then how are their eyes lead around the page and what engages the reader and hopefully, continue to look through the design.

Layout structure

Take a long look at a layout that is nicely designed. The positive and negative space, contrast due to scale and tones, textures, and when broken down — examine the thought behind the design. Sometimes, everything will be laid out just right for balance, flow, and eye-catching graphics. Then an element is added, or the copy or headline is made longer or shorter which will throw the composition out of balance. A trick is to squint at the design and see what needs to be adjusted. Sometimes when unexpected elements are added to a composition, the premise is gone, and the layout is awkward. If it just does not work, then the graphic artist will have to start over. The overall structure should support all the elements in one cohesive layout.

Throughout history the visual arts have had a number of different compositional layout "tricks." While these guidelines are not required, they save time and effort.

One popular layout used by catalog and magazine artists is a grid. The placement of the various elements in columns, margins, and in specific areas for text image keeps a consistent structure from page to page and especially across a series of pages. This continuity through the invisible structure of the elements of a design creates a visual structure for the reader that aligns the elements for simplicity, unity and legibility.

IMAGE 2-16

Graphic Designer: Neal Hettinger

Magazine covers have a great deal of information to grab readers. The grid helps organize that information.

Practicum} The Adobe stock photograph required the image area to be enlarged at both the top and bottom to bleed beyond the page trim. The stamp tool, generative fill, and brush were used to produce a seamless image. The contextual toolbar was prompted to incorporate trees in the background. The spot healing brush corrected sections of the slide that showed the retouching strokes.

There are multiple types of grids based on their structures such as, column, baseline, manuscript, modular and hierarchical. There is no rule that a grid has to be vertical and horizontal. Bauhaus designers rotated grids to rebel against traditional design.

To generate a symmetrical page grid , divide the page into columns and rows using dashed lines on their own layer so they can be hidden from view. Many designers utilize six to nine columns for a website, whereas three columns are typically used for a letter-sized page. The intersection of the lines provides focal points that capture the viewer's attention.

Numerous graphic artists use an asymmetrical grid in which certain columns are proportionately narrower than others. To set the grid, divide the print design page into thirds both vertically and horizontally. Configuring the parts is more straightforward when utilizing picas rather than inches. Elements may occupy multiple blocks.

IMAGE 2-17

Graphic Designer: Neal Hettinger

A busy two page MMA magazine advertisement incorporated numerous images that required adjustments to the background to improve type readability (not drop shadows). The image was positioned in a grid to draw the reader where the lines intersect (circled in magenta). The gutter did not fold where the logo on the vertical bumpers was positioned.

The concept that compositions become more dynamic when divided into thirds vertically and or horizontally is known as the Rule of Thirds. To draw a reader's attention to certain elements, they are placed at the points where the vertical and horizontal lines meet and create focal points.

Image Focus

Graphic artists approach images as either an eye-catching element or as the explanation of the design. The picture will be made up of values which are light, medium and dark tones.

The images usually fall into one of two categories — photographic or illustrative. When creating an image with artificial intelligence, the first decision is whether the image is a photo or an illustration. Photographs are images created with a camera but can also be artwork that appears to be a photograph known as photo real illustration.

To give depth to an illustration, the visual technique Chiaroscuro is used which adds directional light and a shadow in an attempt to give dimension to an object. The opposite technique is where the articulated shape of an object or subject does not have a light source and is either a solid or a texture with boundaries.

Cropping for visual impact

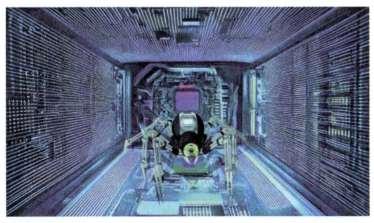

IMAGE 2-18
Created with Firefly and Adobe stock image combined and retouched in Photoshop.

Cropping is when the edges of an image are trimmed to produce an interesting visual or for the image to fit a given space. Photographs, drawings, type, sketches, paintings, or shapes can all be cropped for emphasis. In visual communications, the designer wants to get a viewer to stop and look at the composition and cropping the artwork can greatly improve its attraction. This skill requires practice and trying to look at the crop for the "first time." Creatively removing the uninteresting parts of an image will help the viewer immediately grab their attention.

IMAGE 2-19

Cropped in on the computer bug. Lightened and added highlights to spider to increase contrast.

Upon initial examination of the image, what immediately captures the viewer's attention? What areas did they consider to be unimportant? By generating interest, how can an image prompt viewers to quickly focus on a design?

When cropping the image, the commercial artist might need to enlarge a portion of it. Pixelation can occur when a computer enlarges an image. This is not a matter of concern if the image is a vector file since there are no pixels. A graphic artist can scan a drawing or sketch at a large scale to allow the viewer to see the details and strokes, depending on the rendering quality.

Each image is a story with a single message. The visual artist wants to emphasize something about an image. When you crop an image, it can:

1. Make it have more impact
2. Make the image more pleasing
3. Create an emotional response
4. Make the image more personal
5. Create a sense of tension

One skill that is not obvious is how to crop images for effect. Cropping is not required to be performed in a square or rectangle. Graphic artists will enhance the image by showing less with a masked shape, such as a circle, oval, or star. A cropped image has the potential to enhance the design and layout. Zooming in on an image or allowing a portion of it to extend beyond the shape's boundaries can achieve depth. This enables the creation of a foreground and background in a two-dimensional image. Utilize a variety of sizes to establish a sense of scale and movement which will create contrast. Designers rotate images to attract the viewer's attention.

IMAGE 2-20

Image cropped in and put into a shape for interest.

Design Virtuosos

All graphic designers should study the well-known and obscure designers in their field. The product of graphic designers surrounds everyone from the obvious such as advertising, corporate identity, and packaging to the obscure such as labels on bottles, the bottoms of chairs, and greeting cards. Whether a creative professional uses the term commercial artist, graphic artists, or graphic designer to define themselves, they are focused on one goal—attract the viewer enough to read the message.

The successful creative professional has the ability to creators eye-catching and memorable designs and should be studied. Graphic designers should study the historically famous commercial artists as well as the present-day innovators to learn techniques and if possible, the processes established by the successful graphic artists. The list of effective and pioneer graphic designers is well over a hundred but here is a short list to investigate.

Saul Bass

The trailblazer of motion picture poster design, opening movie credits, packaging, and company logos broke every project down to that basic goal as the first step in the process. He was the first designer to create dynamic movie credits, and his graphic posters were aimed at informing the potential viewers about the subject of the movie.

He utilized shapes and symbolism in his design of corporate logos and advertisement solutions. Mr. Bass had the simple concept, "Design is just thinking made visual."

Paula Scher

Ms. Scher's style cannot be characterized since she adapts it for the subject's audience. Some have tried to define it as a cross between pop art bad fine art but there is no denying her visual design is memorable and attractive. She adapts her style to a multitude of different company brand identities. Her portfolio includes sophisticated logos such as The New York City Ballet and Tiffany & to rule breaker logos such as The Public Theater brand.

Paula Scher definition of a successful design solution is how the viewer discerns the message. Her impressive list of projects includes brand and identity materials, packaging, publications, and maps.

Milton Glaser

Considered to be one of the most impactful graphic designers in the United States, Milton Glaser's influence on graphic design still continues. He believed "the poster's role is to convey information from a source to an audience in order to move that audience to an amplification or change of perception that produces an awareness or an action."

Along with Reynold Ruffins, Seymour Chwast, and Edward Sorel, he founded Pushpin Studios, which provided direction for world graphic design. Mr. Glaser and Clay Felker founded the New York magazine, which served as a model for city publications. He was an instructor at the School of Visual Arts in New York City. Glaser also founded a publishing design firm that has designed over 50 periodicals. The trademarked "I love NY" logo is likely the most imitated graphic design in the world.

His accomplishments in the field are numerous. Milton Glaser did not limit himself and applied his craft to logos, brochures, signage, posters, magazines, restaurant graphics, and annual reports. He relished challenges.

Peter Max

Similar to Andy Warhol, Mr. Max enjoyed taking the everyday visuals and making them visually appealing with bright colors, flowing images, and loose hand drawn type. He is known as the icon for pop art culture since his designs mirrored the spirit and energy of the movement. In 1967, Peter Max designed the "Summer of Love" poster, which inspired hundreds of thousands of nonconformists and free spirits to converge on Central Park in New York City. His philosophy was "My life's journey has been an odyssey through time and space, filled with vivid moments, abundant with color, dazzling with sights, and vibrant with euphonic sounds."

Mr. Max's psychedelic and pop art pieces are vibrant. He has designed advertisements, posters, and even the exterior graphics of Southwest jet airliners.

John Kosh

English designer and typographer Mr. Kosh is known for his adaptability and iconic creations. His understanding of type has made him a renowned art director, album cover designer, graphic artist, and multimedia designer. Kosh's stature as a graphic artist rose while designing for the Royal Ballet and the Royal Opera House. His typography and design reputation allowed him to work on album covers for a long list of recognizable musicians such as the Beatles, Rolling Stones, Linda Ronstadt, Jimmy Buffet, and the Eagles. Never one to limit himself, Kosh saw opportunities in motion graphics in the 1990's and started designing animation of for TV and film credits.

Learning Library Exercise: Report On Two Graphic Designers

Due to the variety of products, services, events, graphic artists have developed different styles. There are a number of graphic designers who are considered leaders in the field. To learn the styles and to develop different approaches, you need to study them.

1. Write a report on the graphic designers that you find interesting and follow their activities. As your career advances and to improve your craft, study additional designers that you can add to your notebook at a later date.

2. Select your two favorite graphic designers. Include examples of their work and explain why you chose them.

3. Your report must be typed, 250 to 350 of your own words, complete sentences, correct punctuation and grammar, include examples of their designs.

References

1| Simpson, J. (2022, April 14). Finding Brand Success in The Digital World. Forbes Agency Council. www.forbes.com/sites/forbesagencycouncil/2017/08/25/finding-brand-success-in-the-digital-world

2| Barrington, C. (2024, July 22). 30 Mind-Blowing Stats and Facts about Logos! Embryo, a Digital Marketing Agency. www.embryo.com/blog/30-mind-blowing-stats-and-facts-about-logos

3| McLachlan , S. (2023, April 5). 85+ Important Social Media Advertising Statistics to Know. Hootsuite Blog. www.blog.hootsuite.com/social-media-advertising-stats

Using the elements

Learning Objective

In this chapter, the student will be able to identify the five components of strong graphic design solutions. They will be able to articulate the creative thinking process. The learner will be able to provide parts of design.

Professional terminology

EPS: When created as a vector file, the data retains details when scaled.

Face: A specific font design based on structure.

Foundry: A company that specializes in the creation or distribution of typefaces.

GIF: Sized for web, small file has limited colors used for static and animated graphics.

JPEG: Reduced file size for web with some image detail lost but has full range of color.

Letterforms: The visual representation of an alphabetic letter.

PDF: Cross-platform data that displays a document without the file that generated it.

PNG: Compressed larger web file without loss of image detail.

Raster graphic: Picture made up by a grid of pixels.

Readable: Type that is easy to interpret and quickly understand.

TIFF: High quality large image file used for detailed photography and printing.

Typeface: A set of designed characters created as an alphabet, punctuation, and glyphs.

Typesetter: A person who creates and sets the attributes of text.

Typography: The art of arranging, creating, and stylizing fonts to set a tone for the design.

IMAGE 3-1
Clients will try to get you to undervalue your work.
AI Practicum}

Firefly prompt 1: Cartoon of middle aged guy writing a company check isolated in an expensive office. Prompt 2: Cartoon fingers on hand crossed. Upscaled and revised in Photoshop adding hands, using content aware to fill in spots, Created speak bubbles in Illustrator, added type Arial Rounded.

The basics

A graphic designer rarely begins a project with the intention of creating an uninteresting solution. Most designers are in the graphic arts to express their creativity. Sure, they would like to make money, but graphic design is not the career to get rich. However, graphic design is one of the few professions that consistently pushes the boundaries of innovation from decade to decade. A graphic designer must enjoy learning and applying new techniques.

It is remarkable that individuals without any formal training believe they are the best graphic designers. Occasionally, they can creatively solve an assignment without learning the steps, but they will eventually fail. They probably think they can dance the waltz without learning the steps. Clients will also try to bargain with graphic artists to lower their fee and promise to make it up on another project. That may be the plan, but the money is rarely forthcoming.

Readers operate subconsciously on these design precepts in the Western world:

- People read from left to right.
- Readers start at the top and work down the page.
- Pages in a publication or website are related.
- Closeness connects while distance separates.
- Big and dark elements are more important.
- Small and pale elements are less important.
- People read lowercase easier than all caps.
- Everything has a shape, including emptiness.

Given the same pictures and copy, five designers, each with their own unique sensibilities and preferences, would create five different designs. But given a single message to get across, the client would expect the designers to develop comparable or equivalent solutions.

A graphic designer must consciously and subconsciously evaluate, dissect, and categorize everything they see. The artist's mind must routinely build a library of ideas and solutions for inspiration. This foundation will be beneficial in evaluating a design solution to determine whether it is a quality solution or an unattractive layout.

Habitualization is a term that refers to how people become accustomed to seeing the same things over and over, such as graphic design solutions. All designers need to overcome this disregard and critically evaluate all visuals for their techniques, styles, colors, patterns, textures, fonts, and other elements, mentally storing these ideas for future designs.

R.A.S. (Reticular Activating System) for graphic design is where the brain familiarizes itself with information as people develop, so it can filter out useless details. Given the abundance of visual messages, designers must sift through the clutter to uncover valuable, imaginative, and innovative solutions. Designers designed this junk for a purpose.

IMAGE 3-2
There is always room for more knowledge.

Overworked or unfinished designs fail to capture the attention of the viewer. By studying and critiquing well-crafted designs, professionals are able to recognize when a solution is creative or just a standard layout. The design principles and rules remain the same whether it's a small can of beans, a magazine, an animated billboard, or a website. All of these pieces need to be engaging and memorable.

Students who only observe captivating designs are likely to forget them unless they participate in discourse, expressing and elaborating on their observations. They must consider the suggestions of the listener too. Beware of being an armchair expert. Graphic designers should explore their environment. They should be open to novel concepts such as visiting the zoo to examine the various posters and informational handouts. They ought to travel to a bus stop and assess the marketing environment. When exploring a furniture store, they should closely observe the hang tags. They should scrutinize all the signage when they travel to an airport. Students for the graphic arts must attend and take note of the visual graphics at musicals, cinema, and art exhibitions. It should become second nature to thoroughly critique all graphic components within a fast-food outlet, including the external drive-through area, and evaluate the menu design.

IMAGE 3-3
Graphic Designer: Neal Hettinger
Billboard concept for cosmetic company.

Graphic designers must broaden their outlook. Remember the greater the range of references, the greater a designer's ability to communicate with all ages, professions and lifestyles. It will allow them to properly design a message to succeed. Graphic designers should be wary of the accuracy in web search results, blogs, postings, and artificial intelligence research. Always check the sources and facts.

Compelling graphic design

The top left corner of every page or spread is a valuable starting point because readers look there first. Exploit the reader's natural habits by placing the logo or starting a headline in that hotspot. The purpose of design is emphatically to have inviting areas of space. An overabundance of information can build a design that is impenetrable.

IMAGE 3-4
Graphic Designer: Neal Hettinger
By constantly developing their knowledge, graphic designers are not limiting themselves. They can design mustard labels or billboards or anything that presents a creative challenge.

Form is related to function which is directly defined by content. The design must consider the user experience. The design should not be limited to 2 sides of a page if the elements are better organized by folding the page and having four panels. Should the viewer feel relaxed or stressed? Relaxed design would use cool colors, comfortable fonts, eye-catching photos, centered or flush left type, possible a grid system, with plenty of leading in the content.

Stressed design would put the images in hard geometrical shapes on a palette of warm or irregular colors, and the fonts would be readable but not ordinary. If the project is for a quiet vacation spot, then the solution may use colorful, heavily retouched image(s), nice blues and greens, a comfortable font such as Goudy Modern Regular with a little extra kerning and leading for the subheads and quotes. The function decides the form.

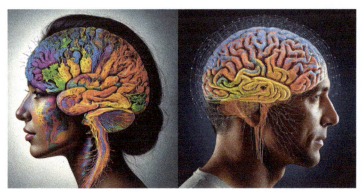

IMAGE 3-5
Practicum} Firefly prompts: map of the creative human female / male brains.

Develop a work map

Yogi Berra once stated, "If you are uncertain about your destination, you will ultimately arrive at another location." This is true for design, and while "happy accidents" are intriguing, presenting a client with a layout that is unrelated to their requests is not engaging. Novice designers rapidly grasp an idea and move forward caught in the swell of creativity. It is unsurprising that upon completion and review of the client brief, they find that the design fails to resolve the issue. Innovative designers who have acquired experience have established procedures for addressing a variety of projects.

Mentally organize

Visual structure and organization elements within a design are essential for a graphic to communicate. Organize elements so all parts fit together to make unity, or an integrated whole. Find design unity in the elements' commonalities. Organize elements by their shared subject matter, shape, or color.

One approach to starting a design is to create a layout and then upload the elements. One variation of this system involves positioning the components adjacent to a blank page, allowing for easy insertion without impeding the design's progress. Some designers put everything required into a layout and then delete or edit what is not vital.

IMAGE 3-6

Practicum} Firefly prompt: Elf on ladder putting words and images into a vintage filing cabinet in a magical vault of filing cabinets; looking up point of view; magical pixie dust floating around; adventure, art, fantasy, imagination, fairy-tale; goblin carrying scrolls. In Photoshop blended goblin with pixie dust, gradation set on multiply, and high pass set at 100 with soft light blend.

Graphic design file types

In addition to the software editable file formats such as PSD, INDD, and DOC labels, graphic designers use a number of types of image files for website and print design. The final result decides which one is appropriate for the final mechanical.

TIFF file format

This high-quality format for pixeled images is commonly used in photography, art printing, graphic design, and publishing, where high-resolution images are crucial. There is no image quality lost during compression of a TIFF (Tagged Image File Format) file. However, these detail capabilities tend to create large file sizes which makes them unsuitable for web use but great for high-end printing and archival purposes. TIFF images can have a very high color depth such as 16-bit or 32-bit, making them suitable for images that need a broad range of colors and shades. Similar to Photoshop, TIFF files can contain multiple layers and store metadata like color profiles and does support transparency

GIF file format

A GIF file supports both static and animated images. In GIF (Graphics Interchange

Format) the "g" is pronounced like in the word general per the format inventor Stephen Wilhite. This format has the ability to support simple animations with combining multiple frames into a single file. GIFs are popular for short, repetitive animations on the web as well as buttons, banners. Short clips for quick-loading images on social media, messaging, and memes use GIFs.

To keep the file size low for the internet, GIFs use a 256-color palette in 8-bit color, which limits the ability to display complex, high-quality images like photographs. The format is useful for simpler images such as logos, icons, or low-color illustrations. GIFs support 1-bit transparency, which means a pixel is either fully opaque or fully transparent. Gradations are not supported like other formats.

JPG file format

This type of file reduces file size while maintaining most of the image quality. JPG (Joint Photographic Experts Group) files compress image data by discarding some of the image information. This results in smaller file sizes but can lead to a reduction in image quality, especially if the file is compressed too much or edited repeatedly. This format works well on photographs or images with smooth gradients of color. It's widely used for digital cameras and online images because it strikes a good balance between quality and file size.

JPG does not support transparent backgrounds. It is designed for full-color images where the white area is not clear but has the background color white. For options on the type of quality for an image, JPG has levels of compression. Higher compression results in smaller file sizes with lower image quality, while lower compression maintains better quality but creates larger files.

PNG file format

The PNG (Portable Network Graphics) file was created as a non-patented alternative to the GIF format. PNG files are commonly used for images on websites and social media because they offer compressed image data without losing any quality and preserving the original details. These files support transparent backgrounds which is extremely useful in internet design. This is useful when placing images over different backgrounds in internet design. PNG files can display millions of colors, making them suitable for complex images like photos or detailed illustrations. This format does not support animation or CMYK printing files.

EPS file format

As primarily a vector graphics file format, EPS is used in professional graphic design for logos and illustrations, since the image can be scaled without degradation in quality. EPS (Encapsulated PostScript) files store vector graphics as mathematical equations and can be opened and edited by a variety of vector graphic software. EPS files are preferred in professional design and printing for creating high-quality, scalable logos, illustrations, and other designs that need to be output at various sizes and maintain perfect clarity.

PDF file format

Adobe created the PDF file format that is readable on a Mac, Windows, Linux, mobile devices and on other PC software. This file type is used by printers since the fonts can be embedded and colors are consistent. The layout is preserved across the platforms and operating systems. To be able to adjust the PDF file for the press, a printer may ask the designer not to embed the fonts but send them as separate zipped files.

Portable Document Format (PDF) can be static or dynamic with fillable forms, click actions that take the user to different pages, add signatures, play a video, and other options. A PDF file can require security with passwords to view only and passwords to interact.

PDF's have multiple compression options that can adjust the size and quality of the data in the file based on the intended use. This format is popular since it retains the visual and type without rearrangement across platforms and software.

IMAGE 3-7
Good design dictates one element must dominate all the other elements.

Five components of strong graphic design solutions

Emphasis

Effective design requires one element to be the most significant within the overall composition. This visual technique directs the viewer's attention towards the most significant aspect of the composition, usually the primary message or focal point. Designers attain emphasis by manipulating aspects like size, color, contrast, shape, or location to establish a distinct hierarchy and focal point.

The best approach is to decide on an element that should be emphasized which would suggest a starting point for the viewer. By prioritizing and recognizing the most essential information or visual elements first, it facilitates the clear and successful communication of the key message. Emphasis can define the message or use the pictures to tell the story. It can motivate the reader to stop and read a layout. Graphic artists emphasize with color to show what is important.

Jan Tschichold was one of the earliest practitioners of the then-revolutionary asymmetrical style. In his 1928 book, Die Neue Typographie, he explained expressive hierarchy is more powerful when its size is reinforced by rational grouping and positioning.

IMAGE 3-8

What could this line signify: a seismograph, a lie-detector, or a heart monitor.

Lines

Lines are essential components of graphic design due to their ability to perform a variety of functions that enhance the visual allure, flow, and structure of a design. A path creates a line with moving point in space that has no thickness and extends in both directions. Lines are adaptable components of a layout that facilitate visual flow, movement, emphasis, and communication. They make a substantial contribution to the overall design by influencing the manner in which information is conveyed and perceived.

Graphic designers enhance the visual and functional aspects of their work by integrating various types of lines, resulting in compositions that communicate effectively and are visually appealing. The motif of lines can function as a border around content and images, thereby assisting in the isolation and highlighting of specific elements, such as text, images, or sections of a page.

Designers frequently generate grids, using lines to arrange content and align elements in an organized and well-balanced manner. Employing horizontal or vertical lines delineates sections of content in websites, publications, and brochures. Incorporating diagonal or curved lines can achieve dynamic movement and enhance the energy of a design. Bold or thick lines can highlight specific regions. Arrow lines can be used to highlight call-to-action content or buttons.

IMAGE 3-9

Lines have energy.

Lines can generate textures or patterns within a design. Employing varied line weights or repeating lines can create visual interest in a composition without becoming overwhelming. We frequently employ hatching and cross-hatching to enhance the dimension and shading of illustrations and texture areas.

In both minimalist and intricate designs, lines are indispensable for delineating shapes or figures. Designers employ contour lines to establish the boundaries of objects, thereby enabling them to either stand out or merge.

Designers employ convergent lines in a one- or two-point perspective to generate depth in flat, two-dimensional designs. This is particularly beneficial for the creation of authentic scenes or the addition of a sense of distance and dimension.

Vertical lines can symbolize power, growth, or strength, while horizontal lines frequently symbolize quietness, tranquility, or stability. Diagonal lines may stimulate movement, action, or transformation.

IMAGE 3-10

Texture immediately evokes a sensation or reaction by the viewer.

Textures

Design is further enhanced by textures. To a composition, they bring depth, realism,

47

and emotion. Graphic designers can enhance the overall impact and functionality of their work by carefully incorporating textures.

This component can improve the static quality of flat designs by mimicking the texture of real-world materials, including wood, fabric, and stone. They create the illusion of depth, which enhances the appeal of a design. Despite the fact that observers are unable to physically interact with a design, textures may trigger a tactile sensation. The visual representation of roughness, softness, or smoothness creates the illusion of contact, thereby providing a more engaging experience. This implied sensation has the potential to enhance the overall experience by establishing a sensory connection with the audience.

IMAGE 3-11

Graphic Designer: Neal Hettinger

The image of the uniform immediately conveys the thick quality of the texture to Judo players.

Textures can contribute to a brand's identity by providing products and marketing materials with a distinctive appearance. Metallic or glossy textures imply modernity and technology, while natural textures such as grass or sand can evoke the outdoors.

Although flat designs are clean and minimalist, they can appear monotonous or lack vitality. Texture has the potential to add energy by introducing variations, thereby preventing the composition from appearing too uniform or sterile. Subtle texture overlays can achieve a harmonious blend of flatness and depth, providing an appropriate level of interest without overpowering the composition.

Graphic designers can use textures to highlight specific elements of a design. For example, using texture to accentuate a focal point by creating a contrast between the textured and non-textured areas can be beneficial. A rough texture in the background can enhance the visibility of finer elements, such as text or logos, by establishing a visual hierarchy that directs the viewer's eye.

The coherence of compositions can be enhanced by selecting the appropriate texture to reinforce the theme or style they wish to convey. Textures can subtly improve the user experience in web or app design by creating interfaces that are more relatable and tangible. For instance, a button that appears textured or has a subtle shadow may enhance the design's interactivity and increase its click ability. In addition, textures can enhance the efficacy of an interface by increasing its comfort and intuitiveness.

As a background element, texture makes a layout interesting and memorable. If a designer wants to lead the eye repeating shapes and icons in different areas will draw attention.

Color

Because it influences emotions, directs attention, enhances readability, and conveys meaning, color is one of the most potent and essential elements in graphic design. It is necessary for the perception, communication, and connectivity of a design with an audience.

Tones and hues make up this composition. Hues are essential in graphic design as they are the foundational colors and significantly influence an emotional response and the functionality of a design.

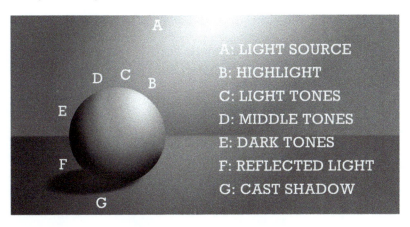

IMAGE 3-12
Chiaroscuro diagram.

Tones are the result of the addition of gray to a hue, which results in variations in the lightness or darkness of a color. They are instrumental in shaping the design's visual appeal, emotional response, and mood. Tones contribute to the establishment of harmony, balance, and contrast within a composition.

In color theory, hues and tones establish the design's attitude and create depth and focus. They distinguish the message from elements, establish consistency and recognition, and improve aesthetics. Color enhances contrast and legibility; it establishes a visual hierarchy; and it establishes a brand identity.

A method to create contrast and depth in a design, utilize brightness with shading. By establishing a light source, the commercial artist employs chiaroscuro which shows highlights with either a gradual blending or a sharp delineation with shadows.

IMAGE 3-13

Chiaroscuro allows graphic artists to create and explore dimension in design.

Color attracts. Lights and darks are seen as tones and can create energy and direct the reader. Vivid, contrasting, and emotionally suggestive colors are especially useful in attracting attention.

IMAGE 3-14

Shaded cones create depth. On white, is the triangle inside the background, or is the triangle on black inside the background.

Shapes

Design is, among other things, the arrangement of shapes. A shape is the form of objects created by an outline or boundary. Balance a large or bright shape against a few smaller or muted ones. Experiment by mentally setting aside the meaning of headlines, copy, visuals, and other elements and treat them as if they were purely form. Shapes exist in the realm of figure and ground only. Grouping and overlapping shapes creates a visually interesting depth. To simplify a design, reduce the total number of shapes by joining or grouping two or three forms.

Typefaces are shapes that can be exploited in display typography and logo design. It is necessary to see the form of letters before complex typographic ideas can be developed based on the visual competition at its presentation location. One option is typesetting content in groups of letters and words. Centered type creates strong profiles.

Areas of white space within type and around columns and pictures forms a shape. Push it in large selections to the perimeter or to the page bottom.

Shape theory

Consumers make emotional judgments about shapes. While these concepts are not steadfast, they are good for the graphic artist to use when designing logos and marketing. Commercial artists use shape as a subtle, subconscious guide in viewers' minds. Shapes have an underlying message to the viewer. Two dimensional shapes are essentially derived from three basic configurations: The square, the triangle, and the circle.

IMAGE 3-15
AI Practicum} Firefly prompt: and drawn circles, ellipses, spheres, that are put together to look like a pillow.

Circular shapes

Ellipses, circles, and spheres are considered soft, comfortable, and safe.

Attributes: cozy, plush, safe, secure and sweet tasting.

Related to pillows, mattresses, and winter coats.

IMAGE 3-16

AI Practicum} Firefly prompt: "hand drawn squares, rectangles, cubes, that are put together to look like a wood box."

Angular shapes

Rectangles, squares, polygons, trapezoids, and cubes are hard and sturdy.

Attributes: strong and durable

Related to bricks, tables, and knives.

IMAGE 3-17

Practicum} Firefly prompts: hand drawn inverted triangles that form a triangle; hand drawn triangles that form a smooth cone and hand drawn pyramids that form a smooth pyramid.

3 sided shapes

Triangles, pyramids, and cones have three sides with three angles and have multiple connotations.

Attributes: tense; risky, leads the eye, balance, imbalance, and spicy tasting.

Related to street signs, pyramids, directions, and movement.

IMAGE 3-18

Practicum} Firefly prompts: upside down inverted triangle floating on blue background falling over and crumbling; ancient Egyptian pyramid; triangle blank yellow triangle street sign with blue sky and clouds in background; copy space; horizontal. Note: AI was unable to generate a 'yield sign" when prompted: create a yield street sign in the street.

Triangles have multiple meanings.

Upright triangles feel stable, solid, and balanced like the ancient pyramids and symbolize greatness or superiority. Inverted triangles feel top-heavy, precarious, and unbalanced suggesting conflict and action. Traffic signs that indicate hazards are triangular, or warnings.

This three sided shape can signify change and is used in many logos. For instance, the three stripes in Adidas's logo create a triangle, which symbolizes a mountain — a metaphor for pushing oneself, overcoming challenges, and being the best, a person can be. Reebok's logo has the "Reebok Delta" which is made up of three separate parts, each symbolizing the physical, mental, and social changes that take place when people push themselves beyond their limits.

Triangles also create movement and lead the viewer's eye in a certain direction. Eyes naturally follow a triangle to the tip. If it is an upright triangle, it will direct the attention vertically. A triangle on its side will move the eye sideways such as on bulleted content. Graphic artists use these shapes as a good directional cues such as directing the audiences' eye toward something.

IMAGE 3-19
Caps are difficult to read since people cannot easily make out the letters based on the shapes.

Text theory

If a graphic artist can think about a page as a three dimensional design, then the side of the building would be the margins. If the type and images are placed at the edge, there is no place for the reader's eye to rest. It is better to have large margin rather than too small of a margin. Margins do not have to be equal, but most individuals are comforted by equal margins. Try a solution where the top and bottom have more space than the sides. If an artist wants to create tension, they can position type near an image or an area of color but not to every edge of the page.

Upper and lower case are easier to read since people can see the shapes of the letters.

Too much or too little space between lines of type makes it difficult for the reader to find the next line of type. Harvard University conducted a study on designing for optimal readability on the internet. It was discovered that type set in all caps reduced readability since the shapes are basically rectangles. Readability is reduced since the words could not be identified by their shapes. The tests found that lowercase and left-aligned type increased readability and comprehension. Unsurprisingly, the study also found that text on a low contrast background made reading difficult. The research revealed that high contrast between type and background can also cause readability problems and suggested that designs with a lower contrast between type and background to be equal to using black on an off-white background.

IMAGE 3-21
Practicum} Numerous Firefly prompt descriptions were used to create three images. Express was used to create the typography but the word CRAP could no be rendered because it violated user guidelines. The elements were combined in Photoshop.

The rules of engaging design

While C.A.R.P. speaks to graphic design in general terms, there is an acronym that specifically addresses how to create engaging design. B.U.L.L.I.T.S. are seven rules or guidelines:

1. Balance:

   If the finished design is difficult to look at, with no space to rest the eye and nothing fits, then the designer has failed. The space, graphics, images and fonts need to visually work together.

2. Use three fonts or less:

   Just because a computer has 1000's of fonts, it does not mean a designer should use a lot of fonts. They should save some for the next design. A company logo does not count as part of this rule—it's really a visual element. Remember a company logo is unique. If the commercial artist uses that same font elsewhere, the logo is no longer unique.

3. Large, medium, and small:

   Try looking at a design that has everything the same size — where do people look and why would they look? If the observer decides it is too much work to try and figure out the message, then perhaps the design was not worth the effort to be laid out correctly. Scale creates a visual hierarchy.

4. Light, medium and dark tones:

   The design should be eye-catching. A marketing piece needs to first get attention and then be memorable. Tones work well when a layout has an image with colors that compliment, contrast, or matches the same colors of type . Type looks better when the family has a bold option which will appear darker than the thinner smaller type.

5. Inspiration from everything:

   Create a mental and physical library of everything that is designed well - even if it is not the complete design but just a small portion.

6. Typos kill a design:

   This rule is an absolute truth — clients are unforgiving and so is anyone else who sees a misspelled word. Use spell check and then read it out loud.

7. Solve the problem:

   If the final piece is a beautiful design that the designer knows other artists are going to ooh and aah over, then the designer needs to throw it away. It isn't that good, and they need to get over it so they can design something really good.

IMAGE 3-22

Graphic Designer: Neal Hettinger

This three-dimensional wrap around project had many considerations that were similar to smaller 3D designs such as packaging: It should display a continuous story on all sides; The textures and colors should be consistent; and the images needed to

use scale to be interesting. To be successful graphically as a building certain features could not be changed: The graphic posters were going in windows so a grid design had to be use; a visual was needed to draw the viewer on both sides of the building; scale must be exaggerated; and it must create curiosity from a distance.

In Time, All Solutions Appear

Design is a process that evolves its solution—uncovering and recognizing design relationships takes time. It's very like the experience of walking into a dark room: it takes time to accustom our eyes to the materials at hand. Design must evolve from basic relationships to more complex, more refined relationships (facing page, top). Start the process by becoming intimately familiar with the content. Read every word of the text. Understand what is being said. Understand, too, why it was written and why it is being published. Then find out who is going to read it and what the reader's motivation and interest is. Finally, develop a strategy for expressing it to the reader's greatest advantage.

Learning Library Exercise — Lines

For this part of the assignment, you will not need a computer. You will need paper or tracing paper and a #2 pencil. You may use pencils and pens of different thickness for this assignment.

Draw the 7 descriptive words below using only lines. Do not draw people, settings, or recognizable images or shapes. The lines should be free form and convey the feeling of the word. Label each of the line drawings by subject. Use one page for each subject.

- Dancing (remember no people)
- Sleeping (remember no Z's)
- Noisy (remember no recognizable images)
- Digging (remember no shovels)
- Dreaming (remember no clouds or sheep)
- Falling (remember no people)
- Scared (remember no screams or wide eyes)

4 Designing with artificial intelligence tools

Learning Objectives

By the end of this chapter, the user will solve marketing projects with Artificial Intelligence prompts. They will be able to explore the ChatGPT options. The reader will be able to summarize how to use Adobe Photoshop contextual task bars.

Professional terminology

Artificial intelligence: A mechanical intelligence that can execute visual and verbal solutions.

Body copy: Content in paragraph form that communicates the message.

ChatGPT: OpenAI language tool that responds from internet and database sources.

Draft: Ideas that need editing for grammar and spelling before publication.

Format: Size, shape, and use of the design in print, motion graphics, or the internet.

Generate: Using the information supplied to produce a potential solution.

Hi-res: An image quality suitable for printing.

Marketing: A strategic plan to promote a brand's service, event, or product.

Menu: A list of options for narrowing down results.

Paraphrase: Rewording phrases or sentences without losing their meaning.

Photoshop: Adobe tool for digitally editing, retouching, and manipulating an image.

Pixel: Bits of visual information that together compose images or communication.

Prompt: Inputs that direct the AI tools in a direction to produce a solution.

Resolution: The quantity of pixels used to produce an image.

Wordsmithing: Editing and revising content.

IMAGE 4-1

Evolution of graphic design.

Practicum} Adobe stock images combined with icon in Adobe Photoshop. Used mask to soften edges with brush tool 0 Hardness. Duplicated layers and added motion filter.

AI will change graphic design

In the May 2023, Artificial Intelligence, which is referred to as AI, became affordable for nearly anyone that had access to the internet. AI is an emerging technology that presents new job prospects for graphic designers. When designers discuss Artificial Intelligence with individuals, they often find that although many people are familiar with the words, they are unsure on how it works and capabilities. A significant number of graphic designers have valid concerns regarding the potential loss of jobs caused by AI, since it can generate images and produce written content. However, successful designers proficient in Photoshop and other design software can grow their skill set by using AI and be prosperous. Designers who fail to become proficient in Artificial Intelligence may risk losing their jobs.

The invention of moveable type revolutionized the book industry. Computers transformed the commercial design business. The explosion of inexpensive stock photography and advancements in mobile phone technology had a significant impact on professional photographers. Photoshop had an enormous effect on retouchers. Advancements in technology will continue to occur, requiring creatives to continuously master new technical knowledge and incorporate it into their creative process; otherwise, they risk being left behind.

For a designer, AI serves as an additional instrument to enhance and improve the creative process. However, it is important to understand that Artificial Intelligence, just like any other software, has limitations. Content creation is based on word prompts so you will need to know more than the average layman by defining solutions with marketing and sales terms. For image creation you need to know design terms and how to verbally describe photo, picture, type ornamentation to assist in the image creation. Artificial Intelligence generators are continuously developing with wider results. This chapter is only an introduction to AI tools. Once a designer delves into AI, they will discover many different options and solutions.

By mastering the skill of utilizing accurate word prompts to generate an image and subsequently modifying the image to align with the desired design, a graphic designer will be on the cutting edge of AI technology. Artificial Intelligence is a highly sought-after term for graphic design job openings. Several affordable Artificial Intelligence options have become available. Google Lab SGE (Search Generative Experience) through Chrome will create images once you register with the Lab. The browser Microsoft Edge has an image creation through Bing. One of the better AI image generators is Adobe Firefly.

Graphic designers with minimal writing skills have various choices for content generation. However, it is important to note that they will still need to revise and improve the written material. While the use of AI content generation may be sufficient for the layout stage of a design, the designer may need the services of a copywriter. An effective workflow consists of using an overall AI content generator such as ChatGPT and applying that content to a refined material generator to another AI tool for content editing such as Quillbot. The generated content may have inaccuracies, excessive wording, and require wordsmithing to be suitable for a final professional message.

Before a graphic designer can start image creation, they must first master the skill of wordsmithing. Since the primary focus of design is communicating the message to a customer, designers must learn the skill of how to prompt AI imaging.

Creating written content

This book does not provide instructions on how to become a copywriter. To enhance the design content, a designer should consider collaborating with a writer. The overall marketing piece will be enhanced when a collective of visionary individuals participate in a collaborative brainstorming session. Innovative solutions will be stronger when a group of imaginative individuals engage in a brainstorming session.

AI composition tools are advantageous and timesaving for written communication. Keep in mind that it is susceptible to errors. It is advisable for the designer to take notes on any significant terms that are discussed during customer encounters. A component of the process should involve conducting an internet search using these terms to identify additional phrases. The message must emphasize the benefits of the service or product and address the issues that consumers are experiencing. Select words that are both actionable and emotive in order to establish a connection with the potential customer. Understanding the broad characteristics of the target market, including age, income, interests, hobbies, and lifestyle, in order to effectively design and write.

Developing a narrative includes ranking the adjectives, action words, and three-to four-word phrases according to significance. Create categories for the descriptions, then reduce the lists to the top 12 elements that are particularly relevant to the goods or services offered by your client. Consider the tone you want to employ for the design as well as the message's intended outcome. Examine the competitors and draw inspiration.

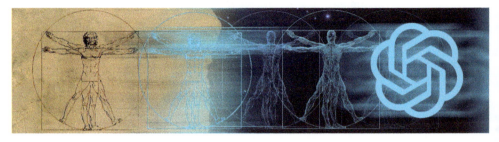

IMAGE 4-2
Image to introduce the ChatGPT AI generation program to design.
AI Practicum} Stock image, Adobe Firefly image, and ChatGPT icon merged in Adobe Photoshop. Used mask and brush tool to soften and blend layers. Set soft light on duplicate GPT layer.

ChatGPT is a helpful tool

Founded in 2015, OpenAI was one of the first companies to provide affordable artificial intelligence. The company became one of the fastest growing online companies in 2023 when they released ChatGPT. About $700,000 is spent by OpenAI each day to run ChatGPT. Subscriptions are their primary revenue stream, aside from investors. Although ChatGPT is free, during peak hours it may be extremely slow or even unavailable. ChatGPT-4 is available to subscribers at all times for $20 a month. Users can also generate text prompt images in addition to creating material, although this functionality is limited unless subscribers buy more tokens. There is a corporate subscription available, but the cost varies based on usage and user count.

OpenAI does not fact check and since the ChatGPT content is from data bases and the internet, errors are extremely possible. Verify the legitimacy since according to Forbes Magazine, there was a personal injury litigation in which a counsel utilized ChatGPT to reference fraudulent cases. ChatGPT is not great with arithmetic or checking for plagiarism. Teachers have tried using GPT to check for plagiarism and AI generation, but ChatGPT remains neutral on whether compositions were written by a human or AI.

The potential for Artificial Intelligence applications appears limitless. AI can be used to generate freelancing contracts for graphic designers and to analyze and evaluate marketing campaigns. There are artificial intelligence systems that can generate visuals and provide advice. ChatGPT services may include a disclaimer such as: "While we have safeguards, ChatGPT may give you inaccurate information. It's not intended to give advice." At https://chat.openai.com/auth/login create a free account.

To avoid creating an account, there is an option to utilize either Merlin or ChatGPT Writer. Open AI will send you an email for identity verification, ensuring that only authorized individuals may access it. Subsequently, you will be required to provide your name and birth date. Subsequently, you will provide them with a telephone number to transmit an additional code.

Demonstration: AI Generation in ChatGPT

Navigate to OpenAi at openai.com/chatgpt and scroll down to the "Ask me anything" a section. If you become a freelancer, the "Teach me to negotiate" section may be of use later but for now scroll down to "Plans" and select "Free > Try on web "which will take you to the prompt field.

Create content for a flyer: 10% discount on gutter guards, expires March 31, Holmes Guttering LLC, 18 years service, Dallas, 10 year warranty.

ChatGPT can make mistakes. Consider checking important information.

IMAGE 4-3

Screen grab of AI ChatGPT prompt window.

In the Message field type: Create ad for Gutters: 10% discount on gutter guards, expires March 31, Holmes Guttering LLC, 18 years of service, Dallas, 10-year warranty.

From those few word prompts, basic sells copy will be generated: Ensure your home is safeguarded! Holmes Guttering LLC presents an exclusive offer: 10% off on Gutter Guards! With 18 years of dedicated service in Dallas and a solid 10-year warranty, trust us to keep your gutters free from debris and your home protected. But act fast! This offer expires on March 31st!

Note that GPT rectified words that were not hyphenated. The wording is slightly inaccurate—the initial sentence gives the impression that you are a security firm. You should consider replacing it with a phrase such as "The affordable way to protect your home from weather damage." Your gutter client informed you in the briefing that the guards do not completely eliminate the need for maintenance. Therefore, it is advisable not to include the statement "keep your gutters free from debris and your home protected" in the advertisement. Conducting research on "gutter guards" and engaging in discussions with your customer provides an advantage in this context, as artificial intelligence retrieves information from the internet without discerning its accuracy. It is imperative to always verify the accuracy of the information.

GPT used an 18-word prompt to write a 54-word advertisement content that should fit into a layout without overwhelming the reader. Now the wordsmithed verbiage would read: The affordable way to protect your home from weather damage! Holmes Guttering LLC presents an exclusive offer: 10% off on Gutter Guards! With 18 years of dedicated service in Dallas and a solid 10-year warranty, trust us to install the perfect gutters for your home. But act fast! This offer expires on March 31st!

As an example of difference distinction between narratives, input the prompt "Create content for a gutter flyer:" followed by the same prompt words to generate sales copy for a flyer. In addition to receiving content, observe that it is providing a verbal flow with a hierarchy

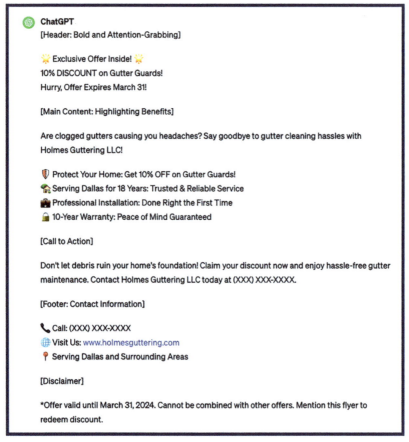

IMAGE 4-4
Screen grab of AI ChatGPT prompt window.

The parenthetical description statements should be deleted. It appears that GPT regards itself as a designer and has incorporated graphic elements. The ChatGPT design concept lacks professionalism and is simplistic. The flyer's design is your responsibility. By enrolling, ChatGPT will retain your history, enabling you to access the content you have requested in the future. To use GPT at a later time, save https://chat.openai.com/auth/login as a bookmark to log in to your free account.

There are numerous AI content writers available, but graphic artists should always check the facts. Marketers use these AI generators to produce content for blogs, posts, social media, advertising, and flyers. They are not recommended for articles and books due to their lack of originality and potential for causing problems. Both free and paid artificial intelligence generators are available for use:

1. ChatGpt has flexible narrative options with 3000 word limit per use.
2. ContentBot has templates with a daily limit of 2000 words.
3. Copy.ai can automate tedious actions. It has a daily limit of 2000 words per month.
4. Jasper AI creates product descriptions, company bios. It has a 7-day free trial and then a monthly charge.
5. HyperWrite creates stories with a monthly limit based on credits.

AI paraphrasing tools can correct typos, grammatical errors, and adjust misplaced punctuation. Five popular AI paraphrasing tools that are available for free:

1. Grammarly spots plagiarism. It has a 150,000 word daily limit.
2. Quilbot can enhance content with a paraphrase limit of 125 words at a time
3. Wordtune can summarize and has a limit of 10 rewrites and AI suggestions.
4. Ahrefs has a search engine optimization site audit tool, and the tool utilizes paid credits.

At QuillBot.com/flow a designer has the opportunity to create a complimentary account by either logging in with your email address or choosing from the provided alternatives. Then, complete the brief questionnaire and navigate to the paraphraser option. Choose a voice from a variety of options including Standard, Academic, Formal, or Creative. However, only the Standard and Fluency options are accessible without subscription. Copy and paste the modified GPT material to the advertising and select the paraphrase button. Specific terms will be highlighted in the color orange, suggesting that they can be substituted with a different term

The cost-effective method of preventing weather damage to your house! 10% off Gutter Guards is a special deal from Holmes Guttering LLC! You can count on us to install the ideal gutters for your property since we have 18 years of dedicated service in Dallas and a dependable 10-year warranty. But act fast! This promotion ends on March 31st!

This new verbiage is a little wordier at 59. You have the option to reword the content by choosing the select "Shorten" option. This function is a subscription option.

IMAGE 4-5
Screen grab of AI created image options with Adobe Firefly.

Using AI tools to create images

Images generated with AI tools such as Firefly are not ready for publication. The images may provide inspiration, but they should be adjustment and revisions by graphic artists. Firefly has generative fill, and the Photoshop contextual task bar's generative fill is highly recommended because of its options. By having greater control and the ability to make adjustments, graphic artists may effectively create the image or effect they envisioned. Firefly is available as part of the Creative Cloud membership, or it can be used for free, albeit with a limited amount of uses. Additionally, there is the option to make payments on a monthly or yearly basis. Nevertheless, it is important to bear in mind that this tool is merely a means to an end. In order to effectively utilize it, graphic artists must engage in critical thinking, strategic planning, and utilize other design tools to complete their concepts.

Begin by selecting words that accurately convey the intended meaning of the message. Document the visual objectives. The objective is to generate a number of solutions that can be imported as layered files into Adobe Photoshop and modified to suit the design and communication.

Go to https://firefly.adobe.com/ and explore the available options. Adobe Firefly is unable create transparent backgrounds on the images it creates so describe the image with simple backgrounds to later knock out in Photoshop. Optional AI generators are available such as Optional AI generators are available such as Midjourney's new AI image which has monthly charges.

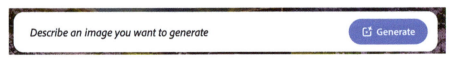

IMAGE 4-6
Screen grab of AI Firefly prompt window.

Demonstration: AI Generation in Adobe Firefly

The design features an illustration portraying robot hands holding a crystal sphere. A potential description for the Firefly prompt could be "robotic hands holding a crystal ball." However, the process of creating an image in Photoshop will require a significant amount of time to eliminate contrasting elements and the background in order to create room for text and add a compelling background. Prompt Firefly to generate "robot hands holding crystal ball with light blue gradation background; copy space focused." Firefly will provide four alternatives for you to choose from in order to proceed. Click on the image to download for possible use later in Photoshop.

IMAGE 4-7
Screen grab of AI Firefly options windows.

To revise the visual, there are choices located on the left-hand tab menu. Choose from the following directions in the menu on the left side of the site: General Settings choose an aspect ratio; Content Type select Art. Effects select Movements and an art style that was discussed in Chapters 9 or 10. The composition should display the reference image for the successive generation. Disregard the images in References; Click the Generate button and select an image or multiple images to download.

This image can be manipulated for the flyer. In Photoshop replace the background with a new background created either in Photoshop, Firefly, or a stock photo. Adjust the contrast, lengthen the robot arms, and give the design a focus. When the image is ready to add the type and show your typography skills. It is advisable to include the disclaimer: The image was partially made using AI tools such as Adobe Firefly and Photoshop AI and was significantly enhanced by human intelligence.

IMAGE 4-8

Screen grab of AI created image options with Adobe Firefly.

Use design terms with AI

Experiment with creating images in Adobe Firefly. Graphic artists can bring design styles into the image creation. In Photo Grid 1 which was prompted with "art deco style robot hands holding crystal ball, space for text" creates a different impression than Photo Grid 2 which was prompted with "Bauhaus style robot hands holding crystal ball space for text." Photo Grid 3 had a different direction and target market with "dark moody photo real robot hands holding crystal ball space for text" than Photo Grid 4 which was "cheerful anime drawing of robot hands holding crystal ball space for text."

IMAGE 4-9
Screen grab of AI created image options with Adobe Firefly.

Demonstration: AI Generation in Adobe Express

Adobe Express can be accessed through the Creative Cloud. This tool is beneficial for generating image posts for social media and internet advertisements by utilizing design callouts to produce artificial intelligence text effects.

Navigate to the Text Effects section and input the desired text into the prompt field. The background can be transparent, which is favorable since it will save time. Remember the fundamental principles of effective design and maintain a straightforward approach. Excessive use of flowery language might reduce the readability of the content block. To eliminate an element that interferes with content, attempt using the Generative Fill Select feature, but the object selection tool might be more effective.

Practice 1: Video title card using artificial intelligence generation.

IMAGE 4-10

Produce a title card to be incorporated into a video commercial with animated motion graphics. Enter the phrase "3-dimensional word NOW with science fiction effects" into the Text to Image prompt field. Adobe Express offers four solutions—select one option to use. From the top panel, select Background Color and choose the option for None. Click the image and on the left side panel choose the Remove Background option. Scroll downward on the left panel to access all the available type effects and choose different textures until the appropriate visual outcome is attained. Click on the download icon located in the upper black header.

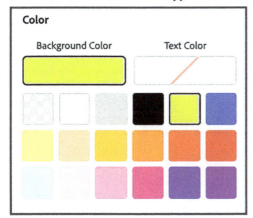

IMAGE 4-11

Practice 2: AI generation of magazine print ad headline.

IMAGE 4-12

67

You want to create an artsy image with just type for a sale advertisement.

Text: On Sale Now | Prompt: 3D splashy secondary colors | Font: Acumin Pro

Note that the font family is not indicated by the prompt. Use the menu on the right to select a font. Download the image to be used later.

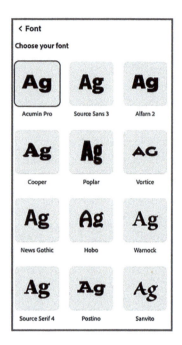

IMAGE 4-13

Exercise 3: Creating an AI generated headline for an EDDM®.

IMAGE 4-14

This direct mail item, known as EDDM® (Every Door Direct Mail®), is specifically created to be eye-catching and dynamic. It is delivered by the USPS to every residence within a particular zip code. Designers often include visual effects and edited pictures into the background. Utilize the provided text prompt below. Select the "Loose" option for the form. Download for future reference.

T: Fourth of July Sale | P: Simple Fireworks primary colors graffiti feel | F: Postino | C: Black

Avoid becoming a graphic artist who overly depends on Firefly (or similar AI techniques for picture generation) to address all design challenges. Visually appealing graphics may capture attention, but they are seldom remembered or effectively convey the brand's message. Graphic designers must utilize artificial intelligence as one of their many tools in order to fulfill their need for creativity and take pride in their creations.

Demonstration: AI Generation in Adobe Photoshop

Practice 4: Resize and retouch an AI image.

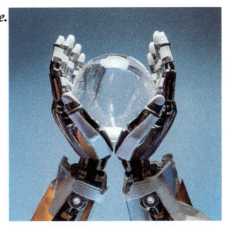

IMAGE 4-15

Artificial intelligence tools do not know how to add areas for type and backgrounds where the type will be readable. Even though the prompt states save room for content, AI does not understand the end goal and assumes the image is the final step. Designers will need to clean up the image created earlier in Adobe Firefly and add a background using Artificial intelligence generated by Photoshop. If you have forgotten some of the steps in the directions, refer to your Photoshop textbook. Hopefully, you have held on to all your software books for later use.

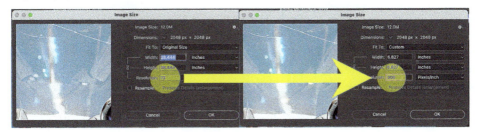

IMAGE 4-16

In Photoshop, open the AI robot hands file and select the "image size" option. Disable the resample option and increase the image's dimensions from 72 to 300 pixels per inch to optimize the artwork for printing. To maintain quality while enlarging the image, it is possible to increase its size by a maximum of 120%. Utilize a mask to eliminate the background. To highlight any areas where the mask removal was unsuccessful, add a gray layer as a background.

IMAGE 4-17

Practicum} Areas to clean up in Adobe Photoshop. Use clone stamp tool, spot healing brush, healing brush adjust contrast and increase saturation.

To enhance the image, employ several tools such as the clone stamp tool, spot healing brush, and healing brush. To increase the appeal of the image, modify the contrast and raise the saturation. Utilize the magnification tool to scrutinize the artwork and identify the specific regions that require refinement. The appearance of this robot picture should possess a level of luster and reflectivity comparable to that of a new automobile. Utilize the lasso tool with a feather value of 2 pixels and choose certain regions to apply a blur effect.

Practice 5: Generate and retouch

IMAGE 4-18

Screen grab of Photoshop AI generation window Contextual Task Bar.

Open a new file with dimensions of 9 inches by 12 inches, 300 dots per inch, RGB, and access the contextual task bar window. Key in the Mac Command-A or PC Control-A shortcut to select the entire layer, and then click on Generative Fill. In the prompt field enter the phrase "looking straight up into outer space with streaks of blue, violet, and orange colors" and select Generate. Examine the options and adjust the prompt until the background artwork is engaging. Transfer this artwork to the Robot file dragging or copying and inserting it into the layers.

Create a new layer and Prompt: galaxy background with stars with star glow. On another layer, in the center of the crystal ball place the letters AI, use filter spherize, add colors, select a few of the different layer blend modes. Retouch, knock out, and mask the images to develop an eye-catching picture with room for the headline at the top and body copy with call to action and logo at the bottom.

IMAGE 4-19

AI Practicum} Created image with Adobe Firefly for robot hands holding globe. In Adobe Illustrator created characters AI as bands of color, merged all elements in Adobe Photoshop. Used mask and set layer with overlay. Flatten image, duplicated and ran high pass on top layer. Set layer at 90% opacity and soft light.

Demonstration: AI Generation in Adobe Illustrator

Practice 6: AI generation of Flat Design Style cartoon cityscape design.

IMAGE 4-20

In the Illustrator navigation bar under Window options open Properties table to access the artificial intelligence vector tools. Select the Text to Vector Graphics and choose Icon which is under the Styles section. Specify to keep the vector image Minimal and in the prompt input "create a city park logo with sun and clouds."

Practice 7: AI generation of a drop cap for children's book.

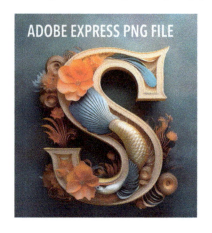 

IMAGE 4-21

Utilize two distinctly different artificial intelligence algorithms to generate a dropcap "S" for the initial page paragraph of a book. Utilize the provided prompt and description to create the letter 'S' using Adobe Express, and subsequently use the same wording in Adobe Illustrator. Note that the Express files provided are in the PNG format, which presents certain limitations such as a maximum usage size and challenges in adjusting and revising them. The Illustrator file offers a vector format that allows for easier manipulation and usage at larger scales. However, the Illustrator design is somewhat basic. For future use, download the picture files.

T: The letter with flowers and 3D and a fishlike texture | Choose a text effect

Practice 8: AI generation icon for company logo.

IMAGE 4-22

AI Prompt 1: The lowercase y with steel 3D on a white background
AI Prompt 2: The lowercase y with shiny steel dimension on a white background

In the Adobe Express and Illustrator software implement the artificial intelligence options to create a logo icon based on the letter 'Y.' Enter each of the provided prompts into both AI programs generators. Note that Express supplies a more dynamic solution which is difficult to adjust and revise. The Illustrator file provides a vector file but not eye-catching. Download the image to be used later.

Demonstration: QR Generation in Adobe Express

QR codes are prevalent because of their usefulness in marketing. The codes can take shoppers to website landing pages or input contact information into a digital address book. Marketers realize that using mobile phone cameras to scan codes is a cost-effective method of making it easy for potential customers to record a website without having to write it down. Graphic designers have many applications for QR codes, including vehicle wraps, tattoos, packaging, jigsaw puzzles, contests, and event marketing.

To create a website-directed QR code, in Adobe Express select QR Generator, which will open a window. After entering the website domain, select open in editor. Basic designs are available, or eye-catching codes can be developed through the personalization of the style and color to match a company's brand.

1. Enter the URL including the https.

2. Select style and follow the prompts on Dots, Border, and Markers.

3. Open in editor and select the Image to open the image editor.

4. Select Effects>Duotone>Custom where you can use a provided color or select a custom color. Remember the QR code needs contrast to be scanned.

5. Resize to 1080X 1080px

6. Add a brand

7. Download.

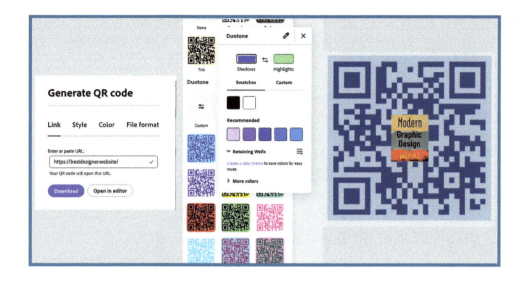

IMAGE 4-23

Learning Library Exercise — Layout AI creations with InDesign

1. Using InDesign, on letter sized pages, put your name and date on the top left of each page. Choose a font that is readable but represents your personality.

2. Import your AI creation 1-8 from this chapter. Consider space and scale in a visually pleasing presentation.

3. In a short paragraph, discuss how you would update and revise the designs for each AI creation, as well as which software you would use, such as Photoshop or Illustrator.

4. Export the InDesign file by creating a print quality pdf.

Typography is more than a pretty face

Learning Objective

In this chapter, the student will be able to classify the different typestyles. They will be able to explain the use of upper and lower case type. The learner will be able to reproduce how to create focus on the message.

Professional terminology

Ampersand: The symbol representing 'and' derived from the Latin "et".

Cursive: Writing where individual characters are joined together to form individual words.

Display: Typeface used in headlines that are strong or eye-catching.

Drop Cap: A stylized initial letter or character that assists readers' navigation.

Embellishment: An attractive feature or decorative element used in design or typography.

Filigree: Delicate ornamental dividers and borders formed to separate content and space.

Flourish: An elaborate flowing curve on a character.

Gutenberg: Credited as the first Western inventor to print using a press and moveable type.

Italic: A sloping or angled typeface used specifically for emphasis or differentiation.

Lowercase: Shorter non-capital letters with ascenders and descenders to improve readability.

Phonetically: Letters with a direct relationship between sounds and symbols.

Phonograms: Symbols for vocal sounds.

Sans serif: Characters without the short finishing lines on the end of the strokes.

Serif: In certain typefaces, the little projections that begin or end a letter stroke.

Uppercase: Capital letters.

IMAGE 5-1

Example of fonts as images.

AI Practicum} Two artificial intelligence images were generated with Adobe Firefly. The selected settings for the first option included art, Bauhaus, and weird lighting. The prompt requested designs featuring the phrase "alphabet styles and colorful." The selected settings for option two were art, specifically the Bauhaus movement, and a focus on brilliant color. The design would need various font faces in distinct font styles, together with a bright background and in 3D artwork. The final prompt was "font faces in different font styles and colorful background, 3D illustration, copy space focus." After being retouched, it was placed beside the first option using Adobe Photoshop. The first option's alphabet's background was removed, and the remaining image was adjusted for brightness, contrast, and exposure. The layers were duplicated and merged to apply the High Pass filter with a value of 100 and adjusted the layer to soft light mode with an opacity of 100%.

Fonts have different faces

Visualize a movie title that resembles a font made to look like a crayon. Upon viewing this movie title, individuals are likely to perceive it as a production specifically targeted towards children. A daring and adventurous pirate movie would necessitate typefaces whose structure, weight, and form elicit that same feeling. Typefaces create an emotional reaction that is influenced by its color and size. The reader will subconsciously link past experiences with typefaces.

Designers should detach themselves from their reactions and bias to a specific font by selecting the most suitable typeface for the composition. They cannot presume their reaction to a font is universally shared by others. An essential aspect of being a typographer involves understanding the historical context and purpose behind the creation of a font. To learn every font and know its origin is not practical. Fonts can be categorized, which helps in selecting the appropriate font. Once a designer understands why and when a font was created, it is easier to narrower down the options to an appropriate font. Understanding the history of writing is crucial in determining the appropriate design or font for an historical context.

Designers struggle with three key areas when trying to solve a problem: Fonts, Colors, and Space. Expert designers do not rely on guesswork when it comes to typography. Selecting a font is not a random or careless decision. The primary function of typography is communicating a message such as recording an event, warning of a weather movement, discussing a political rally, or teaching from a textbook. The message dictates the font family.

If the page is filled with type, the designer may want to use a condensed font to occupy less space and create the illusion of a smaller amount of text for the reader. People tend to dislike reading excessive amounts of content. If the intention of the composition is to communicate a sense of elegance, it might be advisable to use a wider font that is not tightly letterspaced. Another option is to add more pages or edit the content to less words.

Fonts can be viewed as a sort of texture to create an emotional response, but it is essential for the font to effectively communicate information. Language consists of both oral communication and written expression, requiring anyone who wants to write or type, must use some type of font. When people communicate verbally, they can utilize intonations to provide clarity to words and provoke responses by adjusting the volume and pace of their speech. To a degree, fonts are the same. They communicate semantics and syntax based on the structure, weight, size, color, and case. Using all uppercase letters is shouting message at the reader. Small barely readable type such as a copyright indicates to the reader that this information is required but not important to the message and be read.

The importance of font choice in graphic design cannot be stressed enough since people react differently to fonts. Typefaces can make text appear attractive, compact, or easy to read by reducing the length of the content. Knowing typographic history and context helps designers make informed choices to narrow down the options. To communicate effectively, like vocal tones, typography should be used to help relay a message rather than seen as a decoration.

Example of Roman writing on a tablet with illustration of Legionnaire to grab attention.

Practicum} Adobe Stock searched for illustrations, jpeg, horizontal orientation, and include people. Search phrase: "roman soldier in front of cracked wall."

Fonts have a history

Studying history is often dreaded by new graphic designers. To determine the appropriate font for a layout, a designer should possess a certain level of understanding on the historical background of the font.

Written communication has been around since the Neanderthals utilized cave paintings to record events. These graphics have transformed into symbols that are now in use. For instance, a heart represents affection or compassion, while an iron symbol on a clothing label indicates that the garment may be safely ironed without causing any harm to the fabric.

It is quite likely that the Egyptians were the first civilization to abandon the use of rudimentary symbols in their communications. They created sound drawings to depict words and syllables that have similar or comparable sounds. Over a span of 3000 years, they progressively adopted the usage of phonograms, wherein a symbol represented a vocal sound, as a method exclusively dedicated to representing syllables. The Egyptian writing evolved into the form known as hieroglyphics. These phonograms were the next step before forming a word.

The next stage in the evolution of writing was brought about by the Phoenicians. They were businessmen who engaged in commerce, becoming the forerunners to modern entrepreneurs. In Egypt, they made cash investments, engaged in trade in Crete, and conducted sales in Athens, for the purpose of financial gain. The Phoenicians had a clear need for an alphabet, although they did not require the elegant and ornamental phonograms used by the Egyptians. The Phoenicians placed record keeping as their highest priority. As a result, Phoenician writing did not utilize decorative embellishments, was very easy to read, and quick to write down. The Phoenician writing system was solely alphabetic, embellishments This alphabet was the initial application of a phonetic system. This alphabet was the first implementation of a phonetic system.

When someone has difficulty reading a word, they have been taught to sound it out by each letter a method known as pronouncing the word phonetically—as the Phoenicians did. While transacting business in Greece, the Phoenicians also shared their business-oriented alphabet.

The Greeks subsequently introduced vowels, new characters, and curved shapes to the evolving alphabet. As the Western alphabet developed, its visual characteristics emerged. The Latin alphabet originated from Greek letterforms and was passed on by the Etruscans, an ancient civilization in Italy.

The Romans modified and assimilated the Greek alphabet, as did the Greek deities. Capital letters were developed by the Romans specifically to create signs. Monuments and structures have carved these formal letterforms onto their surfaces. Important manuscripts frequently used these letterforms. These letters, engraved in stone, follow the same principles as handwritten letters.

The Romans made contributions to our alphabet through the development of handwriting. Cursive writing was developed with the intention of expediting written communication. Imagine a Roman general sending a message to a centurion by having a scribe carve out the message in a stone or wood tablet. They needed a faster way to communicate so they devised a new method of writing known as cursive on papyrus, wax, and clay. Cursive derived from the Latin term running hand was a more efficient way to communicate. Today, we utilize this form of writing when we are not engaged in texting but rather transcribing onto paper. This faster style of writing enabled the hand to draw connected characters to compose a message.

Calligraphy developed from cursive, although this does not imply that the letters are consistently joined together. Scribes and monks devised techniques to adorn and refine the alphabet, transforming it into a form of artistic expression. The early calligraphers discovered that by looking at the page itself, rather than just the words, it could be perceived as a texture.

The form of the letters along with weight, structure, color, and proportions could create beautiful graphic image as well as communicate a message.

A graphic artist with a knowledge of font history understands when it is appropriate to incorporate symbols into their designs. For example, when designing an advertisement for a music event, a graphic artist might use symbols like a G clef. Similarly, when creating a logo for a Greek playhouse, they might choose a font that resembles the style of that era, such as a Trajan-style font.

IMAGE 5-3

AI illustration of Guttenberg in press room set in the 1400s.

AI Practicum} Two AI images were created with Adobe Firefly. The settings for the first image included art, Art Nouveau, and acrylic paint. The prompt read, "Painting of old German Johannes Gutenberg looking at a page from a printing press, copy space focused." The settings for the second prompt included elements of art, Art Nouveau, and acrylic paint. The prompt was "Painting of an old printing press shop in the Middle Ages, copy space focused." We retouched and merged the image using Adobe Photoshop, eliminating the Gutenberg background with a mask and object selection tool, positioning the image against the press room backdrop, making two brightness/ contrast adjustments, and adjusting the exposure by -4.

Printing press changed communication

Prior to the development of cursive writing, the first form of writing consisted solely of capital letters. Due to their linear nature, these marks were more amenable to being incised into wood or sculpted into stone. The development of lowercase letters occurred with the introduction of wax tablets and papyrus leaves. These mediums not only accelerated the process of writing, but also had the advantages of being more cost-effective and convenient for transportation. The development of parchment and subsequently paper facilitated more efficiencies in terms of time and expenses.

IMAGE 5-4

Example of a calligraphic page designed by scribe in the prepress era.

AI Practicum} Three artificial intelligence images were created using Adobe Firefly and Photoshop. The initial settings in Firefly encompassed art, the Middle Ages, and calligraphy. The initial image's trigger phrase was "ornamental calligraphy on parchment." The second artwork had filigree, flowery embellishments, and earth tones in its settings. The given prompt was "a decorative frame for a Bible during the Middle Ages, displayed on a cork board." The third artwork showcased a fusion of painting, calligraphy, and highlighting. The given prompt was "A letter Q with a textured pattern of flowers." In Photoshop the background was knocked out and photo of cork board edges blended with photo of parchment, retouched edges, added color on center with Gaussian noise blur. Adjusted the brightness/contrast and adjusted the exposure.

In addition to these forms of communication, methods of writing also underwent development. During the Middle Ages, quill pens were introduced as a replacement for sharpened reeds, enabling better control for calligraphy and drawing.

Johannes Gutenberg is renowned for inventing the printing press, however, among designers, he is most recognized for his innovation of moveable type. This technology gave rise to a novel sector known as printing. Printers necessitate the keen eye of a designer to carefully arrange and select typefaces.

Before to the invention of the printing press, only the church leaders and very rich nobility could afford a Bible. Monks devoted lifetimes to transcribing the Bible. The scribes meticulously transcribed the Bible onto parchment or vellum, painstakingly reproducing it letter by letter, word by word, and page by page, resulting in an accurate copy of the Bible. It is estimated it took up to 48 months to write a Bible. Each page was a work of art with the color, calligraphy, and filigree.

IMAGE 5-5

Example of pages in the Gutenberg Bible.
Practicum} The Adobe Stock image search was conducted using the following parameters: image, jpeg, horizontal orientation, and the search term "Gutenberg Bible."

Despite printing the Bible with a press, publishing was not significantly faster, as it took approximately 3 years to print the entire Bible. However, it printed hundreds of pages per day. Consequently, over the course of three years, Gutenberg was able to print hundreds of Bibles to sell. To make sure people could read it and therefore purchase it, he designed the characters to imitate the script used by scribes. He designed over 240 characters to include text, punctuation, initial caps, and decorative borders. Gutenberg created heavier type for the different books and chapters.

The printing press transformed the production of the Bible from a laborious process of handwritten transcription to an affordable book that was accessible to upper-class and middle-class readers. Gutenberg manually printed each sheet by spreading it out on the form, rolling ink onto the movable type, and then turning a hand press, which pushed the ink onto the page. Each page was meticulously hung to dry. Around 1455, he published the Gutenberg Bible, which is also known as the Bible. The initial typeface he employed on a printing press was the Bibel font, which was named after the German name for the Bible. He attempted to incorporate crimson into a few pages; however, in the end, he opted for black. In subsequent revisions, he commissioned calligraphers and

A little over 300 years later in 1876, type composing machines were developed by Charles Moore who also invented typewriters. Innovators transformed these machines into what became a Linotype which produced lines of words as single strips of metal. Newspapers and magazines benefited from this faster form of setting type.

Phototypesetting replaced this technique in the 1950's. The production artist experienced numerous sleepless nights due to the need to precisely describe the font type, weight, size, and leading to accommodate a specific area. They would then have to wait for several days to receive the sheet back see if it was spaced correctly. If the typesetting did not fit and if time was a concern, the artist would use exacto knives cut each line to fit. Typeset pages had rubber cement, spray glue, or hot wax put on the back and then rolled onto a type of smooth illustration board or chip board. The production artist would then add crop marks, overlays of ink and rubylith to mark areas for color and images to be placed. During the typesetting period of design, graphic artist had to be very skilled with their hands to draw type and marks for printing made with T-squares, triangles, rapidiographs, and compasses.

The introduction of laser image setup technology in the late 1980s allowed for the conversion of computer files into physical prints on photo paper. In the mid 1990's, artists were able to email files directly to the print shop. The technician would produce negatives to create plates that were utilized on an offset press operated by a pressman.

Currently, designers transmit portable document files (PDFs) to generate metal or paper plates for printing, or to directly send the file to a digital printer by simply clicking the print command. This approach is more straightforward and less stressful, although it does present challenges.

Just as the original pressmen were responsible for the laying of the type and all that entailed, the content is now in the designers' hands. Due to the modern technology of computer design, proofing for spelling mistakes, incorrect grammar, and poorly written content is ultimately the responsibility of the graphic designer. Several people may sign off on a design, but they will assume someone else proofed the content. That "someone" is the designer.

Usage of Type

Graphic designers utilize use the term "uppercase" to indicate capital letters and "lowercase" to represent non-capital letters. The cases used to store movable items inspired these terms. When composing a page, the pressman used two compartments to store type. In order to extract letters from the drawer and use them on the press's surface, the printer positioned the cases in a cabinet in front of the press. Before inking, they pulled the letters and placed them in their correct reverse order on the galley. The capital letters were stored in the top drawer since they were used less frequently, resulting in a lighter box. The pressmen used the capitals for brief lines of text, such as headlines. The cabinet was exceedingly heavy due to the quantity of moveable items in the bottom drawer. Consequently, it is designated as 'lowercase' for non-capital ones and 'uppercase' for capital letters.

IMAGE 5-6

Example of metal type for letterpress printing.
Practicum} Adobe Stock searched for image, jpeg, horizontal orientation, and exclude people. Search phrase: "collection of letterpress movable characters."

For the customer to continue reading after the headline, the body content needed to be upper and lower case. 500 years ago, pressmen realized readers would understand the message if it was upper and lower case and buy more of the book, newspaper, and magazines. It is surprising that many advertisements and posts are all caps today. These creatives are either not concerned about the consumer reading the message and are focused on the aesthetics or do not know realize that the caps will not be read.

Since printing a page with moveable type reversed the letters, they had to be set backwards and from right to left. Therefore, the phrase "pay attention to your p's and q's" emerged. In the western world, people read from left to right and from top to bottom, so designers must consider the layout's visual flow to ensure they lead the reader around the page.

For the public to read newspapers, books, magazines, and selling sheets, the type characters had to be recognizable in different languages. German characters are different than Spanish letterforms which is one reason different font styles were created. Not everyone wanted to learn 240 different characters, so printers looked for ways to shorten the alphabet by focusing on the character's structures and weights.

The first problem word problem was the since th did not sound correct when spelled out. If you sound out the letter T it would be hard tee which is only pronounced that way in about 30% of the words with a T. An H would be a soft aitch. Put the T and H together in the and technically there would be the incorrect sounds of a hard T and soft H. Since this was not the tongue on the teeth sound that used for th, the calligraphers used a different letter.

Since this sound was not produced by placing the tongue between the teeth, the calligraphers opted for a different letter. In 8th century England this sound was represented in the alphabet with the letter þ called a Thorn. Around the time when the printer was created, the thorn was represented by a y. Movies of England in the Middle Ages show signs such as Ye Oldee Shoppe, but the Ye had been pronounced as thee. After a while to save on the costs of fonts, th took the replaced y.

Printers finally gave up and used the th even though it was not correct. It is so complicated that the International Phonetic Alphabet has created their own letters to signify that sound.

IMAGE 5-7

Example of how Latin characters 'Et 'evolved to and ampersand in Latin.
Practicum} Designed in Adobe Illustrator, the typefaces for E and = were Nanum Brush Script, Ampersand was Norman Script, and 't' and crossbar were created from Adage Script.

In order to conserve time and money, pressmen progressively eliminated letters from the alphabet and replaced them with existing characters. The ampersand '&' was maintained as a single character but was used as a symbol. "Et" is the Latin term that is equivalent to "and" in English. Fusion of the letters "e" and "t" was required to create this symbol. This symbol is a convenient option for designers to incorporate into headlines and logos. The decorative elements and ornamental details of the ampersand can contribute to the aesthetic allure of a design.

It is reasonable to assume that all 26 letters of the English alphabet are pronounced identically throughout the English-speaking glob but that would be incorrect. The letter 'Z' is referred to as 'zed' in Canada and England, while it is pronounced as 'zee' in the United States. The term "aunt" may be pronounced as "ahnt" or like the insect, even within the United States. A competent designer evaluates the target audience's use of colloquialisms and vernacular.

Do not assume everyone reads the same and everyone has the same eyesight. Baby boomers (born 1946–1964) and young children also known as Gen A (born 2010–2025) may need a larger type such as 12 points for body copy and they read complete sentences. Generation X (born 1965–1980) may prefer 10 or 11 points while Millennials (1981–1996) like to read 10 point and read phrases. Gen Zers (born 1997–2012) use texting so they are used to reading 8 and 9 points with abbreviations instead of phrases.

A headline can be easily legible with a brief glance, such as, "STOP THAT". Readers do not read individual letters or words, but rather comprehend phrases as a whole. This implies that a designer has the ability to utilize a compact and captivating typeface, enabling the headline to be prominently shown and captivate the reader's attention. Headlines can be compact when there is ample space on the page and minimal text. The negative space surrounding the little headline can be as captivating, drawing the reader's attention and compelling them to pause and read.

Keep headlines short, especially if you are using all caps. "Stop that noise pollution from taking over the city park" is very long and imagine it all caps STOP THAT NOISE POLLUTION FROM TAKING OVER THE CITY PARK. Not easily deciphered so a reader skips it and moves on.

However, the content must be easily readable. Individuals engage in the act of reading by processing not only individual letters and words but also by comprehending entire lines of text. The letters cannot be ornate, unrecognizable, or inadequately spaced. If the lines of text are excessively lengthy or the characters inadequately spaced, it will result in the potential reader losing interest and moving on. Designers ensure that the smaller text remains legible in order to effectively convey the message to clients.

Typographers need to know the medium the design is being used in so they can decide space between letters, words, and lines of type. If it is being printed, they need to be careful about how small they set the letters, so they type does not fill in when the ink spreads during printing.

Imagine a paragraph of just 2 sentences all in caps. Who wants to read that block of text? It is work and the reader will skip it.

STOP THAT NOISE POLLUTION FROM TAKING OVER THE CITY PARK. YOU MAY HAVE NOTICED THAT THE NEW ROAD MAINTENANCE DEPARTMENT

HAS STARTED USING THE CITY PARK FOR STORING THEIR HUGE EARTH MOVING VEHICLES SUCH AS EXCAVATORS, AND BACKHOE LOADERS.

Stop that noise pollution from taking over the city park. You may have noticed that the new road maintenance department has started using the city park for storing their huge earth moving vehicles such as excavators, backhoe loaders. When they start up in the morning not only is everyone in the city park and playground startled and unable to talk to each other, but the homes surrounding the park are pelleted by this onslaught of noise that echoes over the entire four block neighborhoods. When checking with the city council, we were unable to receive a date as to when this practice will be discontinued. Councilwoman Jan Eyre Payton thought it could be two years before they find a better location, since the areas being developed are near the park.

Although this style is more legible compared to typing in all capital letters, only a small number of individuals are willing to read multiple lines of centered text. Unless the graphic designer is creating a textbook specifically intended for students who are required to read every bit of information for an upcoming test, it is important to remember that all other readers have the option to choose whether to read further or to continue on something else. The designer must ensure that the material is comprehensible.

Reexamine the extensive text. The majority of individuals will choose to read the initial sentence and quickly scan through to the final line because the long-centered lines are challenging to comprehend. The term 'widow' refers to the act of leaving a word without any accompanying context or explanation. Designers should modify the alignment of paragraph breaks to avoid having only one or two words at the bottom. Hyphens should be avoided in flush-left material as they can disrupt the line breaks that the typographer has carefully designed.

When the people read body copy silently, errors can often go unnoticed. However, reading the content aloud allows graphic designers to hear grammatical errors and poorly constructed sentences. Furthermore, orally reading the text can reveal the legibility of the typeface and if the layout, spacing, and line lengths are effectively designed.

IMAGE 5-8

Demonstration of similar concepts with different executions.

AI Practicum} Two artificial intelligence images were generated using Adobe Firefly. The parameters for the first image were configured to art, cartoon, vector, and intense lighting. The challenge requested the use of fantasy-inspired font for the letters G and Ns, with color added in a sketched manner. The configuration for option #2 consisted of artistic elements, a vector appearance, a psychedelic style, and constructivism. The prompt was "Isometric design on white with sculpted 3-dimensional letters G,N,N." In Adobe Photoshop, the photos were merged and incorporated individuals and trees using the Photoshop AI Prompt "small 3D people in modern attire."

Designers must capture the attention of the potential reader in order to entice them to read the content. Utilize a font size for the headline that is the largest or most prominent typeface on the page. Some typefaces are more legible as they are intentionally meant to direct the reader's focus towards the information, rather than being distracting or perceived as overly challenging or time-consuming to read. The fonts that capture a reader's attention are the ones used for headlines and subheadings. Observe the typography on this page. The typeface was selected to be easily readable for viewers accustomed to reading long passages. When youngsters are taught to read, they are primarily introduced to lowercase letters and only a few capital letters.

When selecting a typeface, consider its readability and relevance to the page. The ideal typeface for headlines frequently proves ineffective when used as a 10-point font for body content due to its poor readability. To differentiate between a headline font and a body copy font, the designer can simply read it aloud at both a small and large scale. If the text is challenging to read when displayed at a small size, it is probable that it was specifically designed as a display font. Headline fonts can be all capital letters, while text fonts are more effective when used with a combination of upper- and lower-case letters. As a general guideline, Display fonts are typically chosen for headlines and should be set at a size of 14 points or larger. Text fonts are utilized for content and are typically set between 6 to 12 points.

Sans serif fonts are suitable for headlines, particularly when using condensed or compressed variations. Due to the narrower structure of characters in sans serif fonts, they have the ability to increase the height of headlines and create a noticeable difference from the rest of the material. Sans serif typography is characterized by a simple and angular design, including minimal variation in stroke thickness. Designers set type as capitals sparingly to create emphasis on a headline, and subconsciously tell the reader to "LOOK AT THIS!" They also keep the line of type short to ensure easy readability.

Word usage, spelling, and pronunciation can vary significantly by geographical location and culture. The designer needs to know the history and significance of the letters of the alphabet to correctly connect with the target market.

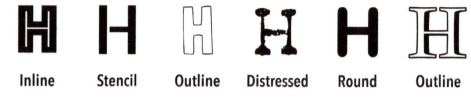

| Inline | Stencil | Outline | Distressed | Round | Outline |

IMAGE 5-9

Type has textures.

Typefaces are not all the same and understanding how factors like type texture, weight, and proportion may captivate a reader serves as an additional technique to engage the viewer and encourage them to read the content. Three primary attributes differentiate typefaces from each other. The stroke widths vary from faint to exceedingly thick, while the letter shapes span from highly compressed to exceptionally broad. Certain typefaces exhibit unique surface textures. These surface textures improve typeface design by providing many options such as outline, incise, stencil, and inline.

Despite attempts to establish a consensus on weight and proportion terminology, none have been successful. Most of the regularly used font terminology indicating the weights of type are Thin, Light, Book, Medium, Demi Bold, Bold, Extra Bold, Black, and Ultra Heavy. Book is an appropriate weight for text in books and Demi Bold is referred to as Demi.

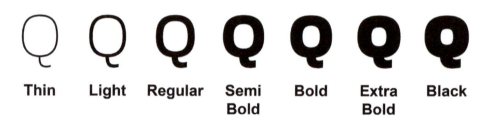

| Thin | Light | Regular | Semi Bold | Bold | Extra Bold | Black |

IMAGE 5-10

For content, font families with many weights are good options.

Proportion in typography refers to the character's width in relation to its height. Generally, the narrowest proportion is described as ultra-compressed. Typically, font descriptions for width are identified as extra compressed, compressed, condensed, regular, and extended. Although typefaces can provide different levels of compression, the expansion widths are usually limited.

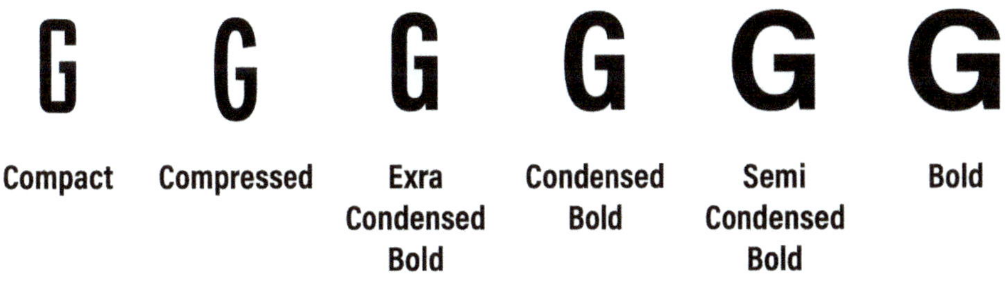

G G G G G G

| Compact | Compressed | Exra Condensed Bold | Condensed Bold | Semi Condensed Bold | Bold |

IMAGE 5-11

Type proportions allow for headlines and subheads to fit on one or two lines.

Although designers typically avoid using full capital letters in body text, starting a sentence with a capital letter is an effective technique to capture the reader's attention. Using one or a small number of letters at the start of a piece of text can convey the overall meaning to the reader.

In storybooks, periodicals, move titles, logo designs, and icons, characters that are taller and wider and wider than the rest of the letters are known as Initial Caps, Drop Caps and Hanging Caps. These special characters can be manipulated and stylized to grab the viewer and allow them to know where to start reading. They can simply be a font that is sized larger, or they can be designed specifically for their medium.

Initial caps refer to when the first letter of a paragraph is enlarged and sometimes styled but stays on the same baseline as the rest of the text. Drop caps go down into the text, occupying multiple lines. This large letter typically extends several lines deep into the paragraph, creating a visually striking introduction to the text. Hanging Caps are outside on the left of the text but need to line up with the first word or part of the word. Although drop caps were typically crafted manually or using specialist typesetting methods, contemporary desktop publishing software frequently include functionalities that facilitate the effortless addition of drop caps to text.

Initial caps add visual interest, enhance readability, and lend a sense of elegance or tradition to the layout. They can be designed in various styles, from simple and understated to elaborate and decorative, depending on the overall design aesthetic and context of the publication.

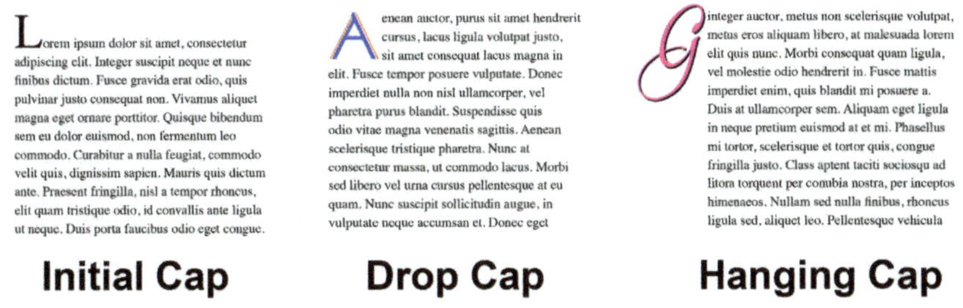

Lorem ipsum dolor sit amet, consectetur adipiscing elit. Integer suscipit neque et nunc finibus dictum. Fusce gravida erat odio, quis pulvinar justo consequat non. Vivamus aliquet magna eget ornare porttitor. Quisque bibendum sem eu dolor euismod, non fermentum leo commodo. Curabitur a nulla feugiat, commodo velit quis, dignissim sapien. Mauris quis dictum ante. Praesent fringilla, nisl a tempor rhoncus, elit quam tristique odio, id convallis ante ligula ut neque. Duis porta faucibus odio eget congue.

Initial Cap

Aenean auctor, purus sit amet hendrerit cursus, lacus ligula volutpat justo, sit amet consequat lacus magna in elit. Fusce tempor posuere vulputate. Donec imperdiet nulla non nisl ullamcorper, vel pharetra purus blandit. Suspendisse quis odio vitae magna venenatis sagittis. Aenean scelerisque tristique pharetra. Nunc at consectetur massa, ut commodo lacus. Morbi sed libero vel urna cursus pellentesque at eu quam. Nunc suscipit sollicitudin augue, in vulputate neque accumsan et. Donec eget

Drop Cap

Integer auctor, metus non scelerisque volutpat, metus eros aliquam libero, at malesuada lorem elit quis nunc. Morbi consequat quam ligula, vel molestie odio hendrerit in. Fusce mattis imperdiet enim, quis blandit mi posuere a. Duis at ullamcorper sem. Aliquam eget ligula in neque pretium euismod at et mi. Phasellus mi tortor, scelerisque et tortor quis, congue fringilla justo. Class aptent taciti sociosqu ad litora torquent per conubia nostra, per inceptos himenaeos. Nullam sed nulla finibus, rhoncus ligula sed, aliquet leo. Pellentesque vehicula

Hanging Cap

Different paragraph caps that attract the reader's eye.

Type as an image

Given the ease of designing type on a computer, many creatives tend to overlook the fact that type can also be an image. Before the invention of letters, images served as the primary medium for communication and conveying messages. Illustrators create types based on images. Effective designers are the ones who do not limit themselves to what the computer can type.

To grab a viewer's attention, try using the type as an image. Designers such as Herb Lubalin and Seymour Chwast did not rely on a typeset font to convey a message with impact. Study designers' in the pre-computer era to learn how the graphic artists created solutions.

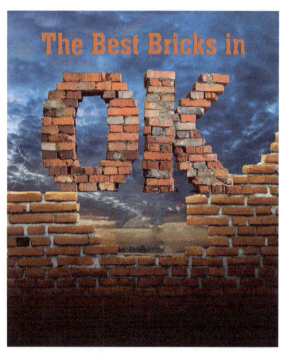

IMAGE 5-13

Graphic Artist: Neal Hettinger

Example of advertisement background demonstrating type as an image.

AI Practicum 4-13} Two artificial intelligence images were created using Adobe Firefly. The initial configurations included of photo and mood light options. The prompt was "the word OK, made of bricks, with space for text. " The specifications for the second artwork were photography and harsh light. The prompt was "brick wall on a stormy night." The artworks were merged in Adobe Photoshop by blending the photos using masks, adjusting the hue and saturation, and adding a gradient at the bottom to create a legible text area over bricks. The composition was modified to accommodate the subsequent positioning of the text, logo, and call to action.

Use type to create eye-catching images. Many designers draw out a headline, scan the idea, clean it up in illustrator, and drop that image in as the headline. If a distorted or damaged effect is the goal, print out the headline and then fold and wade the page up. After scanning the page, clean it up in Illustrator.

One way to create an eye-catching design is to think outside the computer box. Creatives that can use their hands with their minds have an advantage over designers that can only create with the computer. As an example, a bookstore client wants to run an ad directed at the censorship by officials banning books that are deemed socially unacceptable. A design approach utilizing the stamped word "Censored" has been overdone. "Xs" placed across books has been overused. Do not feel compelled to always solve graphic designs with a computer. Many designers have learned to use their hands and the computer by printing out the words, rip the pages, put them together and come up with a different design solution. When an idea is different and not overused to the reader, the message has a better chance of being remembered. All a designer needs to do is come up with that idea.

IMAGE 5-14

Graphic Artist: Neal Hettinger

Example of a design not relying on computer effects.

Practicum} Printed out 2 pages from InDesign typeset with a heavy sans serif font on white background and a thin weighted sans serif on warm grey background. Then ripped the paper and taped into place allowing for slight shadows. Photographed the composition with a mobile phone camera, cleaned up the image in Photoshop and adjusted contrast to show shading on paper.

The designer's objective is to get the viewer's attention and interested in reading the message. Designing a visually eye-catching solution may seem simple but with over 3000 messages a day bombarding targeted consumers, viewers tend to disregard most messages. Due to digital technology, most designers go directly to the software and try to generate unusual ideas or accidental solutions. Instead, creative graphic artists start with research, then develop thumbnails followed by a comprehensive that is meant to create an unusual design that engages readers.

However, there may be another way to stop the viewer before relying just on type or a pretty picture. Instead of immediately accessing the computer, these graphic artists take the time to truly look over the thumbnails to see if there is alternative method to capture the viewer's attention. Creating an image-based headline by hand or Artificial intelligence can be very effective.

Demonstration: Stylizing Type

You can use any of the main three softwares: InDesign, Illustrator, or Photoshop to change and modify to create a drop cap, logo, and icon. For now, use InDesign and type the letter K at 72 points. Choose a font you can manipulate for your design.

1. Duplicate the letter in case you need to go back to it. Go up to the top menu under Type and select Create Outlines.

Image 5-15

2. Select the anchors and adjust as you want.

Image 5-16

3. You can combine with a shape using Pathfinder. Send the box shape to the back for this effect first. Under Object select Pathfinder and then select Exclude Overlap.

Image 5-17

4. Add a blood drop if you want. Place a clear square behind the K and add a stroke.

Image 5-18

5. Try the other pathfinder options for future ideas.

Portfolio Building Assignment – Stylizing Type

Image 5-19

Example for Assignment 2.

1. Using one or any combination of the Adobe software programs Illustrator, Photoshop, or InDesign, create stylized initial cap letters. Do not copy any of the examples or use AI tools.

2. Using the first initial of your first name, create a drop cap to be used in a book on the first paragraph of Chapter 1. The book is for children, and it is a tale of make believe.

3. Attach a page with the Drop cap and a page with the drop cap in position with the content—remember you are a designer and design the page. You will be graded for font choice, how you changed the font, colors, creativity, content font and alignment.

4. Using the first initial of your last name, create a cap letter to be used with the title of a movie. Do not use the same letter as you used in the Book design.

5. Attach a page with the initial cap and movie title on a page. You will be graded for font choice for the cap and the rest of the title, how you changed the font, colors, and creativity.

6 Typographers make it look easy

Learning Objective

The student will be able to recite the different categories of fonts. They will be able to distinguish serif and sans serif typefaces. The user will be able to diagram the anatomy of typefaces.

Professional terminology

Calligraphy: Freehand lettering usually with a pen or brush that can be decorative.

Family: A group of similar typefaces with weights and angles.

Geometric: Type design based on circles, triangles, and rectangles created with straight lines.

Grotesque: Typographers nickname for the fonts that later became known as sans serif.

Kerning: The spaces between letters in words.

Letterspace: The kerning or tracking of letters in a word.

Monospaced: A font with a fixed spacing for all the characters.

Roman: Letterforms that are vertical and horizontal and not slanted or sloping.

Script: A typeface based on calligraphy and handwritten fonts.

Structure: The placement and relationships of typeface components.

Tittle: The dot over the lowercase "i".

Tracking: Term used by software for spaces between words.

X-height: Invisible line that determines lowercase letter height.

IMAGE 6-1
AI example of fun image of type.
AI Practicum} Firefly prompt: letters of alphabet in different font style.

The purpose of type

While language consists of speaking and listening, to record language you must write and to write you must have fonts. When you speak you can have intonation to clarify your words and you can illicit responses based on how loudly you speak, how fast you deliver your words, and the semantics and syntax. Typefaces can be viewed as texture and have an intrinsic emotional response; the basic purpose is to communicate a meaning. Font choice should never be arbitrary or habitual. It is amazing how a typeface can bring about an emotional reaction. A system to identify typefaces is helpful in choosing not only one font, but deciding what fonts go together.

The length of a paragraph should be manipulated for the reader. If it is more than 150 words, it may not be read. Paragraphs with more than eight sentences will be skipped over more than one with three sentences. The designer should vary the length of paragraphs to allow for space in the design. Graphic designers may think this should be the responsibility of the copywriter, but if the design is not read, the client will look at the layout. If it appears to be almost all type, the designer could use a condensed font and drop the type size down to give the appearance of any easier read.

The width of the content is important in reading as well. Many people do not read each word but read the lines of words. If the lines are too long, they will get lost trying to find the next line to read in a paragraph. Roughly, 50 to 70 characters including spaces in a line of text is the optimal width. A guide is to keep the lines of type to around 14 words in length before a break. With the advent of digitized typesetting and self-typesetting by graphic designers, spacing for easy reading has been lost. If the type is set too tight, the content will be skipped over.

Serif | **The quick brown fox jumps over the lazy dog.**

Decorative | **THE QUICK BROWN FOX JUMPS OVER THE LAZY DOG.**

Script | *The quick brown fox jumps over the lazy dog.*

Sans Serif | **The quick brown fox jumps over the lazy dog.**

IMAGE 6-2
Four main typeface categories using all 26 letters in the alphabet in one sentence.

Type Categories

It is estimated there are almost a million fonts available for a variety of purposes. When designers are scrolling through the multitudes of available fonts from Adobe, Apple, and Google, the task of finding the appropriate structure of type to use for a design project can be overwhelming. Do not settle for something that is easy to use. Take the time to know how the fonts families are defined. Font suppliers and type houses do not use the same categories, but the fundamental definitions are nearly universal.

Serif and Sans Serif are the most popular with Script and Decorative comprising the remaining font varieties. The precise font used to convey the message is the foundation of exceptional designs. Students of typography should try to assess type foundries by counting the number of distinct typefaces they provide. The character attributes of each typeface are determined by their historical usage.

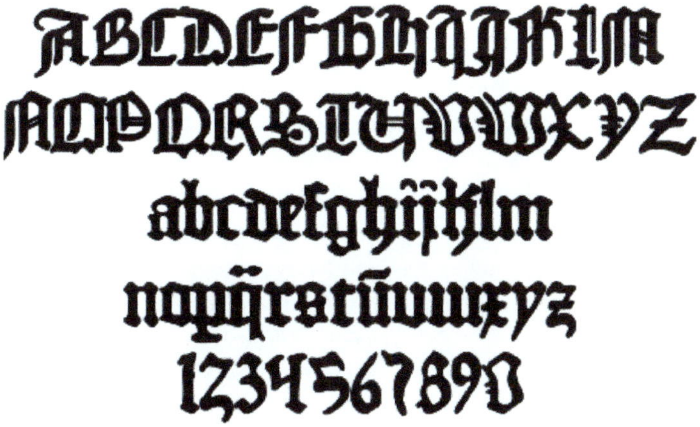

IMAGE 6-3

Bibel font classified as Blackletter in the Script category.

The Serif fonts derive from the old style of writing, painting, and carving letters. To inscribe type was difficult to keep the bottom of the letters to aligned on the top and bottom of each form. Adding horizontal short strokes that project at the bottom and top of each letter makes the letters appear to line up. These strokes are known as serifs and can be added to other parts of the letter at angles to keep the letters uniform. Serif is a Dutch term meaning line. Originally, Serif typefaces were curved, with thick and thin graduations of strokes because communications at that time were written by hand with flat–tipped utensils such as quills and later by calligraphy type pens to shape letters. To keep the ink from splattering, the communicator had to learn how to pull the writing tip and not push the point or it would grab and stick into the paper.

The first type family used for printing was the Bible font created by Guttenberg. It emulated the handwriting of the that time period. Today it is used for newspaper banners such as the Gazette and heavy metal bands.

As a hoax computer wizards quickly fill visual design jobs.

As a hoax computer wizards quickly fill visual design jobs.

As a hoax computer wizards quickly fill visual design jobs.

IMAGE 6-4

Serif typefaces using all 26 letters of the alphabet in a sentence.

In a serif typeface family, there will be roman type which is where the letters are vertical and italic where the letters slant and have severe thick and thin strokes to stand out and be emphasized. Serif italics are completely redesigned type structures that are almost like another font but based on angles. Sans serif families have slanted where the type is leaning with basically the same structure. They may have an italics, but it is not a true italic.

As a hoax computer wizards quickly fill visual design jobs.

As a hoax computer wizards quickly fill visual design jobs.

As a hoax computer wizards quickly fill visual design jobs.

IMAGE 6-5

Sans Serif typefaces using all 26 letters of the alphabet in a sentence.

Fonts that do not have serifs are known as Sans Serif. Sans means without in French. In the late 1800's when Sans Serif started being used, many designers referred to the type without the short lines and thick and thin strokes as Grotesque. They thought the nice undulating strokes with anchoring serifs were beautiful, and when removed created ugly characters. However, Grotesque was considered modern and became very popular. Many typographers still liked the thick and thins or curving ends of the character and used these serif type structures when creating the characters for Grotesque alphabets. Eventually, the designers realized that Grotesque fonts had a purpose, and the term Sans Serif was applied.

As a hoax computer wizards quickly fill visual design jobs.

As a hoax computer wizards quickly fill visual design jobs.

As a hoax computer wizards quickly fill visual design jobs.

IMAGE 6-6
Script typefaces using all 26 letters of the alphabet in a sentence.

Fonts that appear handwritten or resemble calligraphy are known as Script. This category ranges from delicate type for announcements to rough medieval style type such as Blackletter which was used as newspaper banner logos. Now you will see this style used for heavy metal bands.

As a hoax computer wizards quickly fill visual design jobs.

AS A HOAX COMPUTER WIZARDS QUICKLY FILL VISUAL DESIGN JOBS.

AS A HOAX COMPUTER WIZARDS QUICKLY FILL VISUAL DESIGN JOBS.

IMAGE 6-7
Decorative typefaces using all 26 letters of the alphabet in a sentence.

The last category, Decorative, is a catch all for any font style that does not fit into the other 3 categories. Their approaches are distinct and rarely used for body content since Decorative typefaces are usually not readable at a small size. Typographers need to remember these are display fonts which function as headlines and starting points for logos. This style can appear sci-fi, historical, techno, grungy or cartoony. Many have structures that are almost abstract or are rigidly geometric.

In general typographers can choose the correct font categories based on how readers perceive the font styles. To viewers, a clean sans serif font may look more modern, innovative, or futuristic than other categories. Serif fonts may be considered old fashioned but a perfect for a design that needs elegance or a traditional feel. The Script category of fonts range from personal to graceful in design while Decorative fonts are considered creative and attention grabbing.[1]

IMAGE 6-8
The baseline, x-height, ascender and descender lines are fundamental in typeface design.

Type Structure

Typefaces are differentiated by the style of the strokes. Some fonts are geometric and other typefaces curve and undulate. Type can be monospaced where each letter such as an M and a J take up the same amount of space or the font can have proportional letter spacing.

Type sits on an imaginary foundation known as the Baseline which is usually a straight line perpendicular to a page, but the line can be angled or wavy. The structure of typefaces is based on the invisible line known as the X-height which keeps all the lowercase at the same height. The height of lowercase letters is determined by the lowercase x, excluding any ascenders and descenders. The portion of a lowercase character (b, d, f, h, k, l, t) that protrudes over the x-height is referred to as the Ascender. Conversely, the part of a character (g, j, p, q, y, and sometimes cap J) that descends below the baseline is called Descender. Cap Height is the measurement of the uppercase letters from their baseline to the top of characters with a flat tops and bottoms.

The structure of type is the deciding factor in making it readable. It can be set too large or too small but that is the designer's misguided action. Readability refers to whether an extended amount of text is easy-to-read. Legibility refers to whether a short amount of text is instantly recognizable. A typeface becomes less readable as the features become more noticeable. It is a matter of moderation of the features, almost an invisibility. If a very distinctive typeface causes the viewer to stop and notice the differences to normal fonts, that distinctive font is most likely to be less readable than other options.

Readability diminishes if a typeface calls attention to itself through thick strokes, very thin strokes, a strong contrast between the thick and thin letterforms, extremely condensed forms, short and squatly forms, slanted characters, fancy serifs, swashes, or other extreme features. The argument is that the typefaces that are familiar will be more readable than typefaces that are rarely used. For example, the typeface category Blackletter is difficult to read. However, when blackletter was the font, everyone used to read, it was easy for them. Those same individuals would have a difficult time reading this typeface. Since we grew up reading old-style type, we find it the most readable. Consequently, we favor the use of the old-style serif typefaces in body copy. Modern is typically too challenging due to the condensed structure and lack of thick and thin strokes.

The sans serif typefaces category is characterized by taller x-heights and thicker stroke weights, which allows them to be easier to read on short lines of type. They are impactful and attention-grabbing for headlines, subheads, and call-to-actions. If the type style's details are too extreme, they may cause a problem for the reader. Which of the following blocks of content are easier to read?

A typeface becomes less readable as the features become more noticeable. It is a matter of moderation of the features, almost an invisibility. If a typeface is very distinctive, so distinctive that it makes you stop and say wow look at that typeface, it is lower on the readability scale. Readability diminishes if a typeface calls attention to itself through thick strokes, very thin strokes, a strong contrast between the thick and thin letterforms, extremely condensed forms, short and squatly forms, slanted characters, fancy serifs, swashes, or other extreme features.

A typeface becomes less readable as the features become more noticeable. It is a matter of moderation of the features, almost an invisibility. If a typeface is very distinctive, so distinctive that it makes you stop and say wow look at that typeface, it is lower on the readability scale. Readability diminishes if a typeface calls attention to itself through thick strokes, very thin strokes, a strong contrast between the thick and thin letterforms, extremely condensed forms, short and squatly forms, slanted characters, fancy serifs, swashes, or other extreme features.

A typeface becomes less readable as the features become more noticeable. It is a matter of moderation of the features, almost an invisibility. If a typeface is very distinctive, so distinctive that it makes you stop and say wow look at that typeface, it is lower on the readability scale. Readability diminishes if a typeface calls attention to itself through thick strokes, very thin strokes, a strong contrast between the thick and thin letterforms, extremely condensed forms, short and squatly forms, slanted characters, fancy serifs, swashes, or other extreme features.

A TYPEFACE BECOMES LESS READABLE AS THE FEATURES BECOME MORE NOTICEABLE. IT IS A MATTER OF MODERATION OF THE FEATURES, ALMOST AN INVISIBILITY. IF A TYPEFACE IS VERY DISTINCTIVE, SO DISTINCTIVE THAT IT MAKES YOU STOP AND SAY WOW LOOK AT THAT TYPEFACE, IT IS LOWER ON THE READABILITY SCALE. READABILITY DIMINISHES IF A TYPEFACE CALLS ATTENTION TO ITSELF THROUGH THICK STROKES, VERY THIN STROKES, A STRONG CONTRAST BETWEEN THE THICK AND THIN LETTERFORMS, EXTREMELY CONDENSED FORMS, SHORT AND SQUATLY FORMS, SLANTED CHARACTERS, FANCY SERIFS, SWASHES, OR OTHER EXTREME FEATURES.

Type is set at 10/14 which means the type is 10 point in size with leading of 14 points.
Image not actual size.

The absence of serifs and the lack uniformity in the stroke weights of sans serif typefaces for body content can be a challenge for many readers. The serifs in an old-style font can enhance its readability but give the impression of being out of date. People grow up reading upper and lowercase and when presented with body content and long headlines that are in uppercase the target audience will skip it.

Reversed type, which is a light font on a dark background, can be difficult to read. Paragraphs of italic or script fonts can be difficult to read in print. On a monitor, reversed out type may not be as difficult to read. Uneducated designers will use display type as body content not knowing it was never designed to be text, so it is too small and difficult to read.

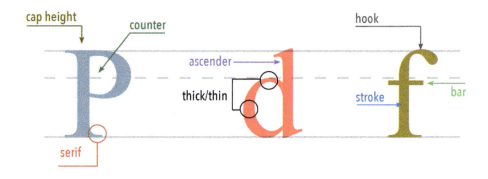

IMAGE 6-10

Letter anatomy on serif typeface.

Type Anatomy

The thick and thin strokes on a typeface along with whether it has serifs or not can create a sentiment for the word. Most layman do not see much difference in type but if they are shown different typefaces in a logo, side by side and ask which one they like, they will have definite opinions.

The art of typography is a painstakingly exact science. Uniformity and precision are necessary for the type to be legible. The height of the lowercase letters should be neither too small which will hinder readability of the words, nor too tall to cause and visually conflict with the uppercase characters.

The vertical line for the letterform is the Stroke where the rest of the letter attaches

Serifs and Bars. A common feature of letters is the Bar which is the horizontal stroke in characters such as A, H, R, e, and f. The partially or fully enclosed space within a character is the Counter such as B, b, D, o, O. A lowercase g in most serif typefaces is a complicated letterform. It has two counters and a Loop which is in the descender portion connects to the Link. Many sans serif g typefaces have just a descender. Without links and loops. The serif g also has an Ear. The end of a stroke in a serif such as a C, or t, or the beginning of serif letter like an a, are called Terminals.

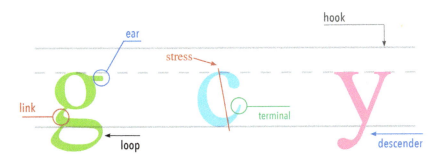

Image 6-11
Letter components on serif typeface.

Typefaces are categorized into families. The term "family" in typography refers to a collection of a typeface's various weights, styles and special characters like dingbats. Typefaces vary based on their weight, form, structure, and style, which allows us to distinguish between them. When choosing a font to use, a family that has many options in weights is preferable. Thin, light, regular, medium, demi, bold, heavy, and black would give the typographer options. It is preferable to choose a family that offers a wide range of weight possibilities. The typographer would have a range of alternatives including thin, light, regular, medium, demi, bold, heavy, and black.

Type structure encompasses various elements such as the x-height, lengths of ascenders and descenders, shapes of counters and bowls, angles of legs, types of serifs, and cap height. Every character possesses a distinct shape that can be either pointed, relaxed, elongated, contracted, or geometric in nature. Type style pertains to the designation of a certain attribute, such as roman, italic, condensed, enlarged, bold, or round.

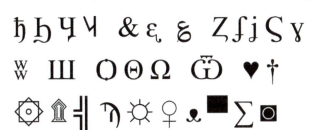

Image 6-12

Glyphs are accessible with InDesign through select dropdown Windows > Type & Tables > Glyphs.

Typesetting responsibly

The goal of a commercial artist's design is to create an effortless reading experience for the intended audience. The fonts are chosen based on their ability to connect with the viewer and the fonts readability structure. Before the invention of computers, a graphic artist would specify the fonts, the weights and sizes, the paragraph width, and the distance between lines of text on paper for the typesetter. This person would be well-versed in punctuation, grammar, and spelling rules as well as the appropriate usage of the English language. Content would be arranged in a printing-friendly typographic structure. Computers have expanded the skill set required of a graphic designer to include Typesetter.

A graphic designer determines the readability of the content by adjusting the leading and character kerning, the spacing between individual letters. The InDesign software engineers assigned kerning control to the tracking feature. If the characters are too letter-spaced, they will be difficult to read. A logotype consisting of one or two words stands out as an exception. It can be challenging to comprehend overly wide sets of lines of text. Alignment, such as justification, can increase the difficulty of reading.

When there are more than two lines of type, designers should avoid negative leading, as this can cause the ascenders and descenders to overlap. Adobe programs typically set the default leading too tight, necessitating an increase of one or two points. Beginning graphic designers should familiarize themselves with several page formatting styles, such as Chicago-style, APA Style, and MLA style, to understand the correct usage of punctuation.

A period is succeeded by a single space. It is essential to type quotation marks and inch marks separately due to their distinct differences. The defaults in InDesign are the quote key and apostrophe key, which are markings that curve. An inch mark and a foot mark must be straight marks and cannot be replaced with a quotation mark when a graphic artist is working on a project that requires measurements. For example, these markings are essential when expressing measurements, such as the dimensions of a postcard that is 4" by 5". Designers have the ability to disable the built-in smart quotes in the InDesign preferences or type inches or feet marks by holding down the bracket keys while holding shift or option/alt. Another alternative is to utilize the Emoji Symbols character viewer on the Mac.

Unlike writing a report where paragraphs can be double spaced to show the breaks, when a designer set the body content type, an em space should begin each paragraph. This em space is typeset by tapping the space bar twice or tabbing a space equal to a capital M. If the designer inserts an extra return between paragraphs in a layout, it will cause the paragraphs to appear too far apart, interrupting the flow. It is important the designer indicates a paragraph break.

Graphic designers utilize the hyphen key in conjunction with the option/alt and shift keys, to enter either an En dash or an Em dash. An em dash, which is longer than a hyphen, indicates a sudden change in sentence form. For example: "He was going to call you earlier — before the meeting — but he got caught up in another one." An en dash, although longer than a hyphen, is shorter than an em dash and is commonly employed to denote a range, such as "8–10 a.m." Although copywriters and AI content generators should possess a strong command of grammar and punctuation norms, it is the responsibility of graphic designers to guarantee the accuracy of the material.

In addition, it is used to replace the phrase "to" in dates, times, or reference numbers such as 8–10 p.m. Previously, the abbreviations "am" and "pm" were written in small capital letters. However, the current convention is to write them as "a.m." and "p.m." in lowercase, with periods separating the letters when used in sentences. Style guides also advise the use of a space to separate the time numeral from the abbreviation. Incidentally, the terms AM and PM stand for 'Ante Meridiem' and 'Post Meridiem', with a.m., indicating the time before noon and p.m. referring to afternoon.

Image 6-13
AI Practicum} Firefly prompts: graphic designer asleep in bed counting little sheep before the start of work; Different fonts with textures for the letter A; Combined and retouched in Photoshop.

Creating and revising fonts

Graphic artists employ various font design software, including FontForge, FontStruct, Inkscape, and Adobe Illustrator. They create individual font characters with a vector design application for logos and headlines. Refer to Chapter 5 for type stylization with Illustrator.

Illustrator generates vectors, rendering it scalable and making it the superior program for typeface development within Adobe design software. Photoshop and InDesign utilize pixels that will degrade in quality when resized. Designers aim to extend the project and employ Illustrator to guarantee that the typeface remains free of pixelation irrespective of size.

When a graphic artist intends to create or modify a design for content, they must efficiently adapt the entire alphabet. FontForge is a complimentary and open-source outline font editor. Visit their website to select and download the most recent version.

Apple does not recognize Fontforge as a registered developer, preventing the installation of the download. The message "FontForge.app cannot be opened because the developer cannot be verified" appears.

Before installing any files downloaded from the internet, the files should always be scanned for malware. Once FontForge has been scanned and cleared, go to the System Preferences. Choose Apple menu > System Settings, then click Privacy & Security. Select FontForge and Click Open Anyway.

Image 6-14

Numerous designers choose crafting their own fonts in Adobe Illustrator and exporting them as EPS files for loading into FontForge. This presentation illustrates the adjustment of a whole alphabet for content type.

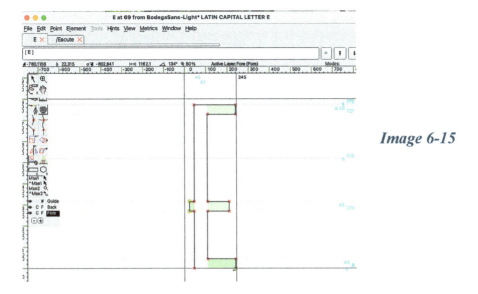

Image 6-15

Once the FontForge menu opens, select New under File. Press the Control button to open the font under change in FontForge, then select Open Font Info under Elements. Give the revised font a name. Select the font to change under File>Import.

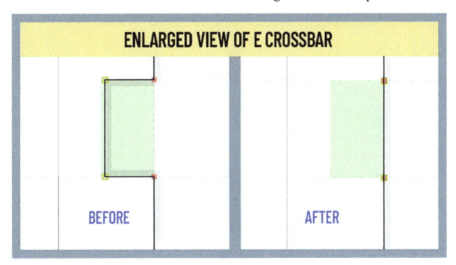

ENLARGED VIEW OF E CROSSBAR

BEFORE

AFTER

Image 6-16

Double click on the letter to revise and make the changes using the various tools provided. On the characters E, F, and H the cross bar will be shortened to line up with the vertical stroke and on the G a point was added to create more of a turn. Close work window and check the alphabet to make sure all the changes have been made.

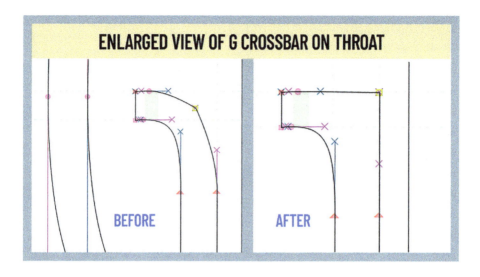

ENLARGED VIEW OF G CROSSBAR ON THROAT

BEFORE

AFTER

Image 6-17

To export go to Elements>Validation>Find Problems. If all is good, proceed with generating the font. Go to File>Generate.

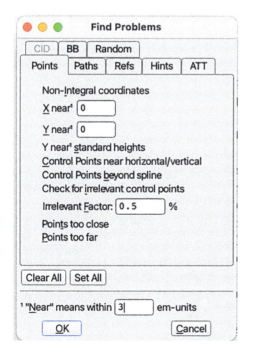

Image 6-18

Choose Open Type which in this case will save the file as BodegaSans.otf which will be saved on the computer. In the Font Book, drag the new font into the All Fonts folder.

Image 6-19

Due to FontForge being freeware, as one would expect its UI (user interface) is cumbersome and not intuitive. However, there are paid programs, such as Fontographer, that are easier to navigate. It comes with a 10-day trial and $499 for a yearly license. They do offer an educational discount.

Image 6-20

The future of typefaces

Rapidly developing technology will enable graphic designers to experiment and learn more about how readers interact with text. There are multiple ideas on where typefaces will be in ten years, and artificial intelligence may have a lot to do with their use.

When computers came out with design software, typefaces had to have a screen file and a printer file. At first internet fonts were limited to approximately 16 choices. For web design to grow, web font files were also created to allow for a consistent marketing campaign by using the same font families.

OpenType fonts are variable fonts which were developed around 2016 by Apple, Adobe, and Microsoft, to allow for a single file to work for all digital design. Designers can actively modify weight, width, slant, and other attributes, resulting in more versatile and adaptable typefaces. Developers will increasingly utilize these fonts to create highly responsive and engaging experiences across diverse platforms and devices. Typographers will likely have greater control over modifying typefaces and changing parameters to align with their choices, whether for aesthetic or accessibility reasons.

Artificial intelligence and machine learning can help create new fonts by examining current designs. Advancements in AI could produce innovative modifications and unique typefaces customized for certain brands or content requirements.

Future fonts may respond to their environment, optimizing readability according to lighting conditions or screen dimensions. An interface could automatically transition to a bolder, more legible typeface in low-light conditions or when displayed on a smaller screen such as a mobile device. Typeface design may progress to meet the increasing demand for cross-cultural communication, using typefaces that adjust to various languages, writing systems, and regional aesthetics while maintaining readability and design integrity.

Designers can design typefaces for energy efficiency, particularly in digital contexts where certain fonts use less power due to their screen rendering. These fonts have the potential to reduce energy consumption by requiring fewer pixels or less computing power.

As accessibility gains importance, viewers could see a rise in fonts specifically tailored for individuals with disabilities, including dyslexia-friendly typefaces and fonts that enhance readability for those with visual impairments or the elderly.

3D fonts are going to be more popular as virtual and augmented reality grow. These fonts will be built for interactive environments, offering new approaches for experiencing and engaging with text. Typography may integrate into virtual environments or augmented reality interfaces, functioning as material objects that can be manipulated.

Master Typographers

Typographer and type designer are two terms that can be perplexing. A typeface designer is responsible for the development of fonts for online libraries and foundries. A typographer designs typefaces and arranges the structure of type into a captivating and imaginative display.

Many graphic designers are weak in selecting the appropriate font. The most effective method of learning and overcoming this deficiency is to study the experienced, successful typographers. All graphic designers should research typography to study the famous and not so famous innovators in the field.

Herb Lubalin

A color-blind typographer, Mr. Lubalin centered his theory of design on how the meaning is communicated from one mind to another. Typography is the key. It is where he started his concepts and ultimately how he reached the destination. Lubalin did not believe that the term "typography" should be used to describe his work. Lubalin was an innovative advertising art director and who established the benchmarks for originality as a publication designer for originality and distinction in the publications Avant Garde and U & lc. His type solutions for Families, Mother & Child, Beards, and show why he is considered a leader of the creative revolution Graphic Expression in place of Swiss modern design. To study and learn more on his design, conduct a search on the internet for "What is the typography of Herb Lubalin?"

Giambattista Bodoni

Italian printer Giambattista Bodoni is known as a pioneer of modern book design in the late 18th century. Mr. Bodoni created a number of clear and simple typefaces, one of which is named after him and is still widely used today: Bodoni. While other styles were being designed based on Oldstyle Serifs, Mr. Bodoni pioneered the creation of the innovative and sleek fonts that are today referred to as Modern Fonts. These typefaces include unbracketed straight-line thin serifs with vertical stresses and emphasis. Not only do his typefaces impact modern design, but many designers also utilize these Modern fonts, mistakenly believing they were produced recently. Calvin Klein and Vogue use the Bodoni typeface for its thin fashion-like lines and sophisticated serifs.

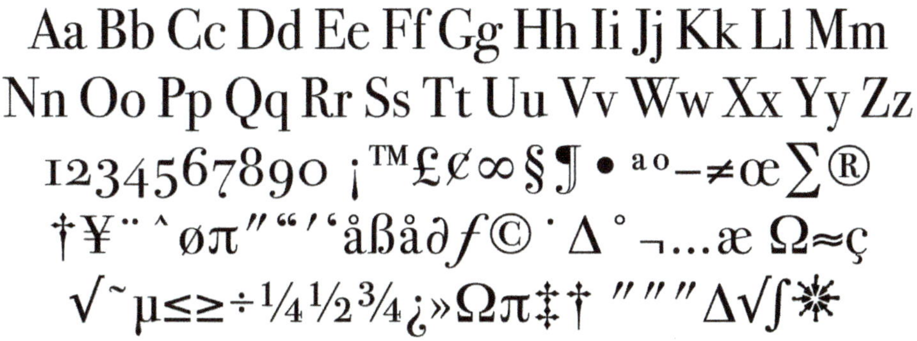

Aa Bb Cc Dd Ee Ff Gg Hh Ii Jj Kk Ll Mm
Nn Oo Pp Qq Rr Ss Tt Uu Vv Ww Xx Yy Zz
1234567890 ¡ ™£¢∞§¶ • ªº−≠œ∑®
†¥¨ˆøπ""''åßå∂ƒ© ˙∆˚¬…æ Ω≈ç
√˜µ≤≥÷¼½¾¿»Ωπ‡† """"∆√∫❋

IMAGE 6-21
Example of Giambattista Bodoni fonts.

Seymour Chwast

As a prominent member of the esteemed "Art Squad," a group of itinerant artists specializing in signage and posters in New York City, Seymour Chwast gained recognition as "The Left-Handed Designer." Alongside Milton Glaser, Mr. Chwast established the innovative Pushpin Studio, which produced groundbreaking artwork that significantly influenced the direction of modern graphic communication.

This freeform newspaper, Pushpin Graphic, was sent to both friends and clients. From its inception, this visually striking periodical caused a stir within the design community. The publication's goal was to push the boundaries of conventional graphic design techniques and integrate design with illustration. The strategy not only efficiently showcased the studio's skills but also had a profound influence on the design and art direction of the late 1950s and early 1960s, particularly in the integration of illustration and design. Chwast and Glaser's organization of all the artwork into a single issue within rounded-cornered boxes marked an interesting graphic development. Other designers promptly adopted these design motifs as design elements in periodicals.

Periodicals such as Vanity Fair, The Atlantic, The New Yorker, and The Wall Street Journal showcase Mr. Chwast's innovative approach. He designed numerous book covers, album covers, packaging, and posters. Chwast created numerous fonts that embodied the 1960s graphic style era, flowing thick and thin with heavy bases. To study and learn more about his design, conduct a search on the internet for "What is the typography of Seymour Chwast?"

Jessica Hische

Jessica Hische has established herself as a talent to study by creating textures and lettering in her designs, capturing a sense of a company's trade. She begins her creative process by always sketching before progressing to formal color models. She imports her designs as a reference, then examines letterforms to construct the design's basic structure. Ms. Hische prefers to begin with basic shapes, adjusting and combining them to create letterforms. Hische's work is more like illustrations of represented typefaces than typeset words and phrases. To study and learn more about her selection of fonts, conduct a search on the internet for "Jessica Hische on Choosing Type."

Steve Vance

The Grammy Award-winning album cover designer, Steve Vance, is also a co-publisher in the Bongo Comics Group, which publishes and produces The Simpsons Comics. He has created cover art for numerous bands album covers, including the Grateful Dead. Mr. Vance worked on home entertainment titles that were campy and B-movie-styled, as well as the ThrillerVideo line. He created a greeting card line that used a comic approach to mock the everyday issues of society. Vance attended Florida State University, where he studied under Mark Witten, a professor who encouraged graphic designers to be creative while identifying the style required to finish a design. To study and learn more on his stylizing of fonts, conduct a search on the internet for "Steve Vance letter portfolio" and "Grateful Dead cover designer."

Exercise— Typographers

This assignment necessitates researching three of the five typographers discussed in this chapter. Provide two or three screenshots of their work and compose a concise explanation clarifying the rationale behind your selection. Copy your photos onto individual InDesign pages for each typographer and include your text below each image.

To take a screen grab on a Mac: Hold the shift-option-4 and drag your cursor over the image you are including in your report. How to take a screen shot on a PC: Press Windows logo key + Shift + S. Press Print Screen (PrtSc). How to take a screen grab on a Mobile Phone: Hold down the 'Power' and 'Volume down' buttons. Devices may vary so if you have problems, conduct a search on the internet for your specific device.

Learning Library Exercise – Font Report

Write a brief report on two of the six fonts listed below. Name the classification and approximate release year for each font below. Refer to the type classifications in this chapter not what you may find on the internet. Then in a sentence, describe what type of design you would use that font on and what specific attributes make the typeface a suitable choice. Remember to write this as an expert using design and typography terms.

Example: The typeface Luminari is an ideal script style for creating a title for a book or movie that takes place during the Middle Ages. The calligraphic structure resembles the strokes made with a quill pen in that time period to form the characters in blackletter.

1. Bank Gothic
2. Commercial Script
3. Caslon
4. Clarendon
5. Duc De Berry
6. Gill Sans
7. Helvetica
8. Onyx
9. Rosewood
10. Zapfino

References

1 | Svaiko, G. (2023, January 12). Font Psychology: Here's Everything You Need to Know About Fonts. Designmodo Inc. Retrieved July 3, 2024, from designmodo.com/font-psychology

Logo design with purpose

Learning Objective

By the end of this chapter, the learner will be able to construct an original restaurant logo for their portfolio. They will be able to explain the purpose of a company brand. The reader will be able to elaborate on 5 Influential logo designers.

Professional terminology

Advertisement: A paid message promoting a product, service, or event.

Brand: A visual identification system that distinguishes a company, app, or business.

Combination Logo: A designed mark consisting of text with an image that distinguishes an entity from its competition.

Direct mail: Postcards and flyers manually delivered by a postal service to potential customers.

Graphic: A designed visual element.

Icon: An abstract or literal graphic element used to represent an object or action.

Legible: A recognizable communication.

Letterhead: Designed stationary with company logo and contact information.

Ligature: Two or more letters in a font family that appear joined when set.

Logo: A unique designed graphic to represent an entity that establishes the brand.

Logomark: Graphic symbol or icon representation of a product, service or function that does not contain verbiage.

Manipulation: A deliberate and skillful alteration of a graphic element.

Monogram: Combining alphabetic characters into a graphic element.

Mood Board: A collection of reference materials such as images and textures to incorporate in a design to achieve a goal.

Stylize: To design an element's appearance to be distinctive and be representative of the subject.

Wordmark: Type graphically designed to represent a company, app, product, service or function.

IMAGE 7-1

A brilliant logo designer should be treasured.

AI Practicum} Three Firefly AI images: Prompt #1 is a ferocious $ is engraved on an open golden treasure chest, fantasy book image; Prompt #2 a ferocious $ is engraved on a golden treasure chest; and Prompt #3 the letters l o g o in 3d. In Adobe Photoshop: Generated background bleed on sides with contextual fill; merged and digitally retouched 3 images together using masks, spot healing brush, and high pass filter.

A company measures success by how many customers it has or their market share. Customers equal profits. Profits mean a company stays in business. A company also succeeds by proving that it performs its chosen business better than other businesses of a similar nature. The logo is a part of that equation. If the logo is more distinctive than logos for competing businesses, then it will stand out in the minds of the customers. Simply using a font as it appears when typed does not result in a creative logo.

IMAGE 7-2

Example of the large companies that utilized Helvetica for their logo.

THE NORTH FACE
Helvetica

JCPenney
Helvetica

Jeep
Helvetica

Kawasaki
Helvetica

TARGET
Helvetica

Panasonic
Helvetica

Knoll
Helvetica

Oral B
Helvetica

TOYOTA
Helvetica

The most distinctive typographic logos contain type that has been modified, manipulated or created by hand. These modifications and manipulations can include interesting or unusual ligatures, letters that interlock or overlap, letters with pieces added or removed, manually distressed letters, substitution of letters with numbers or shapes, flipped or rotated type, letters created from other objects, or letters that create other objects. The word can also use a combination of uppercase and lowercase, combine two different typefaces or combine two varying styles such as roman and oblique. If a typeface in the logo is created, the more proprietary the logo becomes to the company.

A professional logo designer needs to remember the following goals, concepts, and theories to have a successful design. Above all, the logo must be memorable and legible at all sizes and uses.

The essentials of logo design

Logo typography is functional since the design needs to be legible at all sizes. Keeping this goal in mind, the opportunities to develop emotive power to a word, by artistically enhancing the lines and curves are limitless. Typography can be an art form too—or to put it another way, it is a functional medium for artistic expression. The typestyle should be chosen to be unique and create a feeling by the viewer. The font category used the most in modern logos are Sans Serif which includes Futura, Proxima Nova, Helvetica, and Frutiger.[1]

IMAGE 7-3

Example of the large companies that utilized Futura for their logo.

However, most companies want a custom-made font that makes their brand unique. They hire a logo designer to create memorable typeface that cannot be copied by competitors and can be registered as a trademark. Examples of custom-made typefaces for logos are Netflix, Chevrolet, Starbucks, McDonald's, and CNN.

Company logos can be great examples of what can be created based on the structure of the typeface manipulation. Artists and advertisers go to great lengths to ensure that the lettering styles used in the standard formatting of big company logos are exactly right. The size, lines and colors are designed with great care to get a particular feeling across, and associate different subtle emotions with the brand name. Think of some famous logos like Coca-Cola or Dodge. It would be impossible to associate a different font with those companies.

The purpose of a company brand

Company logos are the brand representatives that incorporate images that influence people and develop associations. If you contemplate on big brands like Coca-Cola, Nike, or McDonald's, the one thing that instantaneously comes to your minds is logo. On average, a consumer will take seeing a logo 5 to 7 times before they remember the brand.[2]

Well-designed logos are easily recalled by customers which helps consumers select one product from another because of emotional connection with the company brand. Logos portray brands and they are the corporate pictures since they have that tendency of staying in the minds of the consumers. Exemplary logos never allow their consumers to overlook their brand. When given a choice, shoppers tend to select brands that appear to be visually appealing. This necessitates the need for graphic designers who can create the company's identity through color, font structure, and scale. 75% of consumers judge a brand's credibility based on its logo design[3]

The worse reaction is for the design to be ignored and forgotten. The best response is for individuals to form an opinion on the brand based on the font, structure, texture, and color of the logo. Understanding how the type choices, colors, and scale create an impression is critical for graphic designers. No company wants a forgettable brand or be regarded as completely opposite of the company's product or service. An example is if a pillow company's logo is pointed and sharp, that may make the customer think the pillows are not soft.

IMAGE 7-4

Example of a logo that does not sell the pillow company with design aesthetics. Type is rough, graphic of setting sun competes with night sky.

AI Practicum} Logo design using Adobe Express. Prompts for the background were "bright night sky with stars" and prompt for the type was "text Soft and Sleep in comfortable typeface."

Logo issues created by designers

Amateur designers are responsible for the significant portion of the poorly designed logos used in marketing. Nearly every computer user thinks they can create a logo using the type supplied and finding a stock image for the icon. With artificial intelligence apps, they can layout and write the content. They may not have any formal training, or education, but they somehow feel they are designers. They do not know the difference between and app logo and a company logo.

Many computer typist make company logos that true designers see and chuckle at the clumsy creations. Unfortunately, many business owners want cost-effective results and are unable to see how awful a logo or project is designed. They may even design the company logo themselves or have a friend or relative develop the logo as a favor. They may copy something they like on the internet. The overall cost to place a logo on all the printed materials, marketing communications, internet, and television commercials is expensive.

Establishing the brand is the focus of all marketing at this early point of a company. If a startup company stays in business past the seven-year business bar, then it is considered successful. The amount of money spent to develop a company brand is minimal compared to the expense of replacing the logo with one that is not generic or basic. The average professional logo is not redesigned for 10 years.[3]

Professionally created intricate logos often fall short in their effectiveness for marketing and branding. The logos are constructed on large monitor screens where every detail is observed even though the mark is used in small areas in marketing. The characteristics and the elements of the logo blend together. Graphic artists want their design solutions to be remembered by consumers. One well known acronym borrowed and revised slightly from the US Navy is to follow the principle known as K.I.S.S., Keep It Simple and Straightforward.

The logo assets should be accompanied by a branding style guide. The logo is presented in multiple versions in this guide, each of which exhibits minor variations in construction based on the intended use. The placement, color callouts, space boundaries, and use dimensions would be precisely described in a comprehensive trademark style guide.

Nike, Starbucks, and Quaker have taken decades of repetition in marketing to make their icons immediately recognizable as the companies without the logotype. The swoosh, the mermaid, and the quaker did not become iconic overnight. Many designers make the mistake of creating a pictorial mark as a brand identity such as All About Cha where they assume all potential customers with know the brand and the product.

Graphic designers will have to create outside their comfort circles.
AI Practicum} Adobe Firefly Images combined with Photoshop and InDesign.

Breaking the rules of logo design

Creative people dislike rules and question their use. But graphic artists need to learn the rules before they can break them. Otherwise, the design can just be undesirable rather than effective. Typography is a prime component of design. In order to deliver inspired work to clients, a designer must understand the distinctions in choosing type to be pleasing or complementary rather than ugly or plain. The art of printing and writing has evolved over the centuries, resulting in the establishment of practical rules and guidelines. These regulations may seem restrictive, but their development stemmed from sensible, pragmatic justifications aimed at enhancing customer comprehension.

Learn the theories and guidelines first. Then designers can change them in their own way to add impact to the logo design. The goal is to produce quality solutions that are legible for the reader.

The basic parts of a logo

What we think of today as a logo had its origin with the ancient Greeks and Romans. Early logos were monograms that represented rulers or towns and were found on coins. Monograms continued to be used as logos throughout the Middle Ages for merchants, tradesmen and royalty.

In the nineteenth century, virtually every commercial business had a logo. The Industrial Revolution caused a boom in advertising and logos quickly became an integral part of business. Some of what we consider early recognizable modern-day logos are still in use with some modification. The Coca-Cola's script logo was designed in 1887. The recognizable. Prudential's Rock of Gibraltar was originally designed in 1896. The logo for RCA's dog listening to a phonograph was designed in the late 1800's.

Many logos have hardly changed since being introduced. Audi's logo with the four rings dates to 1932 when four automobile companies merged, and Volkswagen's VW letter combination was designed in 1939. If a logo design conveys the brand in a recognizable fashion, it may be updated but the basics usually continue. Sometimes logos are updated, and the consumer may not recognize it. For instance, Arby's logo was considered dated and not engaging customers. The font was updated, and the iconic cowboy hat was deleted. Sales drastically declined so a stylized version of the hat was included to stop the sales slide.

Examples of iconic symbols include the Mermaid in Starbucks, the smile in Amazon, and the Golden Arches of McDonald's. Conversely, a logotype refers to a specific arrangement

fonts, the creation of color palettes, and the inspiration of a graphic icon. Mood boards, whether they are physical or digital, are visual compositions that encapsulate the final design's style by organizing images, materials, text, and other elements. The designer obtains inspiration from the internet, including Pinterest and Google. At the research stage, the concepts are refined to reflect contemporary trends. Define at least three color schemes and assign each one the mood you are attempting to evoke prior to commencing the design process. Locate logos that are distinct from those of the competition—not for the purpose of duplicating them, but rather for the purpose of serving as an inspiration. The manipulation or texture of a font may be enticing to graphic designers.

Looking through font families that have special characters including ligatures, symbols, icons, and punctuation is one way to get inspiration. Ligatures are when two letters are joined and can be used in a monogram logo.

IMAGE 7-8

Monogram logo example with the ligature created by the letters ff in Adobe InDesign.

Times New Roman was designed in 1932 for the London Times Newspaper as a condensed font to save on ink and paper costs. In addition to the alphabet, Times new Roman has several ligatures and special characters.

The logo design journey

Acquiring an in-depth brief by the client is the responsibility of the graphic designer. Do not ask the client for specifics such as which typeface or color they want incorporated into the design because time will be wasted developing these elements which may not work. The client is not the expert.

IMAGE 7-9

Graphic Designer: Neal Hettinger

An example of a lighting store logo before and after redesigning their logo.

However, it is important to inquire about the message the company wishes to convey through the design, the target market, and the competition. Additionally, inquire about the effectiveness and inadequacy of the competition's logo designs. If it is a redesign, ask about the rationale behind the decision and the extent to which they desire a distinctly different design.

Start with research. Designers who begin their work on a computer and come up with a concept rarely generate five distinct ideas. Inspiration can occur suddenly and spontaneously. It is recommended to have blank paper readily accessible for creating thumbnails accompanied by descriptive notes, font choices, and color palettes. Establish the need of incorporating an icon in conjunction with a typeface choice for the logo. Scale the logo to correspond with the proportions of a business card, letterhead, and website header, taking into account its size as shown on the computer screen. If feasible, print it out.

IMAGE 7-10

Graphic Artist: Neal Hettinger

Example of thumbnails to final rendering for restaurant rebranding.

Practicum} Logo development example for BBQ includes hand drawn thumbnails, loose black and white computer layouts that lead to a final comp in color created in Adobe Illustrator.

Layout small ruffs but do not stop with the first idea that's pops up—it usually is not the best. Explore ideas—it is a must. If you can, put them aside and come back to the conception stage after a few hours or days to look at them with a clear mind.

The presentation should demonstrate a thorough exploration. Presenting a limited number of options will cause a sense of limitation on the choices available for the client. Typically, all of them will be rejected, leading the designer to start over. Presentations of three to seven options will have more success. However, faced with many alternatives, the client may find it difficult to reach a decision. This is not a negative situation. Based on their responses during the presentation, steer them towards two of the available options. Next, instruct the client to showcase printouts in their workplace and identify the most popular logo designs.

After approval, create the final design in various sizes to ensure legibility. It might be necessary to enlarge the small font or remove the icon. Deliver files in different formats and for different uses, such as print, internet, and vehicle wraps.

When proposing a logo development, it is important to state exactly the number of changes incorporated in the proposal. If not, the client will continue to rework the ideas until they become tired of the process. Clients will forget how much they like the original solutions. A restriction on changes benefits graphic designers two ways: The customer understands that ongoing design changes will be more expensive, and it guards against decision fatigue.

The case to hire a professional

For the overall benefits and company marketing, to bypass using a professional on a logo design does not make sense. The logo development budget does not need to be a large expense. 67% of small businesses are willing to pay over $500 for a logo while Only 15% of small businesses are open to paying over $1,000 for a logo.[2]

Hiring a professional company logo designer would help marketers evade problems in future projects, and work to their benefit. The top five advantages of a professional design: the logo will have a professional look; It will be exclusive and memorable; logo files for all uses should be supplied; the company logo would sustain for longer lifespan; and save time replacing it when the executives realize their company is in decline because of the poor branding.

The Harvard Business Review analyzed 597 company logos and concluded that "A well-designed logo can offer substantial benefits to brands."[5]

A company logo design project should start with a creative strategy that includes an overview for the designer of the target market related of the enterprise. The overview is a succinct description of the project that helps to keep everyone focused. A beginning creative designer often skips over this part of the process and presents the client with solutions they do not relate to their company. The creative team can utilize a condensed list of adjectives that will apply to logo to ensure that the final solutions have the right approach.

IMAGE 7-11

Graphic Artist: Neal Hettinger

Project: Revise Logo design for placement on gloves and marketing.

Overview: The Ultimate Fighting Championship® wanted to market their own professional practice gear. The brand should be easily identified but not confused with their on-air fights and shows.

Target Market Aesthetics: toughest fight competition, improve, power, energetic, experienced.

Solution: A two color logo, white and silver was designed with a knocked out thick to thin line to emulate a motion similar to a strike. By cutting across the type, this swash created energy and movement.

Case Study 7B [Full Moon Entertainment Logo]

IMAGE 7-12
Graphic Artist: Neal Hettinger | Art Director Nigel Sherry

Overview: Paramount Pictures video division was introducing different genres and needed a logo for their lower budget horror, fantasy, and sci-fi, films line.

Target Market Aesthetics: B-movie, campy, comic feel, horror, trepidation

Solution: Legible and no color variations on all backgrounds, used blue moon to symbolize witchcraft and scary motif, sharp serif font, complementary sans serif font.

Case Study 7C [Sovereign Storm Solutions]

IMAGE 7-13
Graphic Designer: Neal Hettinger

Overview: A commercial roofing company was expanding their market to encompass a full range of contractor services and needed the brand completely revised.

Target Market Aesthetics: restoration, best, quality, longevity, service

Solution: Inspired by a roof element and created a "crown" of roof trusses. Used a stylized classical font and complementary modern condensed sans serif, with brackets suggested by client to add as a foundation.

IMAGE 7-14

Graphic Designer: Neal Hettinger

Design Steps: Created in Illustrator a number of concepts for style conscious roofing company who wanted a logo that conveyed an elite roofer sense to the design. Final made up of colors and customized type reminiscent of Middle Ages royalty iconography. Crown is composed with the letter W for the owner's last name initial.

Case Study 7D [Ridge Route Ranch]

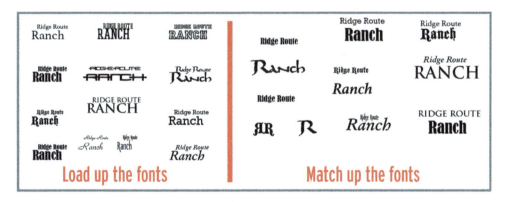

Load up the fonts   Match up the fonts

IMAGE 7-15

Overview: Company opening a "Dude Ranch" with modern facilities near Los Angeles required a brand identity. The ranch offered an old west meets new west experience which included riding trips, petting zoo with cattle such as bison and long horn bulls.

Target Market Aesthetics: different, relaxing, comfortable, memorable, colorful

IMAGE 7-16

Solution: Old style California Western feel to monogram beveled into sheriff badge. Color resembled sunset reflection on textured beaten metallic.

IMAGE 7-17
Graphic Artist: Neal Hettinger

Case Study 7E [Gateway Logo]

Overview: 25-year-old construction company known for rebuilding old structures into modernized tasteful offices needed an updated design to appeal to younger architects.

Target Market Aesthetics: new, sharp, inspired, experienced, passionate

IMAGE 7-18

Graphic Designer: Neal Hettinger

Solution: Old greyscale logo had old columns from bird eye view. Square of a building with stylized columns to symbolize an idea starburst. Used youthful color palette with distinctive modern serif fonts. Letterspaced to support structure of logo.

Case Study 7F [Vergilius Logo]

IMAGE 7-19

Graphic Designer: Neal Hettinger

Overview: A startup chamber music company wanted a logo that was simple but modern.

Target Market Aesthetics: violins, conductor, charming, event, entertaining

Solution: Used conductor wand to replace "|" spacer popular in design, old style serif to contrast compressed sans serif typeface. Greyscale values with warm blue to focus viewer.

IMAGE 7-20

Overview: US company importing coffee from Brazil wanted a standout design for their new product line.

Target Market Aesthetics: natural, jungle, distinctive, not cheap, caring

Solution: As an icon, we recreated a yellow napped amazon parrot the client had photographed at one of the coffee plantations. The illustrated parrot was placed in front of a warm yellow sun with flowing a wood stained-like font. Logo created with Adobe Illustrator.

Influential logo designers

Students of design should study the masters of creating company identities with the appropriate fonts, relevant colors, and impact of scale. Some of the following logo designers focus on the type while others on combination of typography melded with icons. Research and discover how these innovative graphic artists have adjusted and updated their approaches to create contemporary designs.

Paul Rand

Paul Rand, who developed several iconic logos such as IBM, American Express, Ancient Age, Enron, Morningstar, and UPS has a large body of work. He has many quotes but one that nearly every good designer should know: "Most clients are nice clients. It's the people in between who give you the problems: the account executives, the marketing people. They destroy people's work: 'this should be bigger, this should be up here, there should be a sun here with a price.'"

Ruth Kedar

Ms. Kedar is from Brazil which gives her a different slant on her logo designs. Her creative ability as a multi-disciplinary designer and artists starts with her philosophy, "The process always starts with curiosity." She continues to learn and expand into different styles which are always a source of unexpected designs.

Lindon Leader

Known for the FedEx and FDX logos with the infamous arrow, Mr. Leader developed many fresh ideas such as the USA Women's Ski Jumping team brand, Hawaiian Airlines identity system, DoubleTree Hotels and Suites branding strategy, and Disney Land Hotel logo. Note the feel of the type, space, and color scheme and how they relate to the product. Lindon said "…the sole purpose of branding is to facilitate the realization of our client's strategic marketing objectives."

Walter Landor

A German-born American graphic designer, Walter Landor said, "Products are manufactured in the factory, but brands are formed in the mind." He is renowned for crafting designs that have a wide-ranging popular appeal. Mr. Landor established his design firm aboard a ferryboat in San Francisco and long before anyone else, Landor sold himself as a brand. Landor is widely recognized as the designer who originated the concept of Branding. His works were designed to bridge the gap between business strategy and design. He believed a designer must create a comprehensive identity program with clean and dynamic graphics.

Turner Duckworth

Using strong colors to set his branding apart, Mr. Duckworth defines design by three elements: clarity, simplicity and emotion. The new brands must have effective color schemes to match the subjects. Duckworth stated, "If the idea is based on truth, it will always be relevant. Get the idea right, and a logo can last forever." His approach is the work must connect the consumer with emotion for them to act.

Nicole Weber

Nicole Weber logos: www.nicoleweberdesign.com/our-work

An influential logo designer, Ms. Weber resides in the Washington, D.C. area. She not only considers herself a graphic designer, but uses her creative talents as a muralist, and artist. Her use of positive and negative space in her logo design establishes a strong brand identity. Weber's maxim, "I believe in stretching design boundaries in order to make businesses stand out" should apply to all logo solutions. Her logo type not only mimics the company product or service but focuses on being memorable.

Logos with hidden items

Logo designers can have fun using type to create hiding symbols or words in the designs like Lindon Leader hid the arrow in FedEx. Search the internet for these five logos and find the insider joke elements were worked in for other designers to enjoy: Wendy's; Baskin Robbins; Tour de France; Tostitos; and Amazon.

Here are some hints to see if you can find the in-jokes: How many flavors sold; What they sell; A competitor; The word Mom; and People eating. Look at the end of the chapter if you need the answers.

Demonstration: Logo design

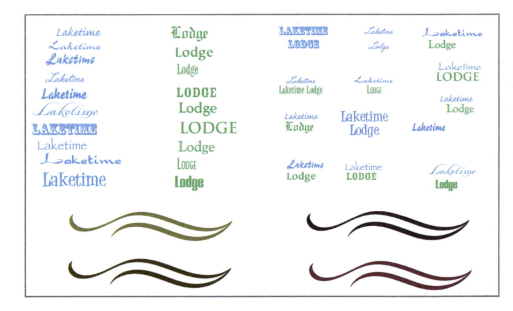

IMAGE 7-21

Brief: Client was considering renting out their large vacation home through the internet. Before presenting the venture to investors, they needed a logo. The house was a large 3-story mansion suitable for sleeping up to 30 people. The multi-million-dollar design was situated a very short distance from a large lake and included amenities such as a jacuzzi, massive deck, outdoor grill, two refrigerators, heated flooring, 4 car garage, and interiors designed as log cabin built for a millionaire. The client wanted to convey the lake feeling of laziness, the old time charm, and in the Airbnb mode but sell it like a high end vacation getaway.

Steps in this logo design:

1. Research Airbnb, Marriott vacation homes, getaways, vacation hideaways, and dude ranches.

2. Establish the goal of the design and how to achieve it based on the message the logo should convey. Based on the client's brief, the logo should relate to a relaxing, rural nature getaway with lavish and comfortable furnishings.

3. Thumbnails

4. Layout out typefaces that may work

Logo development example with Lake Lodge with type exploration after numerous thumbnails.

5. Start putting words together and deleting fonts that do not define the goal

6. Create color palettes with popular colors label based on research and perceptions

7. From narrowed down fonts create typestyle of words

8. Also created in Illustrator some wave like brush strokes.

9. Concept 1: Placed two contrasting but complementary fonts together in

10. Concept 1: Adjusted the characters by adding swashes to connect the type.

11. Concept 1:Extended leg for k into a descender that intertwined in letters below.

IMAGE 7-22

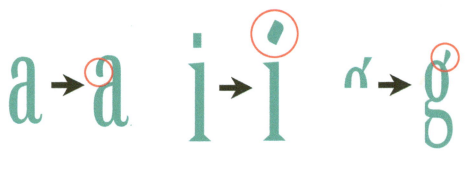

12. Concept 2: Adjusted type to fit a relaxed sensibility of being at the Lake.

IMAGE 7-24

13. Need more so stylized the house.

14. It still was not quite finished so added the setting sun.

IMAGE 7-25

15. Almost finished but the overall elements are not connected. Look at the final concept in Image 7-26 to see the slight but important adjustment to the type..

16. In total 5 concepts were presented. Image 7-26 was the logo selected by the client's board.

IMAGE 7-26

Graphic Artist: Neal Hettinger

Portfolio Building Assignment — Restaurant logo design

Logo Design Overview

Design a color logo with an icon or graphic element. The logo will be used in a marketing campaign including menu, signage, advertising, flyers, website, and TV spots. For inspiration, collect examples of well-designed logos, i.e. search the internet for examples and take screengrabs to store for reference.

Client: Au Bonheur Grand Restaurant

Target Market: Patrons of fine dining at an upscale restaurant that like to spend two to three hours enjoying the multi-course meals.

Restaurant Décor: Spacious seating with tablecloths covering mahogany, decorative dark wood adorns the rooms with soft lighting.

Menu: Geared to higher end tastes with entrees such as a wagyu fillet mignon, served in a classic Blender Béarnaise Sauce with a potato terrine at $93. Fare includes beef, Bluefin tuna, Iberico pork, with McCarthy salad, caviar, special desserts and expensive wines and liquors.

Instructions:

1. Sketch 6 different thumbnail ideas after you do your research.

2. Show to others to get their opinions and then adjust the sketches.

3. Do not use a computer to create the thumbnails.

4. Based on your thumbnails choose two very different approaches and create a color comp of each one.

5. Consider the fonts, colors, layout for the target market's age group, income level, entertainment importance.

6. Use any or all of Adobe Creative Suite programs for the comps.

7. Think how you should present your design on a page and print them out. Recommend one logo on a horizontal format of a letter size page for each comp.

8. Create a print quality PDF for your records.

References

1| (2022, December 12). The best logo fonts and how to choose your own. Adobe.com. Retrieved July 3, 2024, from www.adobe.com/express/learn/blog/best-logos-for-brand

2| Ariella, S. (2022). 20+ Logo Statistics You Need to Know [2023]: Facts + Trends in Branding. Zippia. www.zippia.com/advice/logo-statistics

3| Solomons, M. (2023). 130 logo statistics: Design trends, influence, and business success. Linearity. www.linearity.io/blog/logo-statistics

4| Lauron, S. (2023). Logo Color Schemes: 25 Examples + Tips from HubSpot's Brand Team. Hub Spot. https://blog.hubspot.com/marketing/color-palette-famous-websites

5| Luffarelli, J., Mukesh, M., & Mahmood, A. (2019). A Study of 597 Logos Shows Which Kind Is Most Effective. Harvard Business Review. hbr.org/2019/09/a-study-of-597-logos-shows-which-kind-is-most-effective

Color by any other name

Learning Objective

The user will be able to customize a color palette for projects such as brand marketing, event flyers, and websites. They will be able to discuss the psychology of colors. The student will be able to identify the color modes for final publishing.

Professional terminology

Additive system: Colors applied to a substrate that reflects wavelengths.

Analogous colors: Adjacent hues on the color wheel that will produce harmonious compositions.

Complementary colors: Opposite hues on the color wheel producing contrast in designs.

Cool color: Hues on color wheel mixed with blue.

Hue: The name of a color.

Intensity: The saturation and visual strength of color.

Monochromatic: Using one hue with varying shades and tints in a composition.

Pantone (PMS): A system requiring exact parts of inks be mixed to obtain a color.

Pigments: Substances mixed with oil, water, or other mediums to produce color.

Primary colors: Three hues that cannot be obtained by mixing other colors.

Prism: Refracted surfaces that separate the light wavelengths into seven colors.

Secondary color: Hues created because of mixing primary colors.

Shade: Making a color lighter usually by adding white.

Spectrum: The different wavelengths of colors seen by the eye.

Subtractive system: Colors emitted by an electronic source that interweave the wavelengths.

Tertiary color: Hues created by mixing primary and secondary colors.

Tint: Adding white to a color.

Triad: Three colors that are equal distance apart on the color wheel.

Warm color: Hues on the color wheel that are mixed with red or yellow.

IMAGE 8-1

AI Practicum} Firefly Prompt: font faces in different font styles and colorful background, 3d illustration, copy space focus.

Color in graphic design

In addition to choosing the learning about how to use fonts to create a sense of confidence in the good or service, graphic designers also study color psychology and color theory. What differentiates a good graphic designer from a great commercial artist is understanding how and when to apply color to a design for a planned response.

The color wheel of a traditional painter is divided into three divisions, each containing 12 hues. The first level of colors is known as the primary hues since no other colors can be mixed to create them. Green, orange, and violet are secondary colors that are combinations of the primary colors.

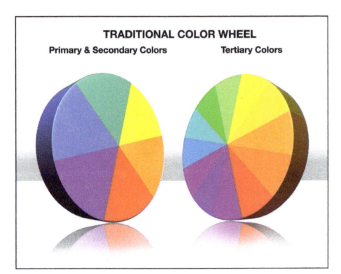

IMAGE 8-2

The basic color wheel with three levels of color.

Practicum} Color wheels created in Apple Numbers and imported into Photoshop for retouching.

The final level, tertiary colors, is produced by combining equal quantities of the secondary colors with the primary colors. The following colors are included: yellow green, yellow orange, red orange, red violet, blue violet, and blue green. When these colors are referenced by visual artists, the primary color is placed before the secondary color.

One of the most widely used instruments for comprehending color is Sir Isaac Newton's color wheel. By projecting light through a prism onto a white wall, he identified the seven primary colors. In one of his publications, Sir Newton arranged the hues on a wheel in the order of their spectrum appearance. Although graphic artists may consult a spectrum to identify these hues, the color wheel is a more practical instrument that can be customized for various applications. The conventional color wheel is the outcome of the process of combining pigments to create paint. Ink pigments are employed in color wheels for print applications, while color illumination is employed in color wheels for computer monitors.

Violet is the term used to define the combination of blue and red in the second level of the color wheel. The prism, which contains violet rather than the non-spectral purple, serves as the foundation for the color wheel. However, a significant percentage of artists contend that this secondary hue should be referred to as purple. It is acceptable for graphic designers to refer to the combination of the blue and red colors by either name.

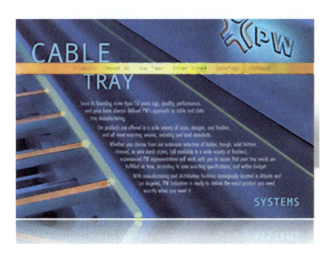

IMAGE 8-3

Graphic Designer: Neal Hettinger

A cable tray company website's landing pages demonstrate how a blue monochromatic approach with a complementary color of orange can make an otherwise less than interesting image have impact.

The 12 fundamental hues on the color wheel produce the highest level of intensity, but they also provide a restricted range of options for a graphic artist. To broaden their choices, they can incorporate black to generate shades, blend in grey to produce tones, or combine a color with white to produce tints. A color's value is its range from darkness to lightness. When a color is applied to a white background, it often appears lighter, whereas on a black background, it tends to appear darker.

The color wheel provides graphic designers with useful relationships between hues.

Visually attractive and creating a sense of harmony and coherence, layouts often make use of adjacent hues, which are known as analogous colors. Colors that are opposite each other on the color wheel are known as complementary colors. Tertiary colors will be opposite one another, and primary colors will be opposite secondary colors.

IMAGE 8-4

Roses created with Artificial Intelligence do not show a difference between violet and purple.
AI Practicum} Roses created with Adobe Firefly. Prompt 1: generate violet rose against a green garden. Prompt 2: generate purple rose against a green garden.

Selecting contrasting hues on the color wheel cause the values to appear brighter. The saturation of a color would be diminished if it were used alone or in combination with an analogous hue in a design. For maximum contrast, use two colors that are complementary to one another; this works especially well when one color serves as the primary hue and the other as an accent. A more harmonious arrangement is the result of a designer's use of complementary colors.

IMAGE 8-5
Process and RGB color circles showing the different relationships.
Practicum} Color wheels created in Apple Numbers and imported into Photoshop for retouching.

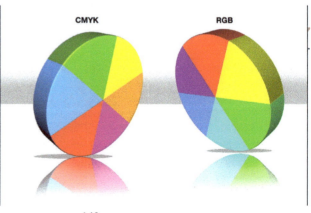

A monochromatic color palette implements one hue with its values and intensities caused by saturation. A triad color scheme is selecting three hues that are equal distance from one another on the color wheel. Triad palettes can give the layout depth with large areas of color that balance the medium spots, and accent colors. Color triads are using related hues on the color wheel, but they are not exact opposites. These triads that use the secondary and tertiary colors have underlying colors connecting them, which express a feeling of harmony and unity in the design for the viewer.

The psychology of colors

Numerous graphic designers contend that color is subjective and, therefore, the scientific results are too general be used when creating a color palette. As an example of the confusion, a darker color may make someone feel depressed or it can create a sense of luxury for an automobile.

Another example is how a worker may perceive a dark-colored box as being heavier than the same box in a lighter color. A tremendous amount of academic research has been done on color theory and responses. It has concluded there is not one proven reaction to a color. As one might logically think, a favorite color for a shirt would be different than someone's favorite color for a house paint. Graphic artists should ignore the theories and studies on color.

IMAGE 8-6

Graphic designers need to know how viewers will react to the colors that they use. The cool hues are on the left side of the color wheel and incorporate blue. Because they tend to recede, these colors can add depth to a design. Cool colors generate feelings of stability, calmness, and relaxation. On the opposite side of the color wheel, warm hues, composed of red or yellow, evoke feelings of passion, energy, and even danger. These hues tend to stand out in the layout.

Red is considered a high-arousal color, often stimulating people to take risks. Blue may trigger feelings of trust, security, order, and cleanliness. Yellow may encourage feelings of optimism, hope, cowardice and betrayal. The secondary colors such as violet and purples may inspire feelings of spirituality, mystery, royalty, or arrogance. Green is associated with nature, health, good luck, and jealousy. Orange may activate feelings of energy, balance, and warmth. The value and intensity of a hue will affect the response as well. Green can have strong reactions. A tint of green in a may attract one person but repel another person.

Age is also a component of how a person perceives a color. Babies and toddlers are attracted to the pure primary colors and not tints. Gen Z favor lime greens, bright oranges, and bold blues as well as black. Millennials prefer energetic colors and organic tones. Baby boomers lean toward pastels of the secondary colors.

IMAGE 8-7
The power of color

Beginning designers often resort to using only black, white, and grey colors. They may argue that this approach is artistic, or different, or a way to attract attention but the facts do not back them up.

Studies have shown the power of color. For instance, in University of Loyola, Maryland research, color was found to increase brand recognition up to 80%. In a comparison of black and white advertisements with the same ads in color, discovered that color designs were read up to 42% more.[1] In packaging design a product has less than a second to get a shoppers attention. Black and white labels grab an observer's attention for less than a second whereas color labels attract customers for more than two seconds.

According to a study by CCICOLOR , the Institute for Color Research, shoppers subconsciously make a decision about a product in less than 90 seconds. Color was the basis for 60 to 90% of the people. In 2003, the Xerox Corporation and International Communications Research conducted surveys with businesspeople that found:

90% Feel color can assist in attracting new customers.

90% Believe customers remember presentations and documents better when color is used.

83% Believe color makes them appear more successful.

76% Believe that the use of color makes their business appear larger to clients.

When graphic design graduates apply for a job, if their portfolio contains mostly black and white type, the interviewer will recognize that the designer is not comfortable using color in their solutions. Experienced graphic designers can quickly discern that the program's software engineer, not the designer, created the colors in a design.

Understanding how we see color

Every given wavelength of visible light corresponds to a specific hue and can only be observed either directly from a light source or reflected off things. Hence, recognizing color is a function of sight rather than a physical sense. For instance, in a room without light, green paint is a liquid, but it could be any color. Based on past experiences with taste, smell, or touch, color optically triggers subconscious reactions and responses.

Graphic designers can create stronger eye-catching visual in their layouts with an understanding of how viewers are affected by their past reactions to color and why they make decisions based on color. From the viewpoint of some manufacturers who ignore color studies, all garage doors would be white. However, people are attracted to color and will pay extra for the option of a hue.

IMAGE 8-8

The medium decides the color system

A simplified explanation of printing with a press, is the process where pressmen roll various metal or paper plates with different colors of ink and then press each plate onto the substrate. These same colors are sprayed onto paper by inkjet printers. Black, cyan, magenta, and yellow are the four inks utilized. The material is dyed with varying amounts of primary, secondary, and tertiary colors to achieve these effects.

The CMYK color scheme relies on a subtractive process in which the ink color is reflected back to the viewer. For example, a green object absorbs all colors except green. Magenta replaces red, and cyan substitutes for blue in the four-color process. Cyan ink permits a broader range of color variations due to its lower intensity than blue paint. The printing process generates a variety of hues and tones by combining varying percentages of the four basic ink colors. When a color is less than 100%, it produces a tint, such as 50% cyan for a light blue and 100% cyan mixed with 80% magenta for a dark blue.

Pantone Matching System (PMS) ink printing provides a more in-depth method of color mixing. Although this printing method is more precise, it can be more expensive. A graphic designer can utilize one or two PMS colors in addition to four-color process printing if they require colors that cannot be achieved through the four basic ink colors. When a six-color press is used a mixture of four color and PMS inks, the printed pieces have more depth because of the ink coverage and intensity of color. Orange mixed with the four-color inks has a brownish value while a PMS orange appears as a mix of red and yellow.

When designing for the internet, films, or multimedia where the images and designs are emitted from a light source, three different primary colors are used. Red, Green, and Blue are the primary colors expressed in values from 0 to 255. The RGB system create countless colors of light by joining them together in process known as Additive color.

IMAGE 8-9

RGB colors are more brilliant and saturated than printed hues.

AI Practicum} AI image created with Adobe Firefly. Settings were photo, digital art. Prompt was "gradients of red, yellow, green, cyan, blue, and violet on a computer monitor."

Black in the CMYK system is the combination of all colors at 100% while black in the RGB system is the absence of any color—visualize the color of a monitor is turned off. White in printing is obtained by using a white substrate for printing and white in electronic sources is devised by an amalgamation of RGB at their full intensities of 255. Another option for electronic light source design is to identifying colors is the Hexadecimal number system. Every color combination has a Hex # which can be easily copied and placed into the design or color palette.

IMAGE 8-10

Graphic Designer: Neal Hettinger

Practicum} Stock photo retouched with motion zoom blur in Photoshop and retouched in areas to allow the typeface to be readable over dark and light areas. Note no gradations, glows, or soft shadows around type to make the words readable. The background was retouched to allow the elements to read without distractions.

Color focuses the audience and client

Color is visually appealing and, when employed effectively, can significantly influence potential customers. Emotional responses may be induced by the values and combinations of tints. In the event that the design is unsuccessful, the client will engage the services of a different graphic designer. The client will want to evaluate the design's success. The designer wants to ensure the method is not limited to soliciting the opinions of a few individuals. Ultimately, the actions by the target market speak for themselves which is why the goal of the marketing needs to be a clear and simple statement without trying to accomplish too many things.

When presenting to a client, instead of saying "we used a shade of blue green" give it a name such as turquoise. For warm colors use the terms chartreuse (yellow green), amber (yellow orange), vermilion (red orange), red violet, for cool colors use purple (blue violet) and turquoise (blue green). The graphic artist wants the client to feel a connection with the color and not think of the hue as a mix of pigments.

IMAGE 8-11

AI Practicum} Adobe Firefly settings were art, digital art. Firefly prompt: clock melting away off a computer desk with warm colors. Photoshop used radial motion spin at different levels for 3 transparent layers.

Coloring time

During the concept stage when the graphic designer knows the creative direction, they do not want to be slowed down picking colors to use and establishing the palette in the software programs. Before starting the comp stage, commercial artists save valuable time by creating a library of different colors, shades and tone as well as color palettes to use ahead the actual design.

Graphic designers begin by conducting research, after which they create thumbnails to generate ideas. If the artist has ideas, they are excited about based on the brief, they will quickly thumbnail them on paper or on the computer with notes. After the research stage, the artist will revisit the thumbnails and consider their relevance. Strong designers determine the message they want to convey, establish a goal, and consider the characteristics of their target audience. Their research will help decide what colors will convey the message and what colors will attract the audience to the design.

One of the three areas of design that graphic artist of all levels of experience struggle with is choosing colors. The top three methods for creating a color palette are image sampling, objective color selection, and using the company style guide's restrictive and limited options. The third method is focused on branding the company and creating a recognizable identity which makes it easy for the graphic designer to choose colors.

IMAGE 8-12

The eyedropper method can provide multiple options.

Since the graphic artist chooses the colors, sampling the image with an eyedropper tool is considered subjective. This type of palette builds harmonious color relationships that are composed of complementary and analogous colors. The highlights are small areas to grab the viewer's attention.

In Image 8-10, the vacation services flyer utilizes a color scheme taken directly from the retouched photograph with the eyedropper tool. This image sampling creates a cohesive and visually pleasing design. For readability, the background trees and road were darkened where the type would be difficult to read. Notice that it did not need outlines or drop shadows. Those old practices are the sign of a defeated designer. Software applications allow us to utilize better techniques.

Building a color library based on their attributes is objective since graphic artists are not bringing in their own personal experiences and opinions. This may the most difficult method of establishing a color scheme. Since the graphic artists are relying on their knowledge of color theories on how people react or respond to hues, this process can be problematic. It is easier to use black or white type if the graphic artist does not have a talent for working with color relationships. For instance, if the commercial artist is working with a product that is targeting a youthful market, they need to devise ways to bring in energetic and vibrant colors

IMAGE 8-13

Image sampling can save time creating a color palette. Note the red-magenta highlight sampled from the flowers at the front door. Depending on how it is used, the color may need to be toned down.

Strong layouts have an elements of subjective and objective design. Commercial artists open their creative right-side brain to visually solve the project. Designers can fall back on the 60-30-10 rule where 60% of the area is devoted to the main color, 30% to the supplementary color, and 10% for spots of the minor color.

Before the master artists started on the canvas, they conducted studies, many of them in-depth in black and white to show textures, values, and dimensions. Once they had several of the areas defined, the artists created a color scheme, which they mixed onto a palette. Instead of stopping their work to create the colors, the palettes allowed the artists to dab their brushes and stroke the canvas. To save time, the artists took the time to create the color palettes at the beginning, before the process and the creative flow.

The graphic design process can apply the same methodology as the old master painters. The graphic artist begins with a blank page and finishes with a design that integrates type, images, colors, and space. The color swatch table functions similarly to the master's color palette. Since commercial artists do not need to worry about their paint mixtures drying, they can create several color schemes to draw from as they work. The creative flow needs to move forward with experimentation and uninterrupted haste. A phone call, for example, can disrupt the thought process and lead to the loss of the solution.

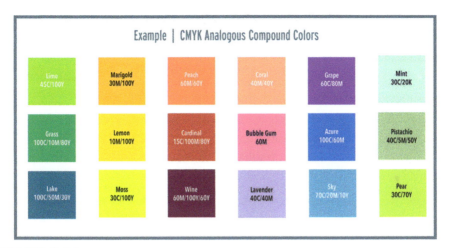

IMAGE 8-14

When noting color breakdowns in 4 color (CMYK) printing, the color callout starts with the order in which the press will print the project Cyan, followed by Magenta, Yellow, and Black and the percentage of that ink in the color. For example, a Candy Red would be 10C/100M/90Y/0K. The 10C equals 10% Cyan and "K" stands for Black. Some professionals with say the term stands for key color but that actually refers to the most prominent color utilized in the design. Educators may refer to the "K" as a shortcut for the term "keyline" which was a thin black line in days of mechanicals that defined the edges of photos, artwork, and colors that before creating the press plates. However, these lines, along with registration marks, fold marks, trim marks needed to be in all four colors at 100% to show up on each color plate.

When a graphic artist loads their color palette, they will adjust the colors to achieve their design goal. With InDesign you can establish palettes such as earth tones, festive hues, and luxurious colors. An earth-tone color palette draws inspiration from nature and consists of natural or neutral hues such as brown, green, gray, and red. While festive hues cold refer to specific holidays, they also refer to parties and celebrations.

Therefore, the colors are strong, vibrant, and intense. Luxurious colors signify elegance and sophistication so a black with a hint of blue may be a choice, metallics such as warm gold, reddish copper, and a cool silver will set off whites and purples. The attributes method is based on research and color theory.

Changing over from manual graphic design concepts and mechanicals has dramatically shifted the color palettes and trends. This shift was made possible by the ability to achieve more precise color results. Previous concepts were created with color pencils and art markers on Canson or presentation hot press boards. Lines denoted the content, while sketches of photographs or illustrations represented the images. Color options were limited and static.

With RGB monitors, digital print design allowed for millions of colors. The limitations of traditional color tools, such as Design markers, were obsolete. This allowed graphic artists to explore bolder colors and use more tints and shades since they could actually see the colors on the screen and not try to guess with film overlays. In the comps, graphic designers would see what colors the press would print.

Design on the world wide web was limited to what most viewers could see on their 216 color monitors and the limitations of transferring data over fax lines. As monitor technology improved with higher resolutions, so did color palettes. They became more dynamic and complex.

Computer programmers and developers and, not graphic designers, handled web design in the early 1990s. The main hurdle was using code to create visuals. When technology improved, graphic artists could create and control the design on the web. Paul Hebron, a noted Los Angeles graphic artist, stated that until websites used a visual program to layout the pages, it would be limited to computer techies.

Developers liked gradations, white or black backgrounds, and reversed type and chose colors that rendered consistently across a multitude of displays. They influenced branding and web design trends. They used highly contrasting colors to grab the "surfer," such as bright primary hues.

With software that graphic artists could use to design, UX, or user experience, became the focus. As technology improved, the speed of downloads allowed print design trends such as minimalism, maximalism, flat art, nostalgia, cultural, and infographics to become part of internet design. Graphic artists can easily customize color palettes for marketing in all digital uses for a consistent message and branding globally.

IMAGE 8-15
Photograph RAW not retouched.

Demonstration: Building an image sampling color palette

This assignment is predicated on the assumption that a client has submitted an image for three different concepts. This problem can be resolved by generating a variety of comps with different fonts, colors, and textures.

Enhancing and retouching the photograph of the heirloom rose requires Adobe Photoshop. Prior to beginning the demonstration, take a snapshot of a flower or rose. Be careful when using stock photographs since they have already been retouched. This picture of the rose was taken with a Nikon camera, not a mobile device. That is the reason the image is sharp, devoid of any graininess or distortion, and has a short depth of field. If you must use a phone camera, it is important to address these potential problems. A RAW file is an uncompressed file that is smaller than a PNG and has more detail than a JPEG.

Part 1 | Retouching

1. Duplicate layer
2. Select the rose only using the Object Selection Tool (Adobe's Artificial Intelligence technology) and the lasso tool to add (shift) or subtract (option) areas, copy>paste to put rose on another layer and then name the layer "rose."

IMAGE 8-16

3. Use the same tools to select unwanted items on the duplicated layer. In this case it would be the hand and textured jacket. Use the contextual task bar and prompt to add background.
4. On the Rose Layer use the dodge tool with a soft edge on the darker areas. Settings: Range is Midtones; and Exposure is 20%. With a smaller soft brush lighten the dark edges. Settings: Range is Shadows setting; and Exposure is 60%.
5. Increase Contrast 50 and Brightness 10 on the rose. Use a clipping layer.
6. Within the clipping layer, increase Saturation +20 and decrease Lightness -5.
7. Hide all unused layers and create a combined layer of all the visible layers.
8. Unsharpen: Amount 200; Radius 1; and Threshold 0.

151

BEFORE   AFTER

IMAGE 8-17

Prepare the image to show the client. Adjustments are based on a flyer image being attractive and not needing the rose to be color accurate.

9. Using Content Aware, add enough image at the top to center rose. Use Content Aware to fill in and open space.

10. Crop squarely to focus on rose.

11. Save as Tiff. Convert to CMYK.

12. Select different areas of the rose light and middle values with the eyedropper tool. Using the background select the dark and middle areas.

IMAGE 8-18

152

Part 2 | Color research

The amount of research on book colors is astounding. For instance, Printivity Insights has current trends of bestselling book covers colors: Mystery use black, gray; Romance soft colors such as pink, red, purple, and white; Fantasy is predominately purple, blue, green, silver, gold; Sci-Fi covers are black, gray, red, green, and purple; Horror unsurprisingly is red and black; Nonfiction can be blue, red, yellow, black, and white.[2]

In another article about colors of books, yellow covers were considered cheap books so do you use it for a nonfiction book. Generally, the least liked book colors for women were orange and brown while a third of those surveyed liked blue the most. Red covers were for mysteries, thrillers, and horror stories while going with the tint of pink usually meant it was a romance book. Green was good for nature and black was highly favored and since it made the other elements stand out, publishers used it a lot. White meant the book was about naivety or purity.[3]

A designer can get too much information which means use some of it but do not argue with your client on the best color.

Part 3 | Creating the color palettes

One of the more difficult color combinations is red and green. When used together, people immediately think of the holidays. Other examples of color associations are black and orange for Halloween and red, white, and blue for patriotic themes. Graphic artists can use the complementary colors of red and green as shown in Image 8-19, to step away for the holiday association.

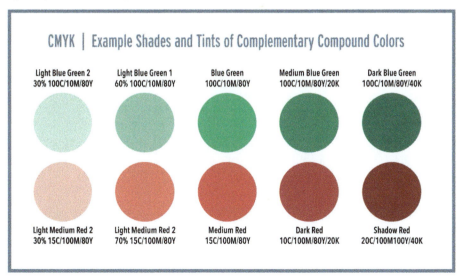

CMYK | Example Shades and Tints of Complementary Compound Colors

Light Blue Green 2 30% 100C/10M/80Y	Light Blue Green 1 60% 100C/10M/80Y	Blue Green 100C/10M/80Y	Medium Blue Green 100C/10M/80Y/20K	Dark Blue Green 100C/10M/80Y/40K

Light Medium Red 2 30% 15C/100M/80Y	Light Medium Red 2 70% 15C/100M/80Y	Medium Red 15C/100M/80Y	Dark Red 10C/100M/80Y/20K	Shadow Red 20C/100M100Y/40K

IMAGE 8-19

1. Set up a Harmonious Palette.

    a. Choose complementary tints and shades of blue greens and red oranges.

    b. Choose analogous colors of violets and yellows.

    c. The color chips are arranged with the colors work well that together.

2. Set up an Objective Palette.

    a. Work with green color chips since the book is about nature, light yellow chips as highlights since the it is nonfiction and vermillion chips to create energy.

    b. Create a base color and texture.

    c. Add a highlight color of amber.

3. Use Image Sampling for a palette.

    a. Using the eyedropper in Photoshop, create different greens, yellows, and red color chips from the entire image.

    b. Lay the colors out as you see their importance in the design using large, medium, and small chips.

    4. Using Greek text, build three different layouts.

Learning Library Exercise – Critique Junk Mail

Building a graphic design library can be expensive if all you do is buy books and subscribe to magazines. These are good options but look around your daily life. A free and easy to obtain method is delivered right to you—check your mailbox. Before you trash this direct mail, look through it and keep the examples that are good. Before you add it to your library folder, stick a Post-it on each one and note down what you liked about design.

For this exercise, you need to analyze and evaluate the font choice, scale of elements, and specific shapes used in direct mail in a critique. Spell check, proof, and read aloud to find mistakes in grammar and context.

1. Photograph 5 different direct mail pieces.
2. Import them into InDesign and add a caption under each with a number.
3. In a text box, add a subhead with a number in an appropriate font followed by three to four sentences in a body content text which comments on the layout and the element choices used for the design.

4. Remember you are a designer so do not just drop the pictures and type on to the page—design the page.

References

1| White, J. V. (1997). Color for Impact. Strathmoor Press.

2| Wiley, N. (2023, March 13). Eye-Catching Book Cover Colors That Sell Best. Printivity Insights. www.printivity.com/insights/2022/12/09/book-cover-colors-that-sell-best

3| Bennett, S. (2023, January 30). How To Judge A Book By Its Colour. Writers Write. www.writerswrite.co.za/how-to-judge-a-book-by-its-colour

Space and the mind

Learning Objective

By the end of this chapter, the learner will be able to defend the importance of space. They will be able to interpret the Gestalt Principles. The reader will be able to demonstrate depth in design.

Professional terminology

Closure: Readers visually fill in the missing gaps of incomplete objects to form a whole shape.

Emphasis: To give prominence to one element over the other parts of a design.

Figure & ground: Humans perceive objects or shapes as distinct from their backgrounds.

Foreshortening: Shortening or distorting an object to give the illusion of depth.

Gestalt Principles: People perceive visual objects according to how they are arranged.

Horizon Line: A visual border where the sky meets the surface of the earth.

Juxtaposition: Two or more elements adjacently placed to contrast their differences.

Negative Shape: The background form around the design elements.

Perspective: Drawing three-dimensional objects in two-dimensional surface.

Positive Shape: The area filled in the design by elements.

Proximity: Individuals see objects that are close together as part of a group.

Space: The area around the placed design components that draws the viewer's focus.

Vanishing Point: In two-dimensional design, lines drawn in perspective appear be three dimensional by meeting at a distant mark.

Volume: The three-dimensional equivalent of the two-dimensional shape.

White Space: The absence of any elements in an area of the design including hues.

IMAGE 9-1

AI Practicum} Firefly prompt: floating blank pages lined up to fly into the vibrant milky way toward the horizon in background; Combined in Photoshop with fake flyers and large page with message.

All visual designs use space

There is a simple method to enhance the professionalism and visual appeal of a given design. Once a graphic designer understands this fundamental principle, they will discover that fully mastering this technique is the most challenging aspect of creative approaches. Any skilled designer knows that maximizing space is an essential strategy when beginning the layout process. It is used by professionals in painting, photography, architecture, civil engineering, vehicle design, and sculpture. Graphic artists embrace it.

Graphic artists view designed space as a combination of positive and negative elements. One way to understand designed space is to visualize a pool. The water is the negative space, while the elements in the pool take up positive spaces. A pool that is stuffed with floats, people, and toys has been transformed from an inviting environment to one that is unappealing. A designer's ability to strategically position large, medium, and small items on the page is the goal for achieving visual appeal. If the arrangement is entirely filled, there is no contrast. The designed space and the elements need contrast.

Space is important for visual balance because it distributes elements evenly across a design. This balance can make a design feel stable and harmonious, enhancing the overall experience for the viewer. In some contexts, especially in luxury branding, the generous use of space can convey a sense of exclusivity, sophistication, and high quality.

Quality oriented stores have an open floor plan with an uncrowded atmosphere, while cost-oriented stores are stuffed wall-to-wall with merchandise. In the former, the shopper will find a good selection, but it is not overwhelming because it signals value. In the latter store, there are stacks of every item because sales volume is this store's goal. If this comparison were made on a scale of loudness, the quality store would be a can bubbling brook and the low-cost store would be Niagara Falls.

IMAGE 9-2
Which bay would you want to traverse?

The fundamental element

Space can be visually defined as the white blocks in a grid, the blank areas on the page, the empty sections created by the elements, or the open parts in a layout. Graphic designers refer to it as negative and positive space. There are several underlying reasons to use space in a design.

Creating a focus and emphasis is part of good design. Graphic artists can highlight specific elements by providing ample space for reading. This draws the viewer's attention to important aspects, such as a call-to-action button, a key message, or a key image. The strategic use of space can guide users through a design, leading their eyes from one element to another in a deliberate order. This flow encourages interaction and keeps users engaged. In user interface (UI) design, space improves usability by making interactive elements easier to identify and click or tap. It helps create intuitive and user-friendly interfaces.

By separating elements, it improves readability and comprehension, making it easier for viewers to process information. In text-heavy designs, adequate spacing between lines, paragraphs, and margins improves readability. A design with well-utilized space appears clean and organized. This cleanliness often translates to a more professional and aesthetically pleasing look, making the design feel more approachable and less cluttered.

Clients will argue that information should occupy all available space. They will request specific elements to be made larger, followed by increasing the size of other elements to emphasize a particular point. If the professional graphic designer fills the entire space, the message will lose its appeal.

An effective layout includes margins that establish a boundary around the design. While margins don't have to be equal, many people find symmetrical margins more appealing. A design can run text up to an image or a block of color, but the graphic artist should avoid extending it to the very edge of the page.

Understanding and utilizing open areas are the one skill novices struggle with since they design on a computer and rarely print out the comprehensive so they can hold it in their hands and really view it at full size. Contrast is the main principle in attracting viewers and Space is unquestionably the most important element needed to achieve contrast.

Do not underestimate design space. A true graphic artist will craft his design to appear to have more space and less elements.

IMAGE 9-3

Graphic Designer: Neal Hettinger | Art Director: Todd Bane

Which ad does the audience want to read? Which ad has a better chance at being remembered?

Depth in design works because of space

Designers strive for their two-dimensional projects to have depth. They will use the traditional technique of adding shadows to type and images. Their hope is the shadows will make the elements leap off the page. Instead, the design looks antiquated. A more effective solution is using the Gestalt principle of figure and ground with space.

The singular intangible aspect of design that distinguishes the amateur from the expert is the utilization of space within a layout. Every phase of graphic design employs this element. The illusion of depth creates spatial organization in an image by establishing a foreground, midground, and background. Content blocks are more legible when surrounded by whitespace. A design attracts clients by presenting a concise message, building in adequate margins, and arranging pieces in an orderly manner that directs attention to the call to action.

When beginning designers evaluate their layouts on computer screens, they will be uncomfortable with the space. Before filling the space, the graphic artist should print the layout to see the design correctly.

If a graphic artist perceives a layout as a three-dimensional design, the margins will represent the side of the building. Placing the type and images at the edge leaves no space for the reader's eyes to rest. It is better to have a large margin rather than too small of a margin. Although equal margins are not necessary, most individuals find comfort in them. Try a solution where the top and bottom have more space than the sides. Try to limit the type to an image or color block rather than the entire page.

Principle of Unity

To communicate a single message, graphic designers must know how to produce visual layouts where all the elements work together. If the parts of a design do not seem connected, the viewer is not comfortable, and the audiences eye will move on. They are attracted to one piece that is the sum of all the parts.

The goal of a design is to present a clear message without the clutter of unimportant and distracting elements. To engage the reader, the marketing piece must be appealing and harmonious. To establish and communicate a brand, the design needs to have a consistent identifying theme with the choice in typography, types of images, palette colors, and use of space.

Gestalt theories lead to cohesive design

Up until the early 1900's, psychologists, graphic artists, and marketers thought the best way to present a message was to load up as much information as possible on a page and people would read it all. The theory was based on structuralism which held that elements by themselves had no meaning. Humans only saw the overall structured system as a collection of elements in relation to other elements and not the individual aesthetics.

A group of psychologists proposed that people see the individual parts of a layout that create whole patterns, and they tested this hypothesis in areas of perception, learning, and understanding. The results, known as the Gestalt Principles, are the basis for effective graphic design communication.

Graphic artists want to signal to the viewer using visual cues. Six Gestalt theories on how the eye and mind use groups of images were developed by the group of German psychologists. The theories describe how people perceive visual objects according to how they are arranged and organized to identify the most important information.

How elements are put together will form coherent idea because they relate to how a viewer's visual systems work. People see the parts of a design in a way that makes sense to them based on the layouts visual arrangement. The design will appear more finished, attractive, balanced, and, most significantly, professional if it adheres to the Gestalt concepts.

1. Proximity

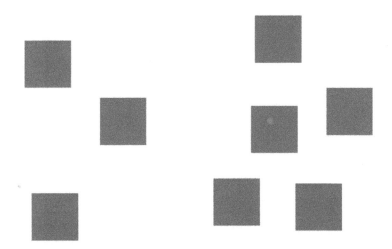

IMAGE 9-4

The viewer sees a group on the right and randomly placed boxes on the left.

In Gestalt psychology, the principle of how people perceive visual objects according to how they are arranged is referred to as Proximity. Individuals are inclined to perceive objects that are close to each other as part of a group. This principle implies that the manner in which we organize visual elements into coherent patterns or groups can be influenced by the spatial proximity or nearness of objects.

When eight squares are arranged in a haphazardly way and not adjacent to one another, they are considered as distinct shapes. Elements that are situated in close proximity are perceived as being more closely related or belonging together than those that are separated by a greater distance. Related elements should be place close together to be perceived as a part of the group. When the eight squares are placed in a tight grid, the layout conveys the impression of unity. Despite the fact that the squares are distinct entities, they are perceived as a group of squares.

IMAGE 9-5
Demonstration of Unity.

When a designer would like to emphasize an element, they can use the principle of proximity. The element that is intended to be prominent can be positioned separately from the group in order to communicate to the viewer that it is unique or different. The viewer will notice that one square more if seven squares are arranged together and one square is not positioned close to the group.

2. Figure/Ground

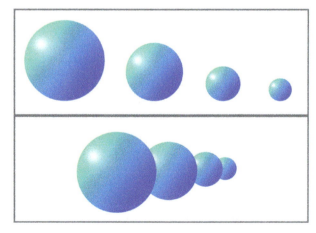

IMAGE 9-6
Note the top image has the same four spheres but the arrangement does not create depth since the spheres do not overlap and are on a horizontal line.

The human eye can distinguish different items in respect to their background, surrounding region, form, silhouette, or shape. Maintaining a correct balance between the foreground subject and the background draws attention and creates a visually appealing layout with the contrast. Dramatically shortening long objects or elements that are closer to the viewer will make them appear smaller will give the illusion of depth.

IMAGE 9-7

Imitation of Escher demonstrating how the eye can be fooled by depth and perspective.

AI Practicum} Firefly prompt: people in different attire walking on staircases that defy gravity and perspective. Retouched areas in Photoshop.

Arranging design elements to set items apart from their surroundings is the process of visual object perception. Artists like M. C. Escher deceived viewers by using perspective in his artwork to create false foregrounds and backgrounds. His staircases used incorrect perspective to make the viewer believe the staircases had no beginning or ending.

IMAGE 9-8

Example of scale for perspective. Witch in foreground, tree in the middle ground, hut in background.

AI Practicum}Firefly prompt: Witch large in foreground in a dark forest with a small hut in the background; focus on hat, blurred face. Retouched and improved with Photoshop.

Larger images tend to come forward on the picture plane, while smaller images tend to recede. A layout can create the illusion of space by overlapping objects, shapes or type. The saturation of color and value creates space. As we look into the distance at mountains, the value and intensity of color decreases. Perspective creates the illusion of space by having one, two, or three vanishing points.

3. Symmetry

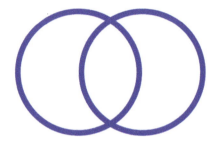

IMAGE 9-9

The principle of symmetry refers to the observation that all the people visually prefer elements that make a complete form with balanced elements, rather than a design made up of haphazardly placed components. When two circles overlap, they are perceived as one structure made up of two circles that create three shapes. The audience desires a sense of coherence. Designers can attain symmetry by ensuring a harmonious equilibrium or cohesive integration of the design elements.

4. Similarity

IMAGE 9-10

When items bear a resemblance to each other, viewers may see them as a collective or configuration known as the Similarity principle. Individual components can be employed to form a unified visual representation. The resemblance among several elements might manifest in their shape, color, size, texture, or value. Logically, unity is achieved when individual pieces exhibit a higher degree of commonality.

Pop Art such as Andy Warhol's Campbell soup cans repeated with color variations employed this concept. The artwork comprises various discrete objects, yet it presents itself as a cohesive whole due to the shared characteristics among all the photos. When producing artwork, pictures, designs, and images, it is crucial to avoid any unplanned or random elements. All pieces are interconnected and should be strategically positioned, taking into account that our eyes naturally seek out connections.

IMAGE 9-11

Adobe Stock illustrations of green artichokes repeated in a line except the final image is replaced with a red bell pepper. The viewer is attracted by the red shape and quickly reads to the right.

Commercial artists can use the principle of similarity to bring the focus to something different in a layout. In a line of green artichokes, the viewers would expect the last image to be the same as the first but by replacing it with a red bell pepper, the viewer skims over the artichokes and focuses on the pepper. Juxtaposition is technique where two or more dissimilar elements are placed close together to emphasize their differences and evoke an emotional response.

IMAGE 9-12

Letter 'A' still reads without leg and the stylized crossbar leads the viewer's eyes.

According to the continuity principle, individuals possess an inherent tendency to seek out repeating patterns and lines. Elements that are arranged in a linear or curved manner are believed to have a stronger connection compared to those that are not arranged in this way. The human brain exhibits enhanced cognitive processing when presented with continuous forms and lines as opposed to fragmented ones.

For instance, when two lines intersect, our perception is that of two uninterrupted lines crossing each other, rather of two distinct lines converging at a single point. The orientation of a line determines the path the track our eyes will follow. If we design the crossbar of the letter "A" as a flowing thick to thin line, it creates a virtual eye path, that directs the observer's gaze toward the end of the line. A commercial artist will use a path, line, or curve a to draw the viewer's eye in a specific direction.

6. Closure

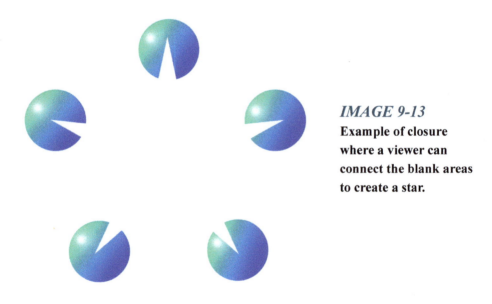

IMAGE 9-13
Example of closure where a viewer can connect the blank areas to create a star.

A psychological phenomena known as Closure is where we tend to close complete lines and objects that or not in fact closed. When an object is incomplete or uses positive and negative space so that it is not completely enclosed, people see the whole by filling in the missing parts. People tend to create a complete object by filling in gaps when parts are missing in a visual image. This is a powerful concept for graphic artists. Instead of showing every part of a logo, the design can be more interesting and memorable by not showing each part which results in the formation of a single continuous image. When a graphic artist uses the Gestalt principles with UI, user interface, the design creates visually appealing and easily understandable compositions.

IMAGE 9-14

AI Practicum} Merged two Firefly images with Photoshop and retouched for effect. Utilized clipping paths and masks. Which Gestalt principles are being used for this visual design?

Overall, graphic designers who can understand the Gestalt theories will create effective and eye-catching layouts. By organizing the elements in accordance with the six basic Gestalt principles, viewers can easily understand and identify the important parts of a message.

Learning Library Exercise — Logo designers

Conduct research on three out of the five logo designers mentioned in Chapter Six. Select two to three screenshots of their work and compose a short statement for each one using design terminology to explain the rationale behind your selection. Make sure that your explanation includes the identity of the graphic artist. Organize your photos on separate InDesign pages for each logo designer and insert text beneath each image.

To capture a screenshot on a Mac, follow these steps: Hold the shift-option-4 and drag your cursor over the image you are including in your report. To capture a screenshot on a PC, follow these steps: Press the Windows logo key plus Shift + S. Press the print screen (PrtSc). To capture a screenshot on a mobile device, follow these steps: Hold down the 'Power' and 'Volume Down' buttons. Devices may vary, so if you have problems, conduct a search on the internet for your specific device.

Self-Quiz

How well are you progressing with this book? As a measurement, you can take the following quiz which covers Chapters 1 through 9. The number in the parenthesis is where the question came from if you need to look up the answer.

25 Questions from Chapters 1–9

1. What is a mood board? (7)

    a. A strategy utilizing the results of ideas and testing to layout a project.

    b. A board where individual characters are joined together to form individual words.

    c. Determining creative strategy by collecting elements through research.

    d. The visual representation of an alphabetic letter.

2. What feeling can symmetry provide the viewer? (2)

    a. Grouping related elements unequally can cause concern.

    b. Provides harmony through balance.

    c. By distorting all the images is an effective eye-catching technique.

    d. Not seeing the creation as a whole to lead the eye off the page.

3. What is a good way to push yourself in the creative process? (1)

    a. Get out of your comfort circle.

    b. Start on the computer.

    c. Copy the masters.

    d. Make everything the same size, color, and tone.

4. When telling a story, what are the 6 W's to include? (1)

    a. Who, what, why, when, where and how

    b. Who, what, why, when, where and time

    c. Who, what, when, where and how.

    d. Who, what, which, when, why and how.

5. Which answer best explains what a 'line' can be used for in visual design? (3)

    a. Amounts of time.

    b. Direction.

    c. The horizon.

    d. All of the answers are correct

6. Which statement is INCORRECT about the creative process and designing solutions? (4)

    a. By focusing on the attributes of an object, person, place, character, topic or theme, product, or service, you can find a characteristic that might lead to an idea.

    b. Doodle, sketch, let your mind wonder.

    c. Brainstorming is not a good method for inspiring creativity since you may get a bad idea.

    d. Stand, sit, walk, move around, play a game while focusing with others on the creative problem.

7. Which statement is correct? (8)

    a. Warm colors recede.

    b. Green is associated with energy and fire.

    c. Black is not a color.

    d. White added to a color makes it a tint

8. What is a good reason to crop an image? (2)

    a. To change the image.

    b. Remove an interesting part of the image.

    c. Focus the viewer on the lack of content.

    d. Create a visual impact and visual interest.

9. Which statement is correct about primary colors? (8)

   a. They can be created by adding the secondary colors.

   b. Children can see these colors better than tertiary colors.

   c. They are complimentary on the color wheel.

   d. There are 5 main primary colors.

10. What may occur to a digital photograph if it is enlarged 500%? (2)

   a. Tassel the image.

   b. Cause the image to pixelate creating a graphic pattern

   c. Cause the image to look too sharp and out of focus.

   d. Make the image subtends too strong.

11. What color can be used to create shades? (8)

   a. Black.

   b. Yellow.

   c. Shading.

   d. White.

12. All 2-D shapes are essentially derived from three basic structures: (3)

   a. The square, the triangle, and the circle.

   b. The cube, the pyramid, and the sphere.

   c. The square, the sphere, and the circle.

   d. The square, the triangle, and the cone.

13. What are the four basic layout principles? (2)

   a. Balance, proximity, repetition, alignment.

   b. Contrast, repetition, scale, proximity.

   c. Proximity, contrast, alignment, repetition.

   d. Balance, proximity, repetition, alignment, scale.

14. Why are lines important to use when creating a design or taking a photograph? (2)

    a. Lines lead the eye around.

    b. Lines are always angular and suggest durability.

    c. Lines used in pairs suggest horizons.

    d. Lines are always calming.

15. Which statement best defines shapes? (2)

    a. A shape is an open, unconfigured area.

    b. The general tone of something is a shape.

    c. They are created either entirely by tones or shades.

    d. None of the answers are correct.

16. When you create a design or take a photo, all the parts are called what? (3)

    a. Graphics.

    b. Elements.

    c. Pieces.

    d. Designs.

17. Which answer best defines a line? (3)

    a. A path created by a point moving in space.

    b. A three-dimensional mark that is without depth.

    c. Always connects 3 visual points.

    d. Lines have to always be seen.

18. What is chiaroscuro? (2)

    a. Adding tints from a specific direction in drawing and painting.

    b. Adding black to grey.

    c. Archaic term for fonts.

    d. Using light and shadow to create dimension on an image.

19. What is an Ampersand? (5)

    a.   Digitally created by electrical bursts into sand.

    b.   Symbol representing the word 'and.'

    c.   Adding sound and vocalization to a digital graphic.

    d.   Famous album cover designer.

20. What is a mechanical? (1)

    a.   It is the concept of the entire ad.

    b.   The final file usually set up as a pdf for printers.

    c.   Tight designs with all the elements and no typos laid out.

    d.   No text should cross the margin, as it could be cut off in post press trimming.

21. In a mechanical what is a 'bleed"? (1)

    a.   Derived from the term for the area used on the side of a page when a scribe had a paper cut.

    b.   When cyan and magenta are mixed together.

    c.   The area around a design that goes past the trim.

    d.   The opposite area of call-to-action text.

22. What are the four Categories of classifying typefaces? (6)

    a.   Serif, Sans serif, Script, Decorative.

    b.   Script, Sans serif, Grunge, Decorative.

    c.   Decorative, Sans serif, Script, Helvetica.

    d.   Decorative, Formal, Serif, Humanist.

23. Who created moveable type? (5)

    a.   Milton Glaser.

    b.   Johannes Gutenberg.

    c.   Paul Rand.

    d.   Wilhelm Steinitz

24. Logo issues (7)

    a. May not have any formal training.

    b. Too intricate and detailed.

    c. Use typefaces that have not been adjusted to fit the brand.

    d. All of these answers are correct.

25. What is the figure/ground principle? (9)

    a. People perceive objects or shapes as distinct from their backgrounds.

    b. Several elements are grouped by their shape, color, size, texture, or value.

    c. In a visual image, people tend to create a complete object by filling in gaps where parts are missing.

    d. People visually prefer elements that are complete.

Design Repeats Itself

Learning Objective

In this chapter the student will be able to characterize the historical art and design movements. They will be able to outline early commercial art. The reader will be able to simulate the Art Nouveau and Art Deco.

Professional Jargon

Catalog: A publication listing products for sale

Character: The letters that make up a typeface.

Culture: Includes collective beliefs, habits, items, and other traits of a group.

Halftone: A screen of a greyscale image for reproduction.

Hand-lettering: Typography drawn for unique and decorative designs.

Impressionism: The 1860s French painting style emphasized light and color.

Industrialization: When an economy shifts from agriculture to manufacturing.

Lithograph: A drawing on limestone using a greased pencil.

Pattern: An arrangement of a repeated decoration or ornament in design.

Periodicals: Publications that are released at regular intervals.

Pictograph: A drawing of an image.

Style: Artists' techniques, include color, form, and composition.

Texture: The tactile quality that creates a sensation of a consistency on a surface.

Vintage: Signifying or having to do with something of quality from the past.

IMAGE 10-1
Artist depiction of old world meets new world using Firefly AI and Adobe Photoshop.

More than an opinion

The emergence of the new industrial era created the need for genuine design expertise rather than just placing information in an area. The long history of graphic design has paralleled significant technological and social transformations in Western society, and the reactions of philosophers, artists, and designers to these changes. Key transformations in the culture encompassed education, social organization, technology, and lifestyles. The increase in reading rates, decrease in production costs, and rise in advertising revenues led to a significant growth in the number of newspapers and magazines. In the United States from 1830 to 1860, publications increased from 800 to 5,000 which marked the beginning of design strategy. Graphic design had to significantly convey the desirability of products to increase consumption which brought about the study of commercial art.

Design movements

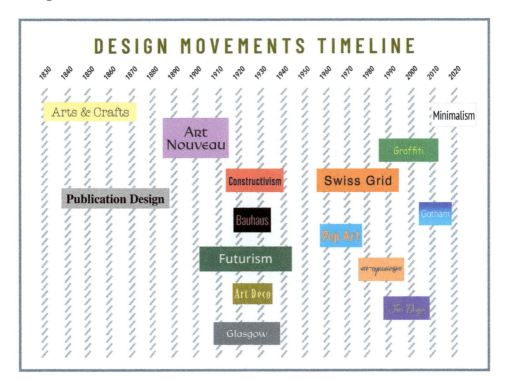

IMAGE 10-2
Approximate time periods for major and some minor art and design movements.

Prior to the Industrial Revolution, printers were designing ads and packaging utilizing small amounts of type with pictographs. Technology changed society and art enormously with the advent of mass-produced products and quality printing presses. However, the designs of marketing were varied and not effective. The need to supply the consuming masses with products reached a plateau in 1856 when Owen Jones, an architect and designer produced an enormous catalog of patterns, styles, and decorations that were used to improve the aesthetics of poorly made packaging. A new profession was created—the commercial artist. Being able to draw type and images was a not a skill possessed by most printers who just guessed at how to fill a space. Ad agencies in the early 1800's did not design ads—they purchased the space for their clients. Manufacturers began to search for successful commercial artists.

Commercial artists learned to stand out and catch the eye of consumers with creative solutions. Before long, ads with drawings and pretty type were the norm so commercial artists needed inspiration. They began to learn and not guess at techniques to attract potential consumers. Commercial artists used paintings with type in the 1880's to sell products which led to the study the of art, the elements and the movements. A designer who only uses what they see in their daily life is limiting their creative solutions. Understanding the history of art movements allows the graphic artist to use a style in a modern project. While this chapter is about art history, it is a chapter for graphic artists to understand the where, why, and when to use visual technique in their creative designs. Art is found in global movements, with influences from different cultures, such as Egyptian, Aztec, and Asian art. This cultural fusion inspires modern graphic designers to incorporate diverse influences, resulting in rich and varied design outputs.

Early Graphic design styles

IMAGE 10-3
Firefly generated old English tavern sign saying Ye Alde Tavern with a lion painted on wood.

Prior to advertising, newspapers generated income by publishing the news and rumors. In the early 1700's, printers discovered a new source of income by selling space in their publication directed at consumers. Advertisements and product packaging design was limited to numerous hand drawn typefaces and type interspersed with extremely decorative borders and typography. This Victorian design style used centered layouts for symmetry and flowing lines since the composition was created by hand.

Graphic design and photography have been closely associated from the earliest attempts to use cameras to take pictures and designers to use those images in a design. Lithographic printer Joseph Niepce created the first photograph in 1826. He started looking at photography by trying to find a way to automatically transfer designs onto printing plates. The strategy of drawing images onto lithographs to print in a design attracted customers for a few decades.

All through the 1800s, advancements in photography technology steadily progressed, culminating in the ability to integrate photographic processes with printing. The New York Daily Graphic made history in 1880 by publishing the first reproduction of an image that displayed a whole spectrum of values. The image was reproduced using a halftone screen that fragmented the image into a sequence of tiny dots, with different sizes producing tonal gradations ranging from completely white paper to completely black ink.

IMAGE 10-4

Photography changed the world as we see it.

AI Practicum} Firefly prompt: create 1800s sepia toned city street. Merged with Adobe stock image of old camera in Photoshop.

Arts and Crafts movement

In response to the glut of mass-produced goods during mid 1850's Industrial Revolution, the English Arts and Crafts design movement grew from Victorian-era decorative art. The movement's design organized the spaces asymmetrically, based on their intended uses. At the time, this idea was unheard of since the prevailing design model called for a box layout with a symmetrical balance. At the movement's forefront was William Morris, who advocated a high-quality packaging design that consisted of purposeful proportioning of space and careful control of type size, type selection, and margins, which increased sales of the mass-produced products. For the most part, The Arts and Crafts movement did not promote a specific style, but reformed graphic design philosophy.

Commercial artists that want to give a concept a retro feel to their design can use the Victorian and Arts and Crafts styles in their solutions. By adding textures and freehand type, the designer can appeal to the nostalgic consumer.

Art Nouveau Movement

IMAGE 10-5

Example of an Art Nouveau poster created with Adobe Illustrator.

Art Nouveau, translated as New Art, was an unconventional design style that emerged in France in the late 800's. The decorative design, characterized by sensuous styling and a combination of geometric and flowing natural shapes with somewhat angular contours, was partially influenced by the linear patterns found in Japanese prints.

The organic design style quickly gained prominence in western Europe and the US between 1890 and World War I. In 1890, the United States was exposed to Art Nouveau through the distribution of Harper's periodicals imported from France and England. Eugene Grasset created cover designs for multiple issues, featuring his images that frequently depicted women in the Art Nouveau style.

IMAGE 10-6

Example of Art Nouveau borders to use in design from Adobe Stock.

Art Nouveau sought to modernize design by moving away from the varied historical styles that were previously fashionable. Artists derived inspiration from both organic and geometric shapes, developing sophisticated works that combined fluid, natural forms with sharper, angular outlines. The movement changed the conventional wisdom of the arts, which regarded liberal arts, such as painting and sculpture, as superior to decorative arts based on craftsmanship. The art world realized that commercial art was more than just handcrafted ornaments.

Modern graphic designers are inspired by the movement's complex patterns, organic shapes, and flowing lines to produce visually captivating works that draw in and hold the attention of viewers. Art Nouveau revolutionized typographic designs by departing from conventional serif fonts and embracing more expressive and ornamental styles. The hand-lettered characters were free-flowing to complement the artwork which has been incorporated into contemporary design. By embracing contemporary materials and technologies, Art Nouveau broadened poster design. It should motivate contemporary graphic artists to experiment and use advanced technologies, such as digital tools, artificial intelligence, and software, to produce memorable designs.

IMAGE 10-7

Example of historical Art Nouveau poster from Adobe Stock.

Commercial artists use modern variations of the Art Nouveau style to depict fantastical and romantic ideas. It may possess an antiquated appearance, prompting graphic artists to modify their color palettes and artwork in order to reduce this characteristic. Art Nouveau typefaces are often ornamental, featuring ornate stroke terminals, slanted crossbars, and occasionally, intricate capitals. The font Bocklin was used in classical rock 'n' roll albums design and P22 Art Nouveau captures the Art Nouveau sensitivities.

Art Nouveau design key characteristics

Overview: Distinguished by its fluid, organic forms and intricate details, it endeavored to diverge from historical styles and establish a completely new and contemporary aesthetic by combining art and craftsmanship. Art Nouveau sought to elevate graphic art to the status of fine art by emphasizing individuality and artistry.

Significance: Organic forms, curvilinear lines, and motifs from plants, florals, and animals were incorporated by artists into the "new art movement." With the objective of reestablishing a sense of harmony and beauty in a society that is becoming increasingly industrialized and mechanized, nature was emphasized. In its captivating designs, it embraced asymmetry, which diverged from the rigorous symmetry of the styles of the early 1800s.

In Vogue: Appeared in the early 1890's.

Origination: Began in Brussels but flourished in Paris.

Influencers: Paul Gauguin, Aubrey Beardsley, and Henri de Toulouse-Lautrec.

Characteristics: Use of sinuous, curving lines that resemble the movement of natural forms, such as waves or vegetation. Incorporates elements from the natural world, such as leaves, blossoms, vines, and trees. The forms are frequently stylized, yet they remain identifiable. The style is extremely ornamental and features intricate patterns. Fonts are hand drawn to be structurally loose and rounded.

Attraction: The quality of fluidity, elegance, and motion that typically directs the viewer's gaze seamlessly throughout the picture.

Production: Employs soft, natural hues such as muted greens, blues, yellows, browns, and golds, including gentle, progressive shading.

Constructivism Movement

IMAGE 10-8
Example of Constructivism design with Adobe Illustrator.

Beginning around 1913, the movement emerged as the most prominent design style following the Russian Revolution against the Tsarist autocracy in 1917. Many Russian graphic artists, in support of the new communist revolution, merged political propaganda and commercial advertising into the constructivism style, creating posters and packaging that aimed to attract buyers to state products. It was a radical and influential movement that sought to align art with the goals of the new socialist society, emphasizing the creation of art for social purposes rather than for individual expression. Constructivism advertising became a means for artists, poets, and others to advance the goals of Soviet society.

People viewed traditional art forms like painting and design as elitist and disconnected from societal needs. In response, constructivism utilized abstract, geometric forms and simple shapes like squares, circles, and lines to create compositions that were dynamic and emphasized the new industrial social order. It is characterized by photomontage images, strong typography, and innovative layouts.

Constructivism's design approach inspires contemporary graphic designers. Constructivism used color to evoke emotion resulting in visually memorable layouts. It is a source of inspiration for graphic artists who are involved in social justice or activism. They utilize posters, digital media, and advertising to advocate causes such as human rights, equality, and climate change.

Modern political campaign advertising design and movie prerelease promotions, such as the Star Wars teaser ads, have been significantly impacted by the potent visual language of Constructivist propaganda. Font families such as Akzidenz-Grotesk, Acumin, and Retro Bold are based on Constructivism fonts.

By merging abstract elements with photography, constructivists pioneered photomontage. Digital graphic designers combine images with graphic shapes, text, and hues, that is similar to Constructivist posters. The graphic artists use similar collage effects and combine photography and graphic textures to generate multi-layered, mixed-media compositions.

Constructivism design key characteristics

Overview: Constructivism graphic design integrated art and propaganda, serving as a powerful instrument for political activism. It used stripped-down geometric forms and modest materials to create rigid angularity, thereby conveying a sense of dynamism and movement. The movement rejected any superfluous decoration.

Significance: An innovative visual language that was developed for the purpose of social change and propaganda. In particular, the dominant color, red, became emblematic of socialism, labor, and revolution, frequently dominating the artwork and posters of the era.

In Vogue: Result of 1917 communist revolution.

Origination: In Russia/Soviet Union.

Influencers: Vladimir Tatlin, Pablo Picasso, and El Lissitzky.

Characteristics: Geometric shapes, drawn with compasses and rulers, featured strong diagonal line. Red, black, white, and yellow used in stark contrast with heavy sans-serif typefaces that conveyed authority and urgency.

Attraction: Raw, functional design with asymmetrical balance where elements appear to be in motion creating tension and energy.

Production: Photographs and graphic elements were frequently combined on white paper to establish a compelling narrative, which was often achieved by utilizing limited ink colors. Posters, pamphlets, and other printed materials were mass-produced in order to disseminate political messages to the broadest possible audience.

Art Deco Movement

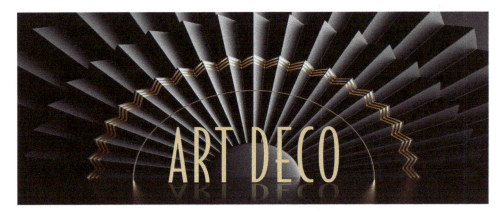

IMAGE 10-9
Website landing page header.
Practicum} Adobe Stock Modern Art Deco style background with Bodega Sans font and reflection design added via InDesign.

From 1920 until the end of the 1930's, graphic artists sought new forms of expression that would speak to the inventive spirit of the age. This approach that evolved into the Art Deco style reflected modern technology. It was characterized by smooth lines, perspectives, shapes, and bright, sometimes garish colors. The patterns were based on geometric forms with designs from technology such as aviation, the radio, and the skyscraper and included chevrons, stepped patterns, sweeping curves, and ornamental sunbursts. Art Deco streamlined layouts with symmetrical trapezoidal and triangular structures.

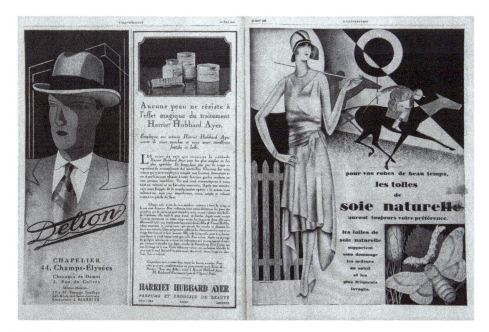

IMAGE 10-10
Example from Adobe Stock of historical Art Deco style newspaper ads.

By using Art Deco style's use of colors, image contrast, and typography, graphic designers create futuristic compositions. Some examples used in the entertainment industry's marketing of recent movies was Green Lantern and Rocketeer. Typefaces of the Art Deco period conveyed a modern sense of sophisticated, distinctive, and decorative forms. These typefaces are still popular today, particularly in designs that evoke a vintage or classic feel while maintaining a contemporary edge.

IMAGE 10-11
Graphic Designer: Neal Hettinger
Example of a concept for a high-end restaurant social post.
Practicum} Adobe Stock modern image with an Art Deco border added in Photoshop to create a sophisticated style to image.

Modern graphic designers manipulate the Art Deco Style of old-world glamour and fashion to create visual layouts that feel fresh and relevant. The lean lines and symmetry of Art deco style can fabricate an elegant visual for consumers. It is versatile and can also add a futuristic or technological component to the design. The utilization of rich materials, intricate details, and bold designs elicits a feeling of luxury that remains highly desirable in contemporary marketing of as lavish hotels, expensive theaters, and affluent apartments. The continued use of Art Deco style is due to its combination of its aesthetic appeal, historical significance, and adaptability, which remains relevant in modern environments.

IMAGE 10-12

Graphic Designer: Neal Hettinger
Art Director: Nigel Sherry

Rocketeer packaging for Nintendo used art deco motif to set the time period for the game.

Art Deco introduced a new style of typography that utilized sleek, sans-serif fonts with geometric shapes and lines. The typefaces have high and low x-lines with diagonal and triangular character shapes. These highly stylized, elongated lettering fonts such as Bodega Sans, Broadway, Metropolis are utilized in branding and luxury packaging where a sense of elegance and vintage sophistication is desired.

Today in graphic illustrations, designers use simplified, elongated shapes to create elegant, modern compositions similar to sleek, streamlined forms of Art Deco. Modern designs often incorporate intricate patterns, metallic foils, and sleek typography reminiscent of the Art Deco period. Much like Art Deco use of color, graphic artist often designs for metallic inks like gold and silver as well as rich color combinations like dark reds, blues, greens.

Art Deco design key characteristics

Overview: Modern graphic design is still influenced by Art Deco's enduring blend of modernity, luxury, and bold geometric aesthetics. The sleek forms of the object exude affluence and sophistication, while its bold shapes and strong lines maintain a sense of elegance and refinement.

Significance: The movement introduced an innovative feeling of elegance and sophistication to design through the utilization of geometric shapes and vibrant colors. Art Deco graphic design promoted customized typography and streamlined images, which became integral to modern graphic design.

In Vogue: At its peak from the 1920's to the 1930's .

Origination: Some of the style elements originated in France but the majority of the movement evolved in Europe and the United States.

Influencers: Romain de Tirtoff, Le Corbusier, and Tamara de Lempick

Characteristics: Defined by the use of bold, geometric forms such as the recognizable sunburst motif, zigzags, chevrons, triangles, and trapezoids, this style accentuates symmetry, balance, and the recurrence of geometric patterns for a polished and organized appearance. It favored extravagant ornamentation, including intricate patterns, sculptural panels, and detailed friezes. Utilized daring geometric sans-serif typefaces.

Attraction: Vertical emphasis and symmetrical layouts are frequently incorporated into the movement's clear lines and modern aesthetic. Decorative embellishments are sometimes used to preserve the balance between modernity and elegance.

Production: Metallic inks and paper printed with heavy rich black and light colored typefaces.

Swiss Design Movement

IMAGE 10-13

Example Swiss style with sanserif type, limited color palette, and grid layout.

Swiss graphic artists pioneered the development of a very influential grid layout style emulated with a structured arrangement of unjustified sans serif type. The grid divided the page up into areas of type, photomontage, and space creating contrast with scale. These innovative graphic designers viewed design as an integral component of industrial manufacturing and sought to achieve impersonal and objective visual communication. They opted for photographic pictures instead of illustrations and selected industrial-looking typefaces rather than those specifically meant for books that were free from decoration ornamental distractions.

Around 1946, a grid style was developed by Swiss designers that celebrated functional simplicity. These mathematical grids emerged as a comprehensible and harmonious method of organizing data and are considered the most defining features of Swiss Design. Grids provide structure and consistency, allowing designers to create well-organized and balanced compositions. The grid helps in aligning text and images, ensuring that the layout is clear and logical.

While grids provide structure, Swiss Design often employs asymmetrical layouts to create dynamic and engaging compositions. This approach to design contrasts with traditional, symmetrical balance by using a contemporary sense of space and elements. This modern method is an organization of elements on an invisible grid to achieve visual unity.

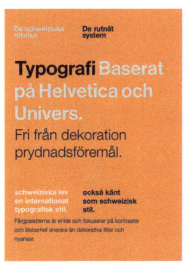

IMAGE 10-14

Swiss Design favors sans-serif typefaces for their simplicity and legibility. In 1957 Helvetica and Univers typefaces were developed to place a strong emphasis on clean simple readable information that has been carried over into modern design, influencing everything from internet application to print media. The typography is set flush left, ragged right for readability and lack of awkward word spacing.

The color palettes are simple and focus on contrasts and legibility rather than decorative filters and gradations. Black, white, and shades of gray are common, with occasional use of bold, primary colors.

Objective photography and images are used to convey information realistically filtering out propaganda and the exaggerated claims of commercial advertising. Geometric shapes, such as circles, squares, and lines, are also frequently employed to create visually appealing and logical compositions.

The Swiss design approach is very similar to the minimalism style popular in the 2010's favoring simplicity and functionality over ornamentation. This minimalism is evident in many contemporary designs, from logos and branding to user interfaces and product design.

IMAGE 10-15

This structurally clean and concise combination of typestyle with space is common for corporate branding. It's simple, elegant appearance lend itself to several applications such as brochures and catalogs, or websites where the grid presents an easy-to-read format to simplify the information that focuses consumers on the product.

Swiss design key characteristics

Overview: Swiss typography and design were a significant 20th-century design movement. White space is crucial for clarity. Isolating elements highlights their significance without creating chaos. White space enhances readability and text emphasis.

Significance: Central to the design were grid layouts to prioritize communication and sans serif typography selected for their modern and legible qualities, often placed asymmetrically, creating a dynamic yet balanced composition.

In Vogue: Emerged in the 1940s and 1950s.

Origination: Switzerland and Germany.

Influencers: Max Miedinger, Joseph Mueller-Brockmann, HR Giger, and Adrian Frutiger.

Characteristics: The design employs a simple yet eye-catching color scheme to guarantee clarity and coherence, frequently displays a strong contrast to boost the visual impact

Attraction: Streamlined by eliminating unnecessary components like ornamental accents so that each piece is functional for easy comprehension. This approach emphasizes a strong neutral structure to organize content, producing a visual flow.

Production: Normally, black ink with large areas of color printed on white paper.

Pop Art Movement

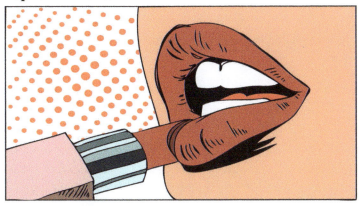

IMAGE 10-16
Adobe Stock example of comic book art based on artist Roy Lichtenstein's style.

Pop Art is widely considered one of the most influential graphic art styles in the United States. The movement commercialized celebrity, materialism, and everyday items and treated these subjects as fine art. It made ordinary goods trendy, converted mass-production into media replication, and reinvented the concept of commercialization.

In the 1960s, the art movement gained prominence. Irony and satire were frequently used in Pop art to comment on and critique the frivolous and commercial aspects of modern culture. Several Pop Art artists created their works using mass-production techniques like silkscreen printing to accurately reflect the mass-produced qualities of the products. Pop artist Andy Warhol's portrayals of Campbell's Soup Cans and Marilyn Monroe, are renowned and iconic examples of Pop art. While Warhol is known as a fine artist, he was educated in pictorial design at the Carnegie Institute of Technology. He worked as a commercial illustrator for publications such as Harper's Bazaar and Glamour magazine, and a graphic artist for Vogue.

IMAGE 10-17
Modern day pop art styled greeting card design. Created using Firefly, Illustrator, InDesign, and Photoshop.

Pop Art in the 1960's was a bold, vibrant, and lighthearted style created by intriguing personalities like artist Roy Lichtenstein. His comic strip art was based on comic books illustrations. Peter Max brought a different style to Pop Art with his free-flowing images and electrifying colors.

Practically every designer, architect, or creative individual has been impacted by the uniquely vibrant and vivid masterpieces. Presently, this graphic approach finds use in feature film posters, tattoo designs, animated TV series, and marketing campaigns targeting cultural connotations.

There are numerous Pop Art style typefaces. Blambot, Comicraft, and CC Biff Bam Boom and most of them are fun. They have energy and are eye-catching.

Pop Art design key characteristics

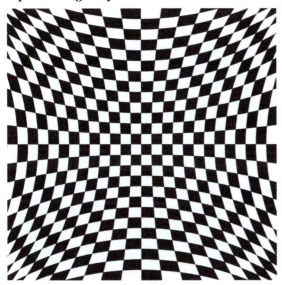

IMAGE 10-18
Pop art had geometrical and fanciful backgrounds from Adobe Stock.

Overview: Pop art draws inspiration from everyday manufactured objects, such as commercials, comics, packaging, public figures, and multimedia. Pop graphic artists reinterpreted this identifiable imagery in their own works of art with elements of humor, parody, and playfulness. Celebrity culture was a key theme and became symbols of broader cultural trends, such as fame, power, and commodification.

Significance: Challenged conventional distinctions between fine art and popular culture by transforming commonplace items and commercial visuals into artwork.

In Vogue: The movement originated in the 1950s and gained prominence in the 1960s.

Origination: Began in Great Britain and gained prominence in the United States.

Influencers: Andy Warhol, Roy Lichtenstein, and Jasper Johns.

Characteristics: Incorporated vibrant, striking colors, imitating the intensity of commercial printing and advertising with forms often simplified or stylized to highlight the object's attraction and beauty.

Attraction: Graphic art pieces conveyed a fundamental critique of consumerism, materialism, and the shallowness of modern society, incorporated irony, challenging society's preoccupation with consumption and celebrities through mass media imagery.

Production: Used commercial art methods including silkscreen printing, stenciling, and mechanical duplication. This adopted the industrial, impersonal aesthetic of mass production and eliminated evidence of the artist's hand from the artwork.

Portfolio Building Assignment– Gestalt Designs

Create images based on gestalt principles

For this part of the assignment, you should use your tracing paper. Below are 4 directions that demonstrate a Gestalt principle. Number each design solution with the corresponding number below and refer to chapter 8 to label which Gestalt principle your solution demonstrates. Each direction has an example - you cannot use the example. Create your own solution. Take photos with your mobile phone or scan the image. Then bring into Adobe Illustrator and recreate them as vector files. Create printer quality PDFS and combine into one pdf. Do not forget to label each design with Gestalt principle you are illustrating.

1. Create a form within a form:

    Draw 2 silhouettes that form an image/shape in the positive area. Example would be drawing 2 faces that create a wine glass between them.

2. Create a focus on one structure:

    Configure multiples of one shape or image to focus on a different image or shape. Do not use basic shapes such as circles, triangles, squares, rectangles. Example would be to draw 5 shapes where 4 are kidney bean shapes and one is a cone shape.

3. Create an incomplete but recognizable image or shape:

    Draw an image that is missing parts, but the viewer will still know what it is supposed to be. An example would be the points of a star, but the center is not seen so you only see the points.

4. Create images or shapes that mirror themselves:

    Draw forms that if you folded the page in half vertically or horizontally, the forms are the same on each side of the fold. An example is concentric circles—a circle within a circle within a circle centered on the page.

Present day design styles

Learning Objectives

The user will apply examples of modern design styles that will enhance average reports such as flat design for government infographics. They will be able to compare Minimalism and Maximalism design styles. The learner will be able to defend the use of Artificial Intelligence in graphic design.

Professional Jargon

Aesthetics: The arrangement of elements in a design to be harmonious.

Aspect ratio: The width in proportion to height of a visual element.

Client: The person hiring the services of a graphic designer.

Composing: The act of combining, arranging, and organizing all the components.

Dynamic: A composition that is not static and expresses energy to the viewer.

Identity: The brand's visual individuality designed for consumer recognition.

Image: A visual representation of a form in photography, illustration, or painting.

Scalable: Able to be changed in size, mode, and shape for different media.

Target Market: A description of the customer group marketing is directed to interest.

Text: A group of written or printed words to form a message or communication.

Visuals: A graphic design term indicating all the elements and components that can be seen.

While graphic designers often associate styles with specific eras, the essence of design lies in its ability to convey a message through any style. If a service wants to push its experience and expertise, the designer may want to use a retro style, such as pop art or art deco. Contemporary literally translated by the Merriam-Webster Dictionary is "occurring in the present." It borrows from the elements of several other styles based on the verbiage in prompts and defining styles and color schemes.

The majority of clients notice design styles after they have been used for years or even decades. Graphic designers should keep up with the latest styles to ensure their solutions remain relevant even after publication.

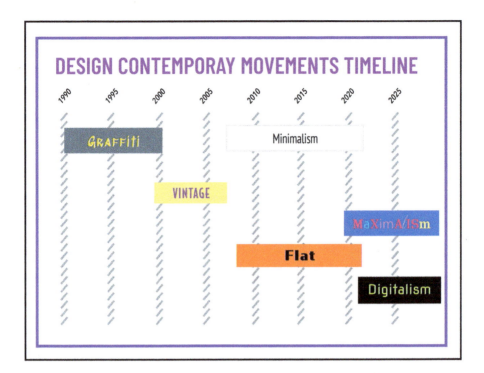

IMAGE 11-1

Marketers typically prefer past styles rather than innovative and eye-catching compositions that are beyond their comfort zone. Clients will opt for a safe approach they have so much that they recognize it. When a client wants a common and widely used design, or worse a template design, the graphic artists need to provide them an option that will stand out along with what the client feels safe choosing.

They bear the financial burden and are ultimately accountable for the success of a campaign. Since their profession revolves around creativity, graphic designers will advocate for a creative approach. The successful graphic artists are the ones who can explain an approach with expected results.

Just as font classifications do not have universal definitions and vary by foundry and software, design styles are not ubiquitous. Graphic designers will classify visual approaches into groups using different terms. Use the following list of basic styles with general descriptions as inspiration when designing a layout.

Contemporary design refers to designs produced from the 1990s to today. This time frame is based on the sudden availability of affordable personal computers. Contemporary graphic artists work in a globally influenced, culturally diverse, and technologically advancing world. Contemporary design isn't a fixed style but rather a reflection of current trends and it is constantly evolving.

Minimalism style

THE JETTA DIFFERENCE

soak in the simplicity

To the outside world we make bathtubs. But inside these walls,
we're here to make your business run as smooth as possible.
That means keeping our deliveries on schedule, our lead times
short, out product line broad, and our customization process
simple. After all, we're in the business of helping people relax.

We start with our customers first.

IMAGE 11-2

Graphic Artist: Neal Hettinger

Example of the Minimalism design style in a brochure spread.

Minimalism emphasizes simplicity through the use of basic geometric shapes and a limited color palette. The layouts are characterized by their cleanliness, with minimal retouching, minimal textures, and a focus on emphasizing a message through space. The design approach is to narrow down the use of unimportant elements. The message serves as the primary focus, resulting in a layout with minimal elements.

Without unnecessary decorations and ornamental components, a design often appears premium and rich. For this reason, higher-end brands frequently opt for minimalist aesthetics. For the shopper, it is easier to recognize the intended message or story with the lack of unnecessary features.

Minimalism is one of the few design styles that strictly uses clean lines and ample white space to create a sense of tranquility and order. In a world filled with so much visual noise, minimalism is appealing to marketers and graphic artists.

Emergence

Similar to most of today's design styles, minimalism is based on past fads. In visual arts, music, and other media, Minimalism was an art movement that began in post-World War II Western art, followed by a resurgence in the 1960s and early 1970s in

American visual arts. Around 2011, it became very popular in the United States for corporate marketing, advertising, packaging, and branding design. Between 2018 and 2019, the popularity of this style declined, and graphic design shifted towards a more maximalist style. However, during the Covid epidemic, minimalist design experienced a resurgence and remains popular for corporate brand identity.

Characteristics

The overall appeal of minimalism to graphic artists is to have a lot of space; the design can only use a few elements and a limited color palette. This simplifies the design process and the creative experimentation. Graphic designers tend to dislike content and opt for smaller typefaces. Minimalism is an uncomplicated approach that avoids trends and relies on fundamental elements such as balance, alignment, easy-to-read fonts, space, simple forms, and simplistic color palettes. The margins are large, and the logos are small in this design technique. The style's structure requires simplicity to communicate a clear and concise brand message. Minimalism generates a sense of visual harmony utilizing symmetrical and asymmetrical balance.

The font size is small to allow for more space. Typefaces are chosen for readability and legibility. The typography stands out since it has less to compete with in the design.

Benefits and Challenges

Many graphic designers embrace the minimalist design style due to its flexibility. The style can be applied across mediums, from print to web projects. They are easily scalable and adaptable, ensuring consistency. Unlike other styles, it fosters a contemporary attitude and is less likely to look outdated in a few years.

The sophisticated layout makes navigation intuitive and enhances the user experience in web design. With fewer elements, websites and apps load faster, creating a more efficient, user-friendly experience.

Some commercial artists dislike minimalism due to its visually cold limitations, which can make the style dull. They believe that the style lacks the personality of a brand and instead concentrates solely on the message or call to action rather than the design aesthetics.

Conclusions

Minimalism creates effective messages that easily fit into different contexts without losing its impact. Its modern, sleek professional design is ideal for corporate design, advertising, and packaging design.

Maximalism style

Maximalism in graphic design celebrates audacity, intricacy, and expressiveness, presenting a strong contrast to minimalism. It flourishes through stratification, powerful imagery, and innovation. It flaunts excellent design rules and guidelines and ignores the need for space.

Graphic artists may incorporate their individual personalities, passions, and artistic influences, resulting in more unique and individualized solutions. The combination of different components can provide a distinctive narrative that emphasizes inventiveness, rendering maximalism a preferred choice for designers seeking to go beyond the boundaries of traditional graphic design.

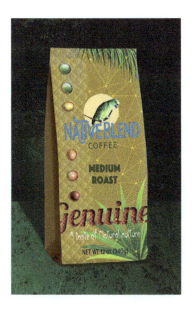

IMAGE 11-3

Example of Maximalism style applied to coffee packaging.

Emergence

After being hemmed in with plain and simple design of minimalism, graphic artists were starving for a stronger visual approach. Maximalism fostered an environment conducive to creative experimentation, rule-breaking, and joyful accidents. Thick strokes take the place of hairline strokes. The page is filled with bright hues, balancing subtle areas of shades and tints with oversized graphics and patterns that extend beyond the trimmed edges. While it can trace its roots back to the 17th century, it gained some acceptance in the United States in the 1960s. It is a style now that became fashionable after the Covid epidemic.

Characteristics

This opulent style urges designers to work with a diverse array of colors, textures, and patterns. This generates visually stimulating and dynamic designs that are vibrant and lively. Maximalist designs generate significant emotional responses through the utilization of striking imagery, diverse materials, and compelling visual storytelling. The complex designs invite viewers to discover a new style of design that is eye-catching. By overlaying multiple design elements, overloading textures, and competing patterns, designers can generate a sense of depth and dimensionality, resulting in a more tactile and immersive experience.

Maximalism frequently employs mixed media techniques. Combinations of digital effects, patterns, photography, and illustrations produce a richly textured appearance. This enables the development of substance and character in designs that are heavily reliant on text.

The designs use vivid, contrasting colors that captivate the viewer's attention. This has the potential to establish a particular mood and generate an emotional response. Unlike minimalism, which frequently employs muted or monochromatic schemes, maximalism permits the use of daring color combinations that can captivate and startle viewers.

This style emphasizes the use of saturated, eye-catching patterns to enhance designs with minimal or no white space. This does not imply a lack of space, but rather a lack of white space. Colors, textures, and shapes fill the space as background elements. Where minimalism cuts out any extra graphic elements, maximalism wants to use it all.

Conclusions

Maximalism is an alternative to the frequently constrained and restrained methodology of minimalist design. It distinguishes itself in a saturated visual environment by providing a wholly unique product. It subverts traditional design principles, prompting audiences to interact with elements that are unconventional, audacious, and vivid. This graphic design style permits more individualized, eccentric, and unconventional techniques for design. Because it's versatile and memorable, it can be used to announce new products, services, and events.

However, the rebellious design limits its use. Maximalism gets attention, but there are a lot of products and services this style does not represent. Corporate identity has limited uses since it frequently employs a diverse selection of intricate and bold typefaces, treating typography as a dynamic and expressive element. Various font sizes, unconventional placements, and a variety of types contribute to the composition's vitality and playfulness.

Graffiti style

IMAGE 11-4

Various graffiti styles can be found to study in locations around cities. Tag graffiti was found under an abandoned pier in Philadelphia and WildStyle graffiti on a wall shown in the upper right.

Graffiti as a graphic design style may be difficult to accept since it was used to deface property. When the use of color, structure, and creativity in typography are examined, it is an energetic attention grabbing element that can be used in design.

A number of recognizable approaches have discernible techniques. The first and most known technique is Tag art. The list includes Throwie, Blockbuster, Wildstyle, and Bubble.

Graffiti and street art are different but for convenience are grouped as one style where street art is more about the image and graffiti is focused on the word or words.

Emergence

If graffiti is considered wall art, it can be traced back to prehistoric cave paintings. Egypt, Greece, and across the Roman empire, people expressed themselves by drawing messages on walls.

The forms of Graffiti that graphic designers emulate and recognize the frenetic designs started in the 1960s in New York City. Graffiti artists "tagged" building walls and transportation with their names that were expressed in experimental almost abstract motifs.

IMAGE 11-5
Looks at the energy in this graffiti arrow compared to a geometric arrow.

In the 1980s graffiti moved into a mainstream elaborate street art that graphic artists recognized as a communication form and began to mimic in their graphic design. It became a popular graphic design style in the 1990's.

Characteristics

Graffiti is free flowing, lacks an historical basis that fills space. White space is negligible and negative space is non-existent. Bright colors with air brushed qualities are the main features.

Some graffiti such as Bubble and Throwie are cartoon like with shading and highlights. Wildstyle is elaborate with sharp 3D edges with complicated details. The typography has an uneven structure and proportions,

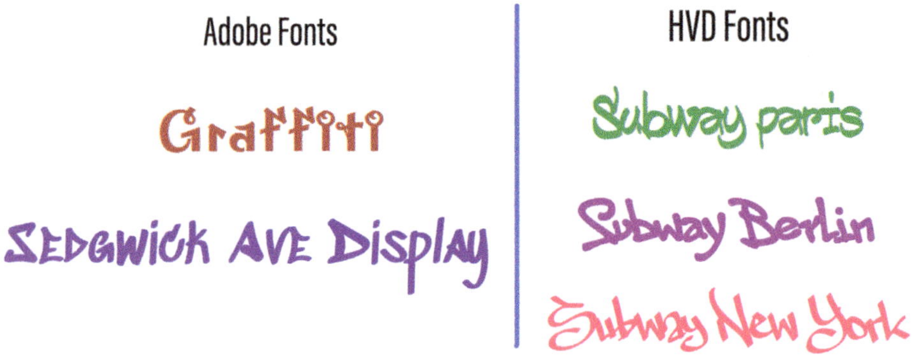

Adobe Fonts	HVD Fonts
Graffiti	Subway paris
SEDGWICK AVE Display	Subway Berlin
	Subway New York

IMAGE 11-6

Graffiti fonts are available from a number of foundries such as Adobe Fonts, HDV, and Google Fonts.

Benefits and Challenges

Some people will always dislike graffiti which narrows the use of it in design. It's market may not be appreciated but it is evolving to be less Decorative and more Script in its composition. Graphic artists should study the energy and flow of the type to be able to apply some of the flavor to their design solutions.

Conclusions

Corporate design may never embrace graffiti due to its history and how observers may react to it but there are marketing situations that should investigate the mannerisms of this edgy style. As younger generations who are more acquainted with the Graffiti style become shoppers, the rebel quality may be a solution.

Digitalism style

There is no widely accepted term for graphic design that utilizes artificial intelligence tools and contextual prompts. It has been referred as artificial intelligence-created design, AI-generated design, or generative design. Graphic artists may even refer to it as contemporary design.

It takes a human mind to prompt the AI generation of an image or design. Understanding graphic design terminology, fonts, colors, and contrast is vital, just like any successful solution. Graphic artists should view it as a valuable time-saving tool, just as they did when personal computers, along with Adobe Illustrator (1987) and Photoshop (1990), became available.

The prompts used to create this book's AI images show that AI is only one part of the solution. To create a cohesive design solution, nearly all the images require revision, retouching, and digital enhancement.

Internet developers and programmers use the popular terms User Experience (UX) and User Interface (UI). When they develop the product with the goal that the user has a good experience — that is UX. When user to computer interaction and communication is easy and visually pleasing on a device, webpage, or app, that is UI. Graphic designers have focused on both of these concepts for decades but used different terms with more aspects. Instead of UX, graphic artists speak about how the design engages the target audience which encompasses more than the visuals. In place of UI, the graphic artist refers to how the viewer responds to the design which could mean forming an opinion, acting on the message, or directing the viewer.

Emergence

Different forms of communication like text messages, search bars, and social media posts have led to digitalism. This style capitalizes on artificial intelligence to create complex images. It is a type of commercialized minimalism that incorporates space, thin, small type, vivid colors, natural textures, display typefaces, and abstract gradients. Designers need to utilize a methodology for designs that address accessibility, gender, age, economic status, location, race, and even religious and political viewpoints. Digitalism is an offshoot of contextual retouching and artificial intelligence-created images.

Characteristics

The appeal of the digitalism design style is the dynamic palettes with energetic images that can be easily produced. AI generated images save time and keep budgets down. It allows graphic designers who have creative ideas but lack the skill to draw, paint, or photograph a setting, to design.

Digitalism embraces bright colors and sans-serif typefaces to communicate information clearly and concisely, allowing for creative freedom.

Benefits and Challenges

The main handicap to AI digital design is the constant updates to the methodology of utilizing the cloud software. Graphic designers need to constantly learn new processes on how to prompt it for the best solutions. As an example, for type a graphic artist would go to Adobe Firefly until it suddenly moved over to Adobe Express. Unlike the design programs of the 1990's, web-based tools can be quickly changed. Software for computers kept revisions down to a few times a year due to the expense of thorough testing, selling, and manufacturing media to manually load into a computer. If an AI online tool is found to have flaws and difficult UI design, it can be revised without major costs typically associated with software development.

AI image generation has flaws—especially with the human figure. It will miss fingers, arms, feet, and distort faces. Graphic artists are using incomplete images without enhancement. A foreseeable result is crowded designs that confuse the reader.

Conclusions

There are a number of negative aspects to Digitalism. A major concern is clients using inferior designs developed by untrained people. The use of online templates and inexpensive graphic fabrications is already a common practice for marketing. As it is, many businesspeople do not know good design solution from an average or worse answer. Print and internet marketing is packed with this type of solution. A second difficulty is the lack of space in layouts since artificial intelligence cannot comprehend the concept of visual space.

AI is expected to be a valuable tool for designers, streamlining the process from brainstorming to final touches. Generative AI is experimental but the combination of 3D and 2D elements in a design is expected to become more common.

Vintage style

While not as prevalent in technology-driven sectors such as app development or UI/ UX, vintage-inspired design is commonly utilized in branding, packaging, fashion, print design, and select digital media.

Vintage graphic design techniques employ retro images, textures, and colors. They invoke the artistic style of the 1950s–1970s with dynamic patterns and fluid graphics. The colors lean towards a psychedelic palette, although a prevalent element is the incorporation of softer pastel hues, stripes, and checkerboards to evoke nostalgia for the fun past.

Emergence

Classic vintage design draws inspiration from past decades such as the 1920s, 1950s, or 1970s, whereas modern designers frequently amalgamate old components with present trends. This produces hybrids that merge retro aesthetics with contemporary fonts, color palettes, or layout methodologies. The style came back into favor in the early 2000's.

Characteristics

Retro color schemes, artisan artwork, and eclectic patterns are prevalent graphic techniques. Prominent vintage design features include 1950s and 1960s typography, muted color palettes, distressed textures, and hand drawn graphics. The vintage style fosters emotional ties, conveying authenticity and featuring a timeless appeal.

Instead of vibrant and stark textures, contemporary vintage designs use damaged, weathered, and muted textures. Script or serif styles with depth continue to characterize typography, but cartoon aesthetics no longer primarily influence it. The design utilizes white space and establishes a visual hierarchy through scale rather than relying on numerous huge objects.

Benefits and Challenges

It frequently permits designs that strive to blend traditional aesthetics with contemporary sensibilities. Vintage styles are evident in digital environments, including website design, social media visuals, and video content. Distinctive branding or advertising materials frequently employ retro features, imparting an "old-school" allure that contrasts with the polished, contemporary aesthetic of numerous digital interfaces. Vintage design is prevalent in packaging, advertising, and restaurant menus.

Conclusions

Vintage design elicits nostalgia, engaging cultural memories and emotions. Brands frequently employ it to cultivate a sense of trust and authenticity, particularly in sectors such as food and beverages, fashion, and music.

Flat style

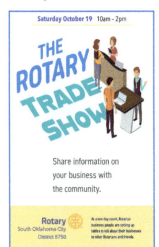

IMAGE 11-7

Example of Flat design. Not all projects have huge budgets and make the portfolio, but the graphic designer still uses the principles to convey the message.

This style is characterized by simplified illustrations that take a cartoon-like approach, but rarely incorporate loose or fun images like a cartoon. Flat design resembles a mix of minimalism, Swiss design, and Bauhaus design, where there are no shadows or attempts at three dimensions. The images, colors, and fonts create an easy-to-follow visual hierarchy.

Emergence

Microsoft's products in the early 2000s contributed to the popularity of flat design. Based on Swiss design aesthetics, the concept behind this design style was to allow the human mind to recognize the images and interpret them accordingly. Unlike photographs, illustrations, and cartoons, they don't elicit any bias or reactions from the viewer. Flat design was also used by Apple, but the silhouettes had a little more styling and attitude.

Characteristics

Rather than employing photography, it utilizes geometrically uncomplicated solid forms to produce drawings of individuals, objects, and locations. Flat design utilizes colors, tints, and tones with minimum embellishments or intricacies. As indicated by its name, it is presented in two dimensions without any effort to convey depth. The design excludes gradients, texturing, embossing, and beveling techniques. White space is essential. This style favors symmetrical arrangements with visual links to the forms.

Recently, the flat design aesthetic has evolved. Graphic artists have incorporated techniques to establish depth through light gradations and shadows. Graphic artists continue to uphold the minimalist, uncluttered layouts.

Benefits and Challenges

The Flat design style can instill in the viewer a sense of luxury and modernism in a product or service. The simplicity of the illustrations allows for their production on a lower budget, eliminating the need for photo shoots. Instead, graphic artists can create the images using AI or manipulate stock vector files. Website design uses the flat style constantly.

The main challenge to flat design is that the visuals look very similar to viewers. Applying the basics of flat design to a project results in solutions that lack individuality. This narrow style provides a limited approach and is considered static by many.

Conclusions

Overall, this minimal approach is popular for advertising and quick marketing solutions. It focuses on usability, which brings life to annual reports, manuals, and computer software design.

Internet design focuses on using straightforward, easy-to-load visuals. The images are straightforward and communicate the information quickly.

Learning Library Exercise – Design Styles

1. Search the internet for the styles discussed in Chapters 10 and 11. Pull examples for your library and place them into InDesign files.

2. Check that the styles in your search results are correct. Art Deco and Art Nouveau are continuously interchanged. Remember that the information you are given from a search engine is information someone uploaded onto the internet who may not be an expert.

3. Divide the guide up into sections that are clearly labeled. Decide an order such as alphabetical or by time and consider adding a table of contents.

4. Mark the design style of each image and make a few notes as to which characteristics define this style.

5. At the beginning of the guide, place a page that has been numbered one through five. List your favorite styles and explain in one or two sentences why that style is a favorite.

6. Years from now, look back at your notes and ranking to see if you still agree with your explanations.

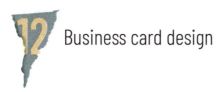

Business card design

Learning Objectives

By the end of this chapter, the student will be able to create a business card. They will be able to determine the paper stock, inks, and bleeds. The reader will be able to analyze the problems with a business card design.

Professional terminology

C1S :   Paper stock term for paper that is coated on only one side.

C2S :   Paper stock term for paper that is coated on both sides.

Cardstock: Paper stock that is thicker than text weight paper.

Coated: A smooth layer on paper that absorbs less ink than uncoated.

Drilling: Punching holes near the edge of paper.

Emboss: Raised graphics on paper.

Finish: The layer above a substrate on stock.

Gang up: Placing multiples pieces on a sheet for printing.

Gloss: A shiny layer on stock or substrate.

Offset Printing: Printing ink onto paper from a printing plate.

Press check: The initial step of printing to determine and color adjustments.

Proof: The printed sample pulled from the press run.

Substrate: The card or paper stock used for printing.

Work and turn: Placing the front and back of pages on a printing plate for one run.

Zip: Compressing one or more digital files.

Vital to business

Opportunities in business can arise either intentionally or by chance. To make sure a potential customer can contact them, business owners and salespeople will have a 2 x 3.5-inch card to hand out. Some individuals may opt for larger cards, but their inability to fit into standard slots can make them difficult to keep on hand for reference. It is important that a business card has easy-to-read and locate contact information, such as name, job title, telephone or cell number, email address, and website URL. A QR code with this information that can be scanned with a mobile phone's camera is becoming standard because it allows for the easy transfer of digital information to phone contacts.

IMAGE 12-1

A business card serves as a promotional tool to remind prospective clients of a presentation, meeting, or chance contact. The layout should be approached by graphic designers as a piece of brand marketing that must successfully convey information. Setting type that is too small or difficult to read is improper.

The design of a business card must convey professionalism, experience, and trustworthiness to a viewer. The graphic artists must select typeface, color, and spatial arrangements that enhance these objectives.

IMAGE 12-2

Example of bleeding graphics onto other cards so each person on the run has a slightly different business card or if they are doubled up, their own cards are different.

Business card printing

A graphic designer must comprehend the printing process before designing the card. For example, the normal arrangement of business cards on a page affects he layout, how they are grouped together and adjacent, restricts the elements that can potentially bleed off the page. If the plan for the card design involves printing each card on a sheet to incorporate elements from the other cards, then backgrounds with solid blocks of color or patterns would be the only areas where bleeds could occur.

IMAGE 12-3

Example of card mechanical set up (cropmarks and bleed not shown).

When producing a significant quantity of cards where the design bleeds for eight individuals, the printer will choose to generate a single plate. The use of two plates would be required to print side A and side B in succession. The pressman will create a "work and turn" plate, which will align the front of one card with the rear of another in order to conserve time and resources. Upon reaching the conclusion of printing one side, the pressman turns the page over and feeds it through, thereby guaranteeing that the front and back are in alignment.

If there are no bleeds, a letter-sized page or sheet can hold 10 business cards. This print run would ensure that each individual receives an identical number of business cards. Nevertheless, certain personnel may not distribute as many cards as others. For example, it is probable that a salesperson distributes a greater number of business cards than a bookkeeper. The designer can configure the mechanical system to produce two or more business cards for the salesperson by simply replicating the card design. The client is satisfied with this arrangement, as it will result in cost savings. Additionally, they are impressed by the graphic designer's capacity to configure the cards without the necessity of a second round of printing.

IMAGE 12-4

Example of setting up card so on the print run John Smooze gets double the quantity of other names.

If the card design bleeds outside the trims, then up to 8 can be ganged up. The graphic designer needs to find out the printing budget before offering this solution.

Bleed layout without bleed and crop marks

IMAGE 12-5

Example of bleed business cards set up on a work and turn layout. Front and back of cards are both on one side. The bleed marks and crop marks should be left off for presentation to client.

Matching color

One of the most irritating challenges in graphic design is the discrepancy between the monitor colors, the inkjet printouts, and the press-printed piece. In the design process, computer monitors use RGB to display colors, whereas the press utilizes CMYK inks for printing on paper. This method cannot reproduce the full spectrum of colors that a monitor is capable of displaying. The translation of digital colors to print inks will lead to a reduction in saturation and brightness.

IMAGE 12-6

If the client is printing a high quantity, it is advisable for the graphic designer to attend the press check. This way the color can be adjusted in spots and increase or decrease the ink coverage.

Practicum} Fire prompt: man and woman examining a press proof in front of a large printing presses, while standing near the press. Photoshop added business cards and transformed the image with the warp function.

Novice designers lack the financial resources to purchase a monitor with the necessary color consistency for professional use. Numerous designers depend on a personal printer; nevertheless, this method is imprecise as it translates laser or inkjet colors into CMYK. Professional graphic artists utilize high-end monitors that allow for precise adjustments in color settings to align with the final printed output. A calibrated, color-accurate monitor with a minimum resolution of 2K (1440p) will closely resemble the final printed product. A 4K display with a resolution exceeding 2160p is currently the most precise option available.

Windows and Macs possess color management applications for the creation and designation of custom profiles. Regularly updating monitors is essential to address the color printouts from different presses and the decline in screen brightness and quality.

A designer's personal printer may lack modification capabilities; yet, the designer should promptly discern where it excels or falters in color and detail. If they utilize the same print shop, they may request a press sample and subsequently designate a color profile for that printer.

IMAGE 12-7

Prolonged exposure to sunlight can result in the fading of screen colors, resulting in less vibrancy.

Practicum} Used two Firefly images. Prompts: computer screen monitor turned toward window with sunlight on it and sunlight on a computer screen monitor. With Photoshop combined the images, added highlight on screen, used lens flare, increased saturation, and set high pass at a of 100.

IMAGE 12-8

Practicum} Firefly prompt: The number 8 in 3D sitting on a white background. Opened in Photoshop and added an inner bevel to "Details" and created a mask for the book text. Paper texture was a photo of a page of white rag bond.

Layout options

Find a business card and notice if the type is too big, if there is too much content, if most of the information is crammed into every inch of space — the type may be spread out to fill all the space. All of these problems are solid reasons for the person not to keep the business card or try to remember the information.

One sided layout

Usually, there are eight items of information to place in this order of proximity:

1. Company Logo
2. Name
3. Job title
4. Director mobile telephone number
5. Company main telephone number
6. Email
7. Address
8. Website

Except for the job title, this list is in the order of the hierarchy with regards to font size and weight. Typeset the readable font between 11 point and 8 points in height.

Two sided arrangement

Having two panels for all the information allows for space and contrast. The client will ask if the benefit of the extra space is worth the extra money. Besides the items listed for the one-sided layout, the two-sided layout could have the company tagline, a QR code, all telephone numbers, and possibly sales copy.

The fun begins with design

Being a graphic designer means being creative and relishing the challenge of developing a visual marketing business card design that stands out. Clients aim to include every feasible feature on their business cards, as they are concerned that they might leave out a critical component that could result in a sale.

Business cards are the initial impression of a company, emphasizing its professionalism. The client will say they understand their business and its success factors. Surprisingly, despite lacking any formal education, training, or experience, these individuals believe they possess a comprehensive understanding of design.

Some businesspeople expect graphic artists to possess a high level of expertise in their respective fields. They have succeeded if the business card is visually engaging and communicates the important information. The graphic artist is accountable for any negative feedback that the design receives. It is imperative for a graphic designer to acknowledge this fact and recommend the most optimal design solution. However, the designer must ascertain whether the argument stems from ego or knowledge. The client retains the final say and is financially responsible, as the designer recognizes. In certain endeavors, the graphic designer needs to surrender control and proceed. The best strategy is to include the unwanted design in the portfolio, satisfy the client's requirements, and receive payment.

The designer's classification as a commercial artist stems from getting paid for their art skill. Commercial artists understand the need for information balanced with space so a potential customers will keep the card and not flip it away. The designer's checklist for business cards includes:

1. Make sure there is visual space.

   Once the concept has been thumbnailed, the next step is to not fit too much information onto a small card. Focus on essential details such as name, job title, contact information, and logo. Use white space to keep the design clean and easy to read.

2. Focus on what makes the design innovative and eye-catching.

   If there is very little contrast between text and background will make the type difficult to read. Ensure that any colored text stands out clearly on the background color or texture.

3. Don't go too large or small with the type (print it out to see it).

   Make sure it is all readable. Text that is too tiny to read nullifies the design. Keep text at a comfortable size 8-11 point size for body text, 12 -14 point for a tagline, and ensure there is a hierarchy in typography for emphasis.

4. Make sure all key information is included and spell checked.

   Forgetting essential information like email, phone number, or website will be embarrassing and possibly costly. Commercial artists include double-checking that all critical contact details are included.

5. Check the QR code is scannable.

   The latest inclusion of QR codes to business cards adds another skill for graphic designers to learn. If the code is too small to scan, it will make the QR code ineffective. Avoid overpowering the design with a large QR code.

6. Include specing the paper stock as part of your design.

   Be careful using low-quality paper that feels cheap or unprofessional as the design will be partially judged by the stock. Choose a paper stock that matches the company's brand personality. Look at samples from the printer to feel the thickness and texture of the paper stock .

7. Follow the brand identity.

   Design components that are inconsistent with your brand's identity, such as varying the colors, typefaces, or alterations to the logo will fail to impress the client. Adhere to the brand rules, including logo positioning and spacing to ensure recognition of the brand.

Given that business cards have been employed as sales tools for over two centuries, the fifth item on this list may present the most significant obstacle. In the limited space, it is a significant challenge to find a means to be both readable and visually appealing. The solution is to adopt a distinct perspective. There are several alternatives, including experimenting with a different stock, employing PMS colors such as metallic inks, utilizing textured paper, and die-cutting the card into a specific shape.

Most educated and experienced graphic designers recognize the importance of research. A review of the graphic artist's own collection of business card will reveal several inventive and creative solutions. However, it's likely that some business cards feature fonts so small that you'll need to use your phone's magnifying feature to read them. These cards tend to have difficulty effectively communicating the information they contain. Some cards printed on stock don't work well. Plastic see-through cards are only legible when placed on white paper. Frequently, the front and rear of a two-sided business card do not appear to be in sync.

Whether the business card is on one side or folds, it must represent the company. Ensure that the logo's type and colors are consistent. This may seem like a straightforward observation; however, it is not uncommon for a graphic designer to extract a logo from a corporation's portal without realizing that there have been updates or that the conversion from a horizontal to vertical format was subpar. Photoshop frequently converts the

RGB-built logo to CMYK without conducting a saturation check.

Presentation

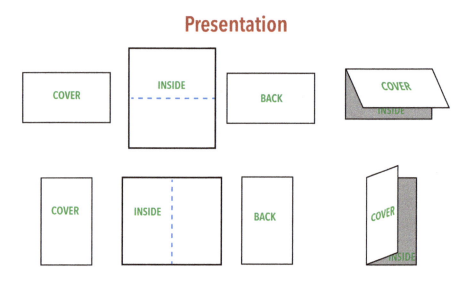

IMAGE 12-9
Folding options

Presentation

The client rarely has the ability to visualize. They may believe they can picture something accurately in their mind, but once a graphic artist explains a design direction based on this premise, communication becomes challenging, and the design fails to meet the client's expectations. When discussing a folding business card, the arrangement for a mechanical and folding dummy differs from presenting it in a comprehensible order.

Begin with a stand-alone cover on a single page, then proceed to separate pages for the interior and the back. This takes the client through how the public will actually see it and the visual flow. Show it at 100% actual size. Presenting it in a printed format makes addressing size and space issues easier, but when displaying it on a screen, it likely won't be at 100% and will instead automatically fill the screen based on the monitor's resolution. When you save it as a PDF, you have some control. The recommended process for on-screen presentations is through an interactive program such as Zoom, Facetime, or Teams, so the graphic designer can control the presentation and view size.

The graphic artist should be at the presentation, physically or online, to judge and record responses. During the revision stages, the client may become bored, focus on minute details, and forget their initial response to the design. The artist can remind the client why they selected a particular concept, preventing them from regressing in the workflow.

Incidentally, this process is the same for all presentations, such as brochures, three-dimensional press kits, packaging, and product branding. By controlling the presentation, the commercial artist can answer questions as the process progresses and clarify any confusion instead of trying to explain after the fact.

To save time, many graphic artists will layout the business card design mechanically, which may confuse the client. In a vertical fold, the left panel represents the back, but the client may mistake it for the cover. The placement of the top panel upside down on a horizontal fold further complicates the visual flow. The graphic designer should design the back panel in the correct reading order—that is, panel by panel.

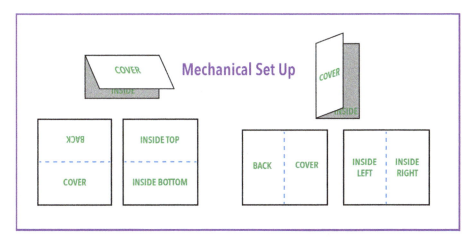

IMAGE 12-10

Layout of folding business card (bleed and cropmarks not shown).

Mechanical configurations

Starting the mechanical process involves communication with the printer to determine their preferred setup. The printer may offer to configure the mechanics if the graphic artist provides the original files. This proposal appears effective, but the designer must still construct the bleed. This service may be deducted from the designer's invoice if the printer bills the client. The printer's fee for the service may be more than the designer would have charged as part of the project.

The printer needs to offer guidelines for constructing a mechanical system that incorporates either a gang-up template or an individual business card setup. The printer can offer paper samples if a press check is feasible. Build this relationship. If the printer calls the designer rather than the customer to address mechanical problems, this can improve the designer's relationship with the client. One potential outcome of collaborating with the printer is that they may refer the graphic designer to their customers.

Lorem ipsum

Lorem ipsum dolor sit amet, consetetur sadipscing elitr, sed diam nonumy eirmod tempor invidunt ut labore et dolore magna aliquyam erat, sed diam voluptua. At vero eos et accusam et justo duo dolores et ea rebum. Stet clita kasd gubergren, no sea takimata sanctus est. Duis autem vel eum iriure dolor in hendrerit in vulputate velit esse molestie consequat, vel illum dolore eu feugiat nulla facilisis at vero eros et accumsan et iusto odio dignissim qui blandit praesent luptatum zzril delenit augue duis dolore te feugait nulla facilisi.

Ut wisi enim ad minim veniam, quis nostrud exerci tation ullamcorper suscipit lobortis nisl ut aliquip ex ea commodo consequat. Duis autem vel eum iriure dolor in hendrerit in vulputate velit esse molestie consequat, vel illum dolore eu feugiat nulla facilisis at vero eros et accumsan et iusto odio dignissim qui blandit praesent luptatum zzril delenit augue duis dolore te feugait nulla facilisi.

IMAGE 12-11
Not a typographical error — it's body content.

When a designer starts laying out a concept, they should use placeholder text and concentrate on the design rather than typography. This allows them to focus on the visual layout. Greek text will let the copyrighter know approximately how many words to write. The most common dummy text is the following Latin essay titled "On the Extremes of Good and Evil" by a Roman lawyer named Cicero. It has been used for over three hundred years.

Known as "Greeking" the content, this text usually cannot be read by clients, so they focus on the design. It gives a pretty good approximation of what English content would look like with ascenders and descenders and the designer can show leading and kerning.

IMAGE 12-12
Inside joke.

Critique Demonstration — Business Cards

To create a compelling first impression with a business card, the graphic designer should prioritize the design concept first. While meticulous attention to detail is crucial during the comp stage, one can postpone it until they have thumbnailed and loosely laid out an effective concept. Beginner graphic designers frequently make similar mistakes in the layout, as shown below.

Critique #1

An example of a business card that requires updating to enhance its professional appearance in order to broaden its services. Beginning graphic designers are not good at understanding visual hierarchy and spatial relationships. They dislike empty areas and will fill each corner with elements. This disrupts the visual flow and muddles the communication.

IMAGE 12-13

Before refinement.

Analysis

Contrast: There is some contrast with the color palette but very little with regards to scale.

Logo: The nicely designed logo includes the pleasing colors of the magenta and chocolate. The logo is emphasized.

Fonts: There are too many typefaces which create a disjointed composition. The placement of the telephone number near edge is not professional.

Balance: Symmetrical balance is comfortable but very busy.

Colors Palette: The interesting colors pertain to the industry.

Space: Spacing is awkward and not visually engaging.

Hierarchy: After the logo, the reader does not know where to go next.

Conclusion: Company has a nicely designed logo, but the business card design did not have the same skill or sensibilities in the design.

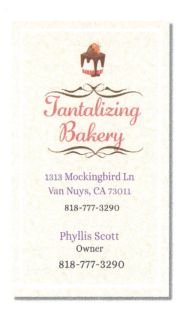

IMAGE 12-14

After refinement. Changed format to vertical to create a visual flow, added a fine filigree texture, focused on the nicely designed brand.

Critique #2

This business card is an example of the information being too small. Branding is strong and could expand to a complete marketing strategy. The brand portrays a competent and dependable utility company.

IMAGE 12-15
Before refinement.

Analysis

Contrast: All elements are the same size with the focus being the center shapes — not the company or the PR director.

Logo: Nice design but not sure if the audience will know it is a utility company. The size could be larger to make sure people easily see it after they put it in a drawer for later communication. The small tagline in caps is not very readable.

Fonts: The audience is an older generation. The type is small and thin and filled in with the black reducing readability.

Balance: Asymmetrical gives the layout energy. However, the multitude of alignments creates confusion as to what is important.

Color Palette: Works well since it is based on logo and the style guide.

Space: Well-planned to allow each element to be located by the reader. QR code is too small to be scanned.

Hierarchy: Developed by position and not size. The reader does not know where to look.

Conclusion: For some reason graphic designers use icons from the web for print marketing. It implies the audience is not smart enough to recognize a telephone number or email address and the icons just add to the clutter. On a mobile website the telephone numbers and email addresses are usually not visible since these type of icons are clicked to dial a number or open the email program. The user can push on the icons on the business card, but nothing will happen.

IMAGE 12-16

After refinement. Kept the branding style but freed up the layout for space, enlarged type and the QR code.

Critique #3

This is a sophisticated layout with strong background colors and shape. Unfortunately, there is too much extremely small unreadable type. The graphic designer should address this issue in the briefing with the client and see if they can print two-sided printing business cards on their budget. In printing it is the paper stock that is the main cost so printing on two sides should be affordable.

IMAGE 12-17

Before refinement.

Analysis

Contrast: The bright background with the white area is eye-catching. The type is black and white and losses the energy of the orange shapes.

Logo: The interesting logo is very small so it appears unimportant.

Fonts: Most of the type is set at 6 to 9 point. Besides the tagline, nothing stands out — including the company or person's name.

Balance: Very tightly set type and leading but the asymmetrical composition works well.

Color Palette: Orange is dynamic and will require to be printed with PMS or it may appear brownish.

Space: Visual space is at a premium in this layout due to the abundance of type.

Hierarchy: The viewer is not lead around to the most important elements.

Conclusion: Going to a two sided card will allow the information to be sized for readability. Of course, as a designer it would be nice to edit some of it but if the client is adamant, there is a better solution as shown below.

Front

IMAGE 12-18

After refinement. Designed a two-sided card to allow for more space and emphasis. One side is focused on the company and the other side on the salesperson. Kept the color palette and graphics to be consistent with the branding.

Back

Critique #4

This business card has design issues, but it did possess many attractive qualities. After a friendly discussion, it was decided the logo could be redesigned, but they did not commit to paying for it unless they approved it. As a company that always provided more than their clients accepted, we agreed to these terms. They had an ampersand to imply that in their list of deliverables to clients, there was always an "and" something else included. The blue watercolor of windows was based on their first project design. The script type indicated they were flexible and blue grey palette implied they were dependable on deadlines and safe on not going over budget.

IMAGE 12-19a
Before refinement.

Analysis

Contrast: Strong in type weight, size and spacing.

Logo: Script was too difficult to read and too small. Not the focal point of the business card.

Fonts: Dated and did not meld with the angular graphics. Stepped flush left content was awkward against the strong line of the bars.

Balance: Asymmetrical added energy and a visual flow.

Color Palette: Limited but analogous tints were compatible.

Space: Planned and logical except for the unwieldy gap between tagline and name.

Hierarchy: After the tagline, everything else was too small to read and did not balance with the logo.

IMAGE 12-19b
Before refinement.

Conclusion: The client needed to see a different design so they would give it a fresh unbiased critique. The card would need to retain the graphics to keep an updated but recognizable brand. Based on the spacing and size of the type on the previous design, the layout went vertical with an easy to follow hierarchy and type was sized between eight and eleven point with the tagline at 12 point. The logo emphasized the ampersand, and the small, jumbled elements were removed. In a few years they might be open to further simplification of the logo.

IMAGE 12-20

Graphic Designer: Neal Hettinger

After refinement. Went vertical for space and flow and kept the bars for branding. Logos was simplified and angular typefaces were selected to follow the graphic elements.

Critique #5

Space for the sake of sticking some space in the layout is not a goal. However, enticing readership and creating a subconscious view of the company as being professional and successful is an achievable goal. This business card is frustrating for the reader to find the pertinent information and contact someone doing business with the company.

IMAGE 12-21

Before refinement.

Analysis

Contrast: Everything is the same size and no space.

Logo: Nice readable brand if it was enlarged This is a different and modern style for a plumber and it will be remembered.

Fonts: Too many typefaces are added to the cluttered layout aesthetics.

Balance: It is symmetrical but not in a good way to assist in reading.

Color Palette: Blue is fitting for the subject and implies competency.

Space: Hardly any empty areas available which adds to the jumbled layout.

Hierarchy: There is none — just unreadable stuff.

Conclusion: Too much information. As a graphic designer, it is a disservice to the client to include everything that should be on a full page ad. The artist needs to work with the client and list the three most important communications for this marketing piece.

IMAGE 12-22

After refinement. Kept the graphic flowing element for branding, reduced the information, utilized a condensed sans serif font, and enlarged the logo.

Critique #6

Just as typefaces sized too small are difficult to read, typefaces too large are also difficult to read. The fonts here range from 9 point up to 16 point with most of the type set at 12 point. Space is non-existent and the overcrowded layout does not present the company well. When a potential customer receives a business card like this example, they may not want to work at deciphering it.

IMAGE 12-23

Before refinement.

Analysis

Contrast: There is very little use of scale to make this card attractive.

Logo: The logo could be smaller with space around it to make it easy to spot.

Fonts: The typeface has been compressed which makes the typeface look odd and creates odd gaps in the wording. Instead of choosing a wideset typeface, the graphic designer should choose a condensed font.

Balance: Sort of symmetrical but with so little space and large type, it is difficult to say what if any balance is in the design.

Color Palette: The shades and tints work with the gold, but the red is out of place and looses any suggestion of sophisticated design.

Space: Pretty obvious that there is no space.

Hierarchy: After the logo, the viewer will go to the red content but after that they will be lost in type.

Conclusion:

The card needed something attract a potential customer. It was printed on thick cardstock to help with rigidity and die-cut around the dollar sign since the message is his clients make money. A QR code would add the salesperson's information to the customer's mobile phone contacts.

IMAGE 12-24

After refinement. Note for presentation instead of the card on a white background, it was angled with a shadow on white marble with gold veins to go with the logo.

Critique #7

 In reviewing the elements of the business card, the logo was a nice design. The waves were an interesting idea, but they were more representative of a marina than a pool company.

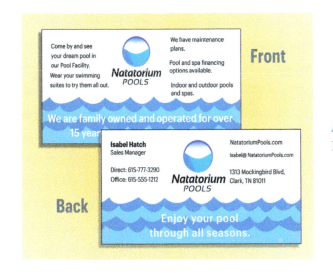

IMAGE 12-25

Before refinement.

Analysis

Contrast: The logo and waves are large medium to catch the viewer's attention, but the type is almost all the same size, color, and weight.

Logo: Interesting logo with almost a smile hidden inside it.

Fonts: Used proximity but the type is small at 7 to 9 point which causes readability concerns.

Balance: Very close to a symmetrical layout.

Color Palette: Blues work but a complementary color in the logo would draw the viewers.

IMAGE 12-26

After refinement. Stylized the waves for a modern appearance and added the complementary color to the blue.

Space: Most of the areas are filled.

Hierarchy: After the waves and logo, it is a struggle for the viewer's eyes to figure out the information.

Conclusion: This layout has a dated feel and the waves ad to the clutter. Since they are trying to sell the relaxing and entertaining nature of pools, a smoother stylized wave would modernize the design.

Styles of business card design

Standard

The approach is clean and simplistic, utilizing minimal color and elements. This fundamental solution focuses on modern, clean fonts with little to no graphics, textures, gradations, or images. Layout is usually horizontal and symmetrical. Contractors, corporate professionals, retail, and service-oriented industries utilize this layout.

Traditional

The form is classical, featuring structured symmetrical layouts and a strong emphasis on the content. Professionals in the legal and medical industries, bankers, investment firms, and consultants use limited color palettes that balance neutral tints and shades with serif fonts.

Innovative

This model occasionally lacks formality and exhibits an experimental quality when it comes to the colors used in typefaces and graphics. These eye-catching, vibrant colors contrast the large open areas and employ unique layouts. The arts, entertainment, creatives, and marketers utilize these colors.

Vintage

The design incorporates popular elements from the 1950s to 1980s, utilizing handwritten and vintage fonts.

Strong primary and secondary colors make up the color palette. Usually, the asymmetrical layout is horizontal, emphasizing textures and patterns over space. Used by professionals in entertainment and for cafes, playhouses, and event centers.

Luxury

The elements are clean, sophisticated, and suggest quality, whether arranged vertically or horizontally. The elements are symmetrically balanced on a rich black or white background, with letterspaced fonts. Some of the typesetting is all uppercase and is usually centered. The logos may be embossed, or foil stamped, requiring a heavy, smooth stock. Used by expensive car dealerships, jewelers, investment consultants, and financial industries.

Modern

It typically features a monochromatic color scheme and sans serif fonts arranged in a straightforward horizontal arrangement. Minimal graphics are used along with space to emphasize. Used by fashion professionals, real estate agents, and universities.

Geometric

Variations of thick or thin sans serif fonts echo the angular and circular elements. This contemporary structured model utilizes simple colors and light backgrounds, possibly ghosted patterns. Architects, software developers, engineers, and the technology manufacturing industry utilize this model.

Green

The type is typically printed in shades of green and blue, or earth tones. The message is that the company is involved with recycling and is an earth-friendly company. Vertical layouts are popular when combined with symmetrical layouts. Engineers, oil and gas companies, organic agriculture and distributors, as well as back-to-nature hotels and tours, utilize vertical layouts.

Interactive

Multiple pages, die-cuts, and embossed stock create a tactile business card with basic color palettes and modern sans serif fonts. Used by salespersons, proprietors, media buyers.

Digital

Artificial intelligence tools may have created the colors, but they are bold and feature strong textures and patterns. Space is filled with color and type. Horizontal symmetrical layouts with sans-serif typefaces. Various industries are gradually adopting this new approach.

Portfolio Building Assignment – Business Card

Create an eye-catching business card from information supplied. You decide what needs to be on the business card and how many sides it needs to have printed. For inspiration, collect examples of well designed business cards (i.e. search the internet for examples and take screen grabs). Analyze the supplied text below and decide what should be on your design based on the client's briefing included after the instructions.

IMAGE 12-27

Visual image created with AI generator Firefly as example of what the restaurant would look like inside to give a graphic designer an idea of what type of patronage would be dining there.

Business card information

Jessica Wister – sales manager, (771) 555-1212, 111 18th Street NW, Washington, D.C., Jesica@ AuBonheur.com, AuBonheur.com

Instructions

1. Use the Restaurant logo you created for the Assignment in Chapter 7.
2. Sketch three to six thumbnails with notations and color ideas.
3. On the computer, recreate one of the thumbnails using either InDesign, Photoshop, or Illustrator into a presentation comp.
4. Design the card with vital information including a logo, tagline, and QR code.
5. Create a tagline with ChatGPT that sells the menu.
6. Build 1 business card comp, 4 colors, bleed, 2 inches x 3.5 inches. Allow a 1/8 inch (.125) bleed but do not include in the presentation.
7. Save a pdf of the composition for your portfolio.

Client brief

Restaurant Name: Au Bonheur Grand Restaurant

Business type/industry: Restaurant | Age of Restaurant: 2 years

Target Market: 15-25 year olds, Patrons of fine dining at an upscale restaurant that like to spend two to three hours enjoying the multi-course meals.

Impression: Spacious seating with tablecloths covering mahogany, decorative dark wood adorns the rooms with soft lighting.

Marketing design

Learning Objective

In this chapter, the learner will evaluate the application of design in a number of case studies. They will be able to Integrate the color trends of next year. The reader will be able to characterize the fundamentals of flyer and ad composition.

Professional terminology

Booklet Envelope: Large envelope that holds an unfolded letter or flyer.

Call to action: Verbiage that inspires the reader to react in a particular way.

Die-cut: A specific instrument for cutting materials into forms or patterns.

Door hanger: Door handle or knob-mounted printed marketing.

Leave behind: Post sales pitch flyers remind prospects of the proposal.

Legal-size: Suitable for printing paper that measures 8.5 inches by 14 inches.

Letter-sized: Suitable for printing paper that measures 8.5 inches by 11 inches.

Letterhead: The header on letter-sized paper with contact info and logo.

Markup: Notes of improvements that should be made to an image.

Rack card: Marketing for foot traffic located on holders.

Sell sheet: Marketing with key points for purchasing a product, service, or event.

Stock: The material used for printing that has different thickness and surfaces.

Tabloid-size: Suitable for printing paper that measures 11 inches by 17 inches.

Tradeshow: An event where companies display their goods and services to potential clients.

Trifold: Marketing piece that folds twice creating 6 panels.

Promotional marketing materials

Several channels exist within the field of marketing to promote information about products, services, events, or organizations. Due to the same creative techniques and principles, graphic designers are capable of producing a wide range of materials.

Professionals follow a seven-step procedure in the creative process: examine the project brief, investigate the problem, devise strategies, generate thumbnails and layout alternatives, analyze the comprehensives, present solutions, including the client modifications, and finally create the mechanical of the design.

IMAGE 13-1

Graphic Designer: Neal Hettinger | Art Director: Nigel Sherry

Two sided sales flyers. Note design style of the image placement with cropping, the repetition of type alignment, and color palette. Flyer printed 4/4 (4 process colors CMYK over 4 process colors CMYK).

Printers lead the design marketplace for business cards, letterheads, and envelopes. Either company will waive the design fee or include it in printing expenses. Although graphic designers have the ability to produce these essential corporate communications, the market for such services is very small. Printing catalogs is expensive, and they have given way to online platforms. Electronic mail has taken over traditional letterheads as the predominant mode of communication. QR codes are quickly replacing traditional business cards.

Print marketing is a lucrative sector within the field of graphic design. Four often used promotions, each tailored to certain budgets and objectives, are flyers, door hangers, trifold brochures, and envelopes. Flyers are single-page designs that may be either one-sided or two-sided and sometimes folded. Their cost-effectiveness makes them suitable for targeted distribution of information about events, specials, or promotions. The increasing popularity of door hangers can be attributed to the rise in postal rates and reductions in printing expenses. They strategically position the marketing materials at the doorstep of the prospective buyer. Although their lifespan may be brief, door hangers provide the brand with immediate exposure to the homeowner, circumventing the competition of a mailbox packed with direct mail. Each trifold brochure can be either inserted into an envelope for bulk mail or distributed directly to the recipient, enabling convenient storage in a pants pocket or bag.

Placing branding and promotional information on the exterior of envelopes can effectively entice consumers to open them. The graphic artist's goal is to create a design that will entice the recipient to look at the contents.

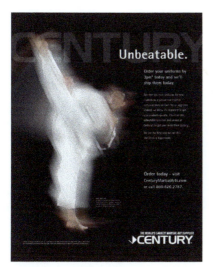

IMAGE 13-2

Graphic Designer: Neal Hettinger | Art Director: Todd Bane

Martial arts company branding flyer Printed 4/0 (4 process colors CMYK only one side). Design focuses on company with flush left content that leads down to the call to action.

Flyer as print media

A client's primary objective is to maximize their return according to their budget. The most effective approach is for the graphic designer and client to engage in a conversation regarding the flyer's goals. These discussions should determine the flyer's dimensions, the number of colors, PMS possibilities, the impact of overlap, and whether to print on both sides.

The paper stock is the most expensive component of printing. A leaflet flier is typically a low-budget print run, as it employs thin, low-quality paper for pamphlets or circulars. As a tactile response, individuals subconsciously observe the thickness and quality of the paper before evaluating the information. The thicker the paper, the more likely the reader will stop to look at the message.

When working on a printing budget, the amount of time the flyer will be on a press affects the budget. The operational cost of a press increases proportionally with its size, but it has the benefit of enabling simultaneous printing of a greater number of pages. A 4-color press is capable of producing CMYK, while a 6-color or higher press can incorporate PMS colors. Alternatively, if the print run is of limited duration, the client may opt for a digital laser printer that copies in a CMYK format without PMS inks. There are limited options for paper stock, and the final quality heavily relies on the thickness of the paper.

IMAGE 13-3

Example of a large printing press.

AI Practicum} Firefly prompt: Large modern printing press in action with bright colored flyers on paper on the production line; front view; industrial technological process. Type added with Photoshop.

Formats

The basic flyer is letter size, 8.5 inches by 11 inches. It can be printed on one side or both sides and is also referred to as a leaflet, sell sheet, or leave-behind. The flyer can be printed horizontally two-up on a page, making each flyer 5 inches wide and 8.5 inches tall, or vertically 4.15 inches by 11 inches. Whether or not the design is affected by the size is based on the area required for a bleed.

IMAGE 13-4

Note how there are 2 flyers printed up on a single letter sized page. The design includes the white margins and does not bleed. This design allows for twice the quantity as a full page flyer.

The door hangers have dimensions almost equivalent to those of a vertical half-page flyer, measuring 4.125 inches by 10.875 inches, and include a die-cut hole for the house doorknob. To obtain precise measurements, the designer should contact the printer and request a template. Die templates are essential for graphic designers since they provide precise markings of the cutting area. The presentation should intentionally show the region as empty to clearly communicate to the client that there will be no content in that location.

IMAGE 13-5

Template on door hanger with areas noted for the graphic designer.

Practicum} On the layout and mechanical the template can be placed but select the layer option for it not to print. It is for the artist's reference only.

The green line indicates the bleed area.

The blue line shows the live area.

The red line indicates the door hole cut.

IMAGE 13-6

Graphic Designer: Neal Hettinger

Door hanger example.

The green line on the template indicates the bleed area. Only unimportant elements such as a background image will pass this line since this area will be trimmed off. The blue line shows the live area for text, logos, elements of importance. Anything not in this area may be trimmed off. The red line indicates the door hole cut. The cut for door hole should include image and background but not anything of significance since it will be cut out.

When designing a door hanger, it's important to dedicate the specific area for the doorknob, ensuring that the viewer can't see what's directly beneath it when they approach the door. The headline should capture the viewer's attention, followed by a concise message. The contact information should be easy to locate.

Graphic artists may be asked to design a marketing envelope and should contact the printer for the live area and the post office for the requirements on printing areas. The trifold brochure is a convenient size for placing into a business envelope which is also known as #10 envelope and measures in inches 4.125 x 9.5. The trifold will also fit into a #9 envelope which measures in inches 3.875 x 8.875. An invitation envelope is 5.25 x 7.25, and a booklet envelope is for an unfolded flyer is 9 x 12.

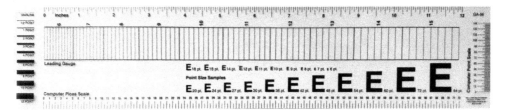

IMAGE 13-7
Clear Graphic Design ruler with points, picas, inches, character size, leading gauge, and strokes.

Understanding measurements

The process of manufacturing hot type involves casting typefaces in a lead bed, known as the body or shank, with additional lead surrounding the characters. Today's font measurements stem from the printer's use of a point ruler to measure the distance between the upper and lower edges of the lead body. While this manner of measuring type is based on an archaic technology, it is so locked into our field of graphic design that it would be extremely difficult to change it now.

In their typography, graphic designers use points and picas as units of measurement. While the units may be compared to millimeters and inches, they are significantly smaller. A pica consists of twelve points, and six picas are equal to one inch. Hence, 72 points is equivalent to one inch. For comparison, a larger millimeter is equivalent to 0.35 points.

Cold type refers to computer typefaces. The digitally generated 72-point type will be smaller or larger than the 72-point hot type since typographers could not measure the bed of lead and had to eyeball it.

There are layout advantages to using picas. When a graphic artist is setting up a trifold brochure by dividing a letter-size page, 8.5 inches x 11 inches, into thirds along the long side, it would be difficult to mark the 3.67 inches and 7.33 inches fold lines.

However, since 11 inches equals 66 picas, the designer folds the design at the 22 and 44 pica marks. It is also easier to divide the short side of the page of 51 picas by three if the design calls for the folds to be along the 8.5-inch side. Instead of 2.83 inches, a graphic artist would place each fold at 17 picas.

IMAGE 13-8

A graphic designer's nightmare client.

AI Practicum} Two images created in Firefly and retouched including t-shirt graphic and speak bubbles in Photoshop.

The function is the design

Because graphic designers often hear the phrase "the function is the design" or similar words of wisdom, they frequently tend to forget them when starting a design solution. The purpose of the marketing piece, target audience, and content being communicated is the final design's function. There are many types of flyers, and all are based on the target audience.

Commercial artists determine the color palette, type of images, font sizes, and typeface based on the characteristics known as demographics. An older audience may need larger traditional type, and a younger reader may prefer a smaller sans serif font. The graphic designer needs to receive a project brief with information on a defined group, which includes gender, age, income level, race, education level, religion, marital status, and geographic location. The design of the flyer is also based on the subject, the distribution and duration of the event or promotion, and how time-sensitive the event or promotion is for flyer longevity.

One of the most common flyers is for specific products used in retail or for product launches. The designer will highlight the commodity, often relying on large, heavily retouched, high-quality images of the product. The typography will present the features, benefits, pricing, and locations to buy the products. Clean, modern fonts will enhance the product's appeal.

Flyers that announce events, such as a music festival, may feature vibrant colors, band names, and photos related to the event. The content will focus on the date, time, location, and key details of the event with large, eye-catching fonts. A workshop flyer may not have had bold colors but will focus on details such as classes, dates, topics, and registration information.

Promotional flyers advertise sales, discounts, or special offers. Images are high-quality photos or illustrations of the products or services. Typography will emphasize a discount or promotional message with bold percentage numbers, promo codes, and limited time offers. For example, a retail store flyer highlighting a seasonal sale will use images of products and have a clear call-to-action for the intended viewer.

Information flyers, such as those distributed at a fundraising charity event, provide detailed information on a specific topic, service, or product and may be presented in bullet points or boxed sections. This type of flyer usually has details on how to register and donate, along with photos of participants. A design needs to use a simple, easy-to-follow layout with engaging visuals such as infographics, icons, and photos. To entice the reader, the typography should use readable fonts with a focus on hierarchy and space. A healthcare flyer could display the services offered, with sections for each service, and direct the eye to the contact information.

Corporations use flyers to present a company's services, products, or brand in a professional manner. Their marketing department usually prefers a Swiss or minimalist design following the company branding guide. The content can be overwhelming, so designers need to consider condensed fonts with the smallest readable font size for the target audience. Companies will want an overview of services or products, contact details, and possibly some form of company mission statement. The design must be professional with a consistent style.

The focus of real estate flyers is to promote properties for sale or rent. Multiple high-resolution images of the property will engage the audience, and the type needs to be readable for the main details like price, location, and contact information. Once again, the content type must be simple and have a visual hierarchy. A landscaping flyer would also have numerous photos of beautiful gardens and lawns, as well as a list of services with pricing options.

A visual hierarchy will consider each type of flyer design to prioritize specific needs. Whether it's drawing a crowd to an event, boosting sales, or raising awareness for a cause, the design choices should align with the flyer's purpose and the target audience to ensure it effectively communicates its message.

A flyer is not an ad

Flyers are primarily used for informational purposes. They are designed to provide detailed information about a specific event, promotion, product, or service. The goal is often to inform, invite, or remind people about something specific. Flyers aim to distribute information directly to an interested target audience, often with the intent of driving immediate action, such as attending an event, visiting a location, or taking advantage of a special offer. Ads appear in multiple various formats including print, digital, broadcast, and outdoor advertising to a potential audience.

FLYER   PRINT AD

IMAGE 13-9

Graphic Designer: Neal Hettinger | Art Director: Nigel Sherry

Pianist Flyer and Ad

Practicum} Note the flyer has more information, less space, and complicated layout compared to the ad. Created with InDesign, Illustrator, and Photoshop.

Beginning designers often mistake the two marketing pieces, flyers and advertisements, as the same marketing projects. The flyer information is generally of interest to viewers and are they typically less likely to disregard it. Ads focus on creating a strong visual and emotional impact to capture attention quickly, since the viewer usually wants to move on.

Potential customers can pick up flyers in person, post them on bulletin boards, distribute them in mailboxes, or leave them in public places. They can also be distributed digitally as PDFs or images via email or social media.

Flyers often contain more details, including dates, times, locations, and specifics about an event or promotion. The content may include bullet points, lists, and multiple sections to convey all necessary information. While flyers are still visually appealing, they prioritize clear communication of information. The design supports the text, with an emphasis on readability and organization. We use visual elements such as images, logos, and color schemes to draw attention and strengthen the message.

Typically, flyers target a specific local audience or a defined group, such as event attendees, customers in a specific area, or participants in a particular activity. Distributing flyers directly to potential customers often takes place in specific locations relevant to the audience, like community centers, schools, or businesses.

Flyers have a limited lifespan and serve specific, time-sensitive events or promotions. Their impact is immediate but limited to the duration of the event or promotion. The impact of a flyer depends on its distribution and how well it communicates its message to the target audience. A flyer's physical presence can prompt a direct response.

While flyers and ads are tools for communication and marketing, they differ in their purpose, design approach, and distribution methods. Flyers are typically more detailed and localized, while ads are often broader in reach, more varied in format, and designed to create a strong, immediate impression.

Designing the marketing pieces

A flyer typically includes several design elements to effectively communicate its message. Start by researching the product or service, as well as the client. Create a list of key words and phrases, begin with the objective and available images, and explore other flyers within the same industry. Research the flyers that go in a completely opposite direction. If one is available, review the corporate branding style guide and consider potential textures for the background and type. Investigate images in stock photography, images from the client's brief package, and sketch out images you can photograph at the client's facility. Next, sketch a few thumbnails with notations for color palettes and potential typefaces.

An engaging flyer design effectively captures attention, conveys a clear message, and encourages the desired action from the target audience. It should have an attention grabbing headline, striking visuals, easy-to-read content, and a layout that guides the reader's eye down the visual hierarchy. The correct colors and typography will ensure readability, along with the quality of the printing.

The color palette should either convey a sensation about the product or attract attention. The tints must be determined by the brand's identity. The intended audience will be able to identify the message by utilizing a consistent color palette. To prevent the design from becoming overwhelming, refrain from employing an excessive number of colors. A subtle background can provide depth, but it is important to avoid anything that is excessively cluttered and detracts from the text and images. The background may be a solid color, gradation, texture, or image that establishes the tone of the overall design.

As previously mentioned, the right amount of space will increase contrast and captivate the audience. Space is instrumental in the organization of content and the establishment of a professional, tidy appearance. Margin and line spacing are frequently overlooked by novice designers, resulting in a disorganized appearance of the flyer.

The headline is the most prominent text shown on the leaflet. The design of the flyer effectively captures attention and provides a concise insight into its content. Employ a conspicuous, prominent typeface, or enclose it by empty space to enhance its visibility. The text should be concise, persuasive, and direct. At times, presenting supplementary information necessitates a subheading highlighted in a smaller font size and with reduced boldness. For marketers, the body copy or text is the most important part of a flyer since it contains the necessary information enabling the prospective consumer to reach a decision. The selection of typefaces can have a substantial impact on the legibility and tone of the flyer. The graphic designer must ensure that the font has been typeset at a readable size and avoid using more than three typefaces. To enhance reader engagement, the written content can be condensed by using bullet points or brief paragraphs.

From the perspective of a graphic artist, the visual elements that enhance the text and create a more engaging flyer are the most critical component. They must attract the reader and promote the product with pertinent photographs, paintings, or illustrations high-quality images that have not been significantly enlarged. The artwork should balance with the space and text.

The flyer's logo and branding represent the company's identity. A commercial artist constantly refers to the company style guide for colors and fonts. At the presentation, the client may feel the designer is not capable of providing a satisfactory solution if the flyer does not follow the guidelines. The logo should be placed in a prominent but not overwhelming position, with the surrounding space drawing the eye.

In order to motivate the reader to execute a particular action, such as visiting a website, contacting a phone number, or attending an event, the visual hierarchy should direct them to the Call to Action (CTA). It should be distinguished by a bolder font or color in the design and be compelling and easily located.

The contact information should clearly indicate who, what, and where the reader can find more information. It may encompass a phone number, email address, website, or social media links. This information should be prominently displayed, accompanied by specific details such as the date, time, and location.

The client will regard every component in the design as important and need to be emphasized. Implementing this approach will result in a design characterized by all elements being the same size and lacking contrast or distribution of engaging space. No individual item will stand out or be easily located.

Trifold brochure design

Defining boundaries for different information on a trifold brochure starts with margins—

the blank space on the left, right, top, and bottom edge and along the folds. Borders, blocks of color, overlays, and bullets can direct the reader to specific information.

IMAGE 13-10

Graphic Designer: Neal Hettinger | Art Director: Taylor Brewster

Mechanical set up with InDesign for printing — not reading.

To set up the comprehensive, review the previous section, "Understanding graphic design measurements." The printer requires a different setup for the trifold mechanical than the client does for the presentation. If a client views the mechanical, they may not understand the arrangement of the cover on the right and the back page in the middle. For presentation, start with a 3D layout and then set up the panels in an order that the client will comprehend.

| Cover | Inside Flap | Inside Spread | Back |

IMAGE 13-11

Presentation is in the order of the reading order of the trifold.

Case Study 13A [The 'create a story' trifold]

Overview: The client is a commercial and residential landscaping and lawn maintenance company. The client needed a new flyer brochure to hand out and mail to potential customers. Additionally, the client needed a door hanger as soon as possible.

Target Market Aesthetics: People who are homeowners, aged 25 and above, reside in middle-class neighborhoods and the metropolitan areas of major cities in Oklahoma, Texas, and Colorado.

Distribution: Each customer estimate will include the trifold, the sales team will hand them out at trade shows, and mail them in a #10 envelope to potential new clients based on leads from the website and phone calls.

IMAGE 13-12
The leave-behind should be memorable and tell a story for the target market. The presentation uses a background to set off the images and compliment the design.

Solution: ProTech's industry is lawn work and outdoor pests; therefore, the choices of type structures were kept light and not foreboding with a humanist San Serif typeface to complement a script display font. We based the layout on the earlier design style established by the door hanger. Given the busy nature of the Adobe stock image, we strategically positioned the main services and logo within a transparent warp shape to capture the viewers' attention. We did not use bug images because they could create a negative reaction in the target market. The design focused on showing a storybook-type outdoor area with smiling faces enjoying the area filled with plants and flowers.

Specifics: Fonts were Hurricane Script with a forest green drop stroke to give an edge to the word "Enjoy;" and Nova Sans; for the text, and Interstate Compressed was used for the subheads; Colors were Lemon Yellow at 100% Yellow with 5% Magenta, White, Forest Green at 100% Cyan, 50% Magenta, 100% Yellow.

Case Study 13B: [The no space flyer]

IMAGE 13-13
The 'before' flyer.

Overview: The Commercial Realtor® team was sending out flyers to new markets but did not receive any responses. They represented high-end properties and felt their art department's design was not relevant to the target market. They printed the flyer on heavy, slick stock to impress potential customers.

Critique: Without a dominating element, the viewer's eye had no idea where to start reading—nor does it want to read all the information Nothing engaged the target audience or informed them what this communication was about. Someone who was already familiar with the information designed it with the intention of maximizing page space. An untrained designer probably did not know thought there was competition for the reader's time.

Target Market Aesthetics: Large market real estate investors looking for mid-market deals for commercial properties.

IMAGE 13-14
Colored booklet envelope to attention with a printed label with a teaser line.

Distribution: USPS First Class in a 9x12 Booklet Envelope. We recommended a custom label for the return address.

IMAGE 13-15

Graphic Designer: Neal Hettinger

The 'after' flyer

Solution: At the creative meeting with the client, we requested a NAI Style Guide. They were surprised to learn that there was one. After reviewing the existing flyer to establish a hierarchy of information importance, our account executive compiled a list of essential and non-essential items for communication. During the meeting, we showed the client the printing prices for one-sided and two-sided press printing in their expected quantity. Having already budgeted the cost of the paper stock, the client realized the increase would be negligible for two-sided printing. This strategy allowed the information to be spread out in the design, creating visual space and utilizing large images to engage the audience. For additional space and readability, our copywriter edited the content.

Specifics: The design used the san serif font Avenir Regular and Avenir Bold, with a color scheme of Ruby red 100M/90% Y/5K, dark Columbian blue at 90C/ 53M/ 15Y and medium grey at 70K.

Case Study 13C [The TOO many words flyer]

Overview: The client was known for out-marketing the competition and disseminating information about the commercial inspection industry on a daily basis. He believed that potential customers could not receive enough fact-based content. Knowing that yellow and black are the most contrasting colors, he used that color palette in nearly all of his

IMAGE 13-16
The 'before' flyer

Critique: The flyer's small type, excessive content, lack of visual hierarchy, and lack of emphasis on the most important takeaway would discourage people from reading it.

Target Market Aesthetics: Commercial investors of high end properties in the Midwest and southwest areas of the U.S. These businesspeople were located in Dallas, Los Angeles, Denver, Oklahoma City, Tulsa, and Little Rock. There were no specifics available for the customer base, such as gender, age, or income level.

Distribution: By mail and prior to starting an inspection, a marketing folder with a description of the areas of the commercial inspection were sent to the buyer.

Solution: The client requested a straightforward fact sheet with content that covered the entire space on the page, not "busied up" with photos and designer elements. Typically, we would avoid dealing with this type of client. We knew from past experiences that regardless of the client's satisfaction with the design, the potential for customers to read it would be low. Nevertheless, this was an important client, so we accepted the challenge. The client agreed that if we could present the flyer information in a visually engaging manner with space, he would be interested. We needed a prominent feature to give the flyer impact. A typographical headline was devised to visually summarize the flyer for the potential customer.

The design integrated broad areas of color and spatial arrangement to separate the groups. Upon reviewing the 31 reasons, the copywriter categorized them into three primary talking points. Using the principle of Repetition, we positioned the primary concerns of the target market, namely reputation, time, and certificates, vertically on the left side. We inserted a call-to-action at the bottom of the flyer. The certification and award logos were layed out on the back side of the flyer.

Specifics: The design used the san serif fonts in regular and bold Berthold Akzidenz Grotesk Condensed and Zurich BT Condensed, with a color scheme of Steel Grey 30C/50K and Cool Grey 11C/17K.

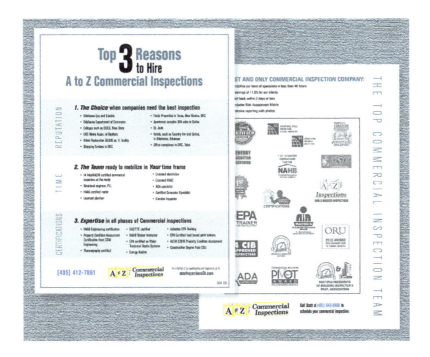

IMAGE 13-17

Graphic Designer: Neal Hettinger

The 'after' flyer

Case Study 13D [The "minimalist" cover]

Overview: While examining the company's marketing materials, the new president felt it needed a design markup. She had us start with the price list's cover. The marketing looked tiered and dated and wanted the popular minimalist style.

Target Market Aesthetics: New homeowners, construction companies, general contractors, plumbers, and DIYers. Audience will want higher end tubs that could function as a retreat after a difficult day. Demographics are 35 to 55 years of age with middle to upper income levels and married.

Distribution: Tradeshows, direct mail, responses to website inquiries, and for the sales staff.

Solution: Focused on smooth, clean lines of tub in modern relaxing Jacuzzi. Retouch for effect.

Specifics: Font used was DIN Regular. Photo was retouched in Photoshop to create a light teal water tone and change the grey wall to a cool tone grey wall.

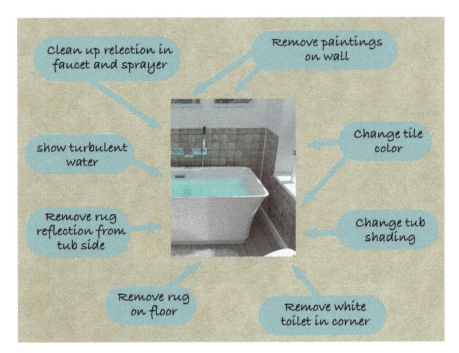

IMAGE 13-18

The markup of areas to be retouched in Photoshop.

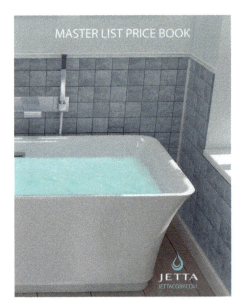

IMAGE 13-19

Graphic Designer: Neal Hettinger

The cover after retouching in Photoshop.

Learning Library Exercise — Color palettes for this year

1. Read articles on trending colors for graphic design this year.

2. Focus on a marketing area such as food labels for grocery aisles, new vehicle flyers for dealers, or brochures for health clubs.

3. Show examples and write a report 150 to 200 words.

4. Check the spelling and grammar.

5. Do not use AI for research or to write the report since it will not be accurate.

Web design fundamentals

Learning Objectives

The student will be able to predict the obstructions to UX design in her/his own words. They will be able to differentiate the parts of a website. The learner will be able to explain the fundamental elements of website design.

Professional terminology

Content: Verbiage in a design.

Copy: Words combined to convey a message or piece of information.

Favicon: A small marketing image that represents website.

Header: Top section of a website.

Hero: A large impactful image that is usually below the header.

Meta: HTML code that describes a webpage's content.

Palette: Compiling colors as part of the strategy for a design.

Unique: Absolutely one of a kind.

Image 14-1

Graphic Designer: Neal Hettinger

Website for working ranch that has locations for filming shows. Note the added UI additions for ease of use such as dot navigation and up arrow button.

Just as in printing, the internet has a history that graphic designers should know and understand. By knowing the past, they can make predictions and prepare for the future of design. 94% of first impressions rely on the design of the website.[1] 75% of viewers base their impression of a company on the website design. [2]

Lawrence Roberts initiated the first instance of two distinct computers communicating with one another in 1965. The digital data was transmitted using packets over a telephone line with an acoustically coupled modem in this experimental link.

The first intranet was created by the Department of Defense in the late 1960s during the Cold War. This intranet was intended to establish a military and research network that would facilitate communication and data sharing among various institutions. This network would provide a way for government researchers to share information. It also had communication capabilities that would remain intact in the event of a nuclear attack.

In 1989, Sir Tim Berners-Lee proposed the idea of the World Wide Web and in 1990 he developed the first web client and server. One byproduct of web technology was electronic mail. An American computer programmer, Ray Tomlinson, was responsible for developing a way to send messages, emails, and having the @ symbol between the user and the host domain.

Image 14-2
Graphic Designer: Neal Hettinger
Example of mobile web page revised from home page for the user experience.

Internet browsers

In the early 1990s, there were only a few applications that could search the internet, such as AOL, without people typing in codes. Then in the early 2000s there were hundreds of apps that could search the internet. Now there are only a few dozen with Google, Bing, and Duck-Duck-Go the major search engines that website designers should use to check website search results. Edge, Chrome, Safari, Brave, and Vivaldi are a few of the browsers that graphic artists should check on their designs to see how they look and operate.

Internet basics

In the top of a browser such as Google Chrome, Safari, and Firefox, the internet surfer can type in an address known as a domain. These words without any spaces are followed by a "." and a domain extension such as com, edu, or org. These domain suffixes now have over 700 options such as .website and .vegas. The list is constantly growing. When a domain is typed into the URL [Uniform Resource Locater], it will be pointed to a server that houses the files for a website which then has an IP address. For instance, in the URL type Google.com or type 74.125.139.100 to go to the Google search page.

Domains are the address of a website, but the actual website is hosted on a server with an SSL, Secure Socket Layer, that was originally created by Netscape. It could transfer data such as credit card information, securely. To hinder website scams, Google required all websites to have an SSL, or they would not be ranked.

Do not try to fool Google or other search engines. Due to unfair and manipulative search practices, companies were penalized by Google in the search results. The Washington Post, BBC, BMW, Mozilla, eBay, and The Home Depot dropped in the results for violations of their guidelines. WordPress is a popular blog program that tried to bend the rules and Google did not show them in any search results for two days. Overstock was banned from Google searches for two months. As a website designer, read Googles guidelines to avoid penalties.

Basics of search results

Web crawlers, referred to as robots or spiders, are automated algorithms employed by search engines to locate and index website information. When a page is indexed, the search engine analyzes the content, keywords, meta information to decide the page's relevance, and 300 hundred other points of reference to store in a database. It will measure the loading speed and mobile compatibility to also decide where it should show up for the searcher.

Google's control over ninety percent of the mobile phone search market led to a monopoly ruling in August of 2024. The division of the market to establish fairness remains unclear, but it will significantly affect website designers. When a client hires a website designer, they anticipate that search engines will find the website.

SEO

Laypeople use the word "search engine optimization" loosely to refer to a variety of topics. In reality, it describes the process of designing a website to enable search engines to index and classify it. This phrase first appeared around 2000.

Search engines like Google use small programs called bots, crawlers, or spiders to collect data from websites. These systems have visited nearly every website on the Internet, gathering information, including codes, links, keywords, and phrases. Search engines manage enormous databases that store the collected data. In essence, these databases include copies of almost all websites and images that are accessible to the public worldwide.

SGE-the next generation

Google continually modifies its algorithms to display businesses in search results. Ten years ago, it was discovered that if companies added blogs to their website, they would show up high in search results. By the time marketers were award of this and had implemented blogs, Google had moved on. Significant effort and resources were expended on blogs that were ineffective and, in certain instances, detrimental due to improper keyword utilization. If a blog had no followers or comments, Google knew it was not relevant.

Search engine optimization specialists attempted to use search phrases like "service near me" to show up better in search results. Once again, Google modified the results by incorporating the searcher's location.

Companies hire website designers, assuming the graphic designers understand how to optimize the site for search engines. Despite having components to address potential visitors' questions, if the site lacks indexing and fast download speed, it will fall to the bottom of search results. Many website designers believe that Google will automatically find the site. This chapter covers a few of the many optimization steps.

Image 14-3
Besides Desktop, mobile, many websites need to be revised for a tablet.

Search engines

A search engine is a software application that assists individuals in locating the information they are seeking online by utilizing keywords or phrases. Search engines are capable of rapidly returning results, despite the presence of millions of websites, by continuously scouring the Internet and indexing each page they encounter.

Google

In May 2024, Google applied for a patent on "Generative summaries for search results" with the US Patent Office. Also in May of 2024, Google phased out most of its human sources used in search results and replaced them with artificial intelligence. A 34-page patent document was approved, and the patent was assigned on September 26, 2024. Artificial intelligence is now being used to enhance the internet surfer's experience. The term for locating a company in search results is now SGE, Search Generative Experience but people still use SEO. Website designers need to understand the proper terminology and the background of searches using Google.

Bing

Microsoft has enhanced its search engine endeavors with its artificial intelligence techniques. However, users can only access these tools through their Edge browser. Bing positioned itself as a search engine that enhances results by presenting a hover pop-up, enabling users to preview the webpage prior to actual visitation. Voice and visual search capabilities are available on Bing.

DuckDuckGo

By portraying itself as an independent internet company, this browser and search engine is able to attract customers belonging to the younger demographic. It does not keep a record of search history, does not store the IP addresses of users, does not exchange information with third parties, does not block advertisements, and does not monitor users. Users run the risk of downloading malicious software, such as viruses, when they visit websites that are contained inside the search results.

SearchGPT

Developed by OpenAI, which invented ChatGPT, SearchGPT blends search engine functionality with generative AI. Web searches sometimes take several attempts to yield relevant results. Each inquiry builds context for the searcher to ask follow-up queries. SearchGPT highlights high-quality material in a conversational interface with various engagement options using AI. To engage users more, they will find more results in the sidebar with source links.

The purpose of a webpage

Every page on the internet serves a specific function, or many functions at once. Most pages aim to provide some form of benefit to users. A firm designs certain pages to inform a viewer about a product or service it offers. Despite Google's impression that the internet serves as a giant encyclopedia, people first turn to the internet for information when they need anything for their home, need a repair, need a place to travel to and stay overnight, among other things.

Webmasters and search engines agree that the internet is a valuable resource. In order to attract individuals, webmasters are required to not only develop websites that provide answers to questions posed by viewers but also designs that are visually appealing and fascinating.

The main purpose of the internet is to share information which can include personal, social, about a company, or about a topic. Websites are created to:

- Share pictures, videos, files or software.
- Articulate a viewpoint or pose inquiries for other users to address.
- Entertain.
- Sell products or services.
- Disseminate news

Types of layouts

Design rules apply to webpages just as they apply to a small mustard jar or a large moving billboard. A visual hierarchy, attention-grabbing visuals, proper use of space, and appropriate scale are essential elements of a webpage design. Due to the nature of web design, grid systems are the easiest to work with, but keep in mind that the area above the fold, which is the part of the page seen without scrolling, is the most important for viewers and for Google.

There are a number of home page design options, but most websites have the logo and navigation menu in a header at the top of the page. Below the header, the most widely used layouts contain:

1. 1 large image or sideshow with a headline above or below the image. Below the image is the copy in 1-3 columns starting with subheads.

2. 3 large images with a headline above or below all three images. Below the images, the copy is in 1-3 columns started with subheads.

3. Headline with content on the left or right side of an image.

At the bottom of the pages should be a footer with details about to the company such as licenses, relevant links, copyright information, webmaster link, and a link to contact the company. The footer should repeat the logo and is an out of the way but visible area to add links the Privacy Policy, Terms of Use and the site map for indexing with the search engines. Since many visitors quickly scan a page, branding top and bottom should remind them the company first and last that they visited.

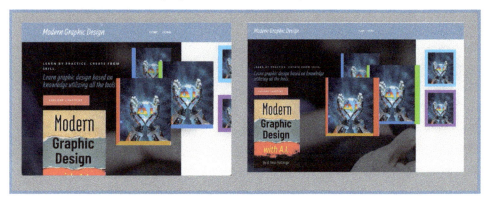

Image 14-4

Example of how elements appear differently based on the size of the screen.

Cannot completely control the layout

Even with limitations, web design can be rewarding and even more than before, graphic designers are getting some control over the visual elements. In 1996 for graphic designers, the web design programs such as Front Page were barely more than typewriters with spaces and returns placing the content and very low quality and resolution digital images. At that time the visual and content design was manipulated by computer developers and programmers.

When someone visits a webpage, they see text displays of the HTML tags and attributes, which define how the page is organized and displayed visually. It is composed of HTML code that makes up everything seen by a visitor.

Web design systems have advanced to provide graphic designers enhanced control over the elements. Web design has a distinct methodology compared to print design. In static print design, a graphic artist positions a picture, selects the typeface, and determines the content size on a page, which remains fixed for the viewer's observation. The concept of "what you see is what you get" (abbreviated as WYSIWYG) is expected. Nevertheless, with web design, WYSIWYG does not equate to what you receive. The dimensions of the website will alter, the user may lack the correct fonts, resulting in substitutions, and the color tones are not standardized.

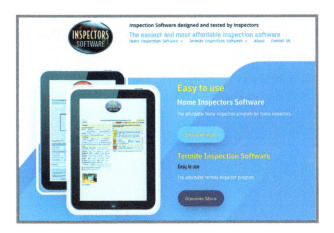

Image 14-5

For internet design, the graphic designer should have at least two monitors of different quality to observe the design online. People have monitors that are 800p and have faded over ten years of use while other users may have a gaming monitor that is relatively new and 1440p. Nuances in color may be seen differently.

Because of age, quality, device, and settings, monitor colors will always vary. The download speed, the age of the device, the browser version, and the availability of web fonts are the primary factors that limit fonts. Depending on the device type, the layout size will vary, with a desktop website appearing significantly smaller on a smart phone. However, it's possible to address each of these concerns to some degree.

The need for speed

Image 14-6

Spinning ball of loading

The primary consideration in web design is download speed. The viewer must download all visible and invisible parts of a website. A sluggish download speed will result in a delayed appearance of the design. The viewer may prefer to leave and visit an alternative website. The browser then caches these components, enabling faster downloads on the user's subsequent visit to the website.

Initially, to use the internet, a web user employed a modem to dial a service and establish a connection. The process took several minutes, and using the phone line significantly limited the amount of material available for download.

Websites have come a long way technically and visually since computer programmers first started developing them for the internet. Download speeds are much faster with DSL and faster modems and computers. But back in 2006, the internet speed was a major concern for building websites. The NY Times wrote an article on how to speed up a website. "The problems are made worse by designers being in Los Angeles or New York, and not, say, Texas, so 'they think everyone has a large monitor and a fast DSL connection,' said Neal Hettinger, co-owner of Lead Pencil Ad Design, a marketing and design company in Manhattan Beach, Calif. He suggests mixing text and graphics on a Web site, with dark type set against a light background for easy reading."[3]

With DSL (Digital Subscriber Line), a high-speed service utilizing telephone lines, websites can accommodate greater sizes, allowing for the inclusion of more images and typefaces. Web designers need to keep an eye on the download speed, as prolonged loading times can frustrate users and lead them to abandon a site. Google indicates that consumers abandon a website if it requires over three seconds to load. However, they are prepared to wait a bit longer if they have a strong desire to view the page.

Contemporary website design has become increasingly laden with visuals and motion graphics. The phenomenon known as the "spinning ball to nowhere" will prompt prospective visitors to navigate away.

Optimizing photos for a website

Image 14-7
Example of options for saving an image. Images on the right show the loss of gradations when converting to Gif. Stats in the lower left indicate the size of a file saved at different settings. A jpeg saved at 2100 pixels is 565Kb but at 1000px it is 32Kb. A 2100pxin a png format is a huge 3.7Mb while the lesser quality gif file is 269Kb.

Adobe Photoshop offers a "Save for Web" feature that compresses photos for online utilization. GIFs are an effective format for producing compact file sizes suitable for buttons and basic artwork. PNGs include significantly bigger file sizes; nonetheless, they offer superior image quality and the capability to include a translucent background, necessitating compatibility with surrounding elements such as color, gradation, image, or texture. JPEGs yield optimal results without detail loss and possess a moderate file size when utilized at higher settings.

Website designers should bring the images into the layout at 100%, compressed for the quality they want or need, and the correct color mode converted with Adobe Photoshop. Do not expect the website design software to convert the images at the best optimization.

One important but overlooked visual to create is a Favicon. This square 500 pixel image is generally a simplification of the logo or icon that visitors will recognize. This image file appears in search results and at the top tab or window and from a marketing perspective, is another communication of the brand. Favicon is the portmanteau for favorite icon.

Image 14-8
Graphic Designer: Neal Hettinger
Example of Web page

Engaging the visitor

Users don't always conduct searches for content. Many users actively seek out photographs, using the alternate attribute to classify them. People with visual challenges can also benefit from these explanations when searching. Although robots are unable to see the photos, alt text provides a description of the image.

Meta tags, which impart information to search engines and robots, are an essential component of search engine optimization (SEO). This code describes the content of a page and indicates its relevance to the user's entered search query. Meta tags have the potential to influence the search engine results (SERPs) of a website.

To foster interaction with visitors, graphic artists will integrate motion elements. Graphic artists utilize several techniques such as drop-down navigation, slideshows, animation, films, and parallax scrolling to establish a relationship with the users. When the images in the backdrop move at a different speed than the ones in the front, the page gives the impression of being three-dimensional and provides a sense of depth. "Parallax scrolling" refers to this particular method.

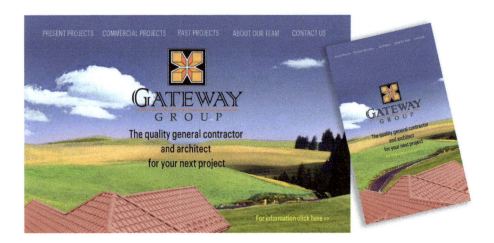

Image 14-9

Sometimes a client will trust the web designer to go against the norms to give them the end result they want.

Top three concerns of website design

Naturally, a graphic designer wants to start by outlining the components of their design concept. However, they must keep in mind that, in addition to the visual design, the user experience and the optimization of the website are equally vital. If a website is not easily available through searches, then it's worth will decrease, regardless of how beautiful its aesthetics may be. Graphic artists should consider the structure and visual flow of the work when they draw thumbnails and write down ideas.

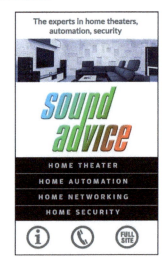

Image 14-10
Example of mobile web page

Users should have an effortless time navigating the website. When the design is overly busy. If users find it difficult to locate items and the website loads slowly, they are likely to leave and visit the websites of competitors.

The consistency of the brand is of the utmost importance in all marketing designs. Establish the color scheme and load optimized photos into the library before starting the element arrangement process. It is necessary to specify the font faces, widths, and text content for each header, including H1, H2, H3, and so on. In order to increase search engine optimization and search results there should be only one H1 word, phrase, or sentence.

The first steps

Before starting a website design, the designer needs to verify with the client the hosting platform with a Secure Sockets Layer (SSL) certificate, domain name, and the sign in credentials to access the server set up.

Secure Sockets Layer is the connection between a browser and a website to encrypt data to be sent securely. Protecting sensitive data, such as financial details, names, and addresses is important to the web designer, the company, and the customer. If credit card information is not sent securely, then the non-compliance fines start at $5000 per month and move higher up to $1000,000 per month. The final penalty is losing the ability to accept credit cards.

The Payment Card Industry (PCI) has set guidelines that businesses must follow to protect and transmit cardholder data. The amount of the fine depends on the size of the company and how long it has been out of compliance.

Web designers do not want or need to be involved with accepting and storing credit card or other personal information. Utilize a well-known third party service provider.

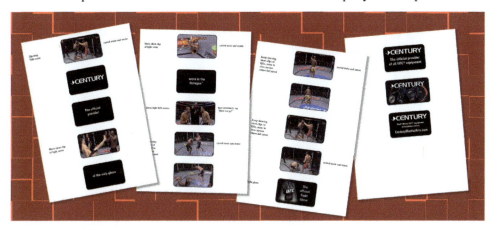

Image 14-11

Example UFC storyboard taken from screen grabs.

With the client, define the websites goals, functions, and features. Some web designers start with a flow chart that starts with a home page a shows the connections to each page or parts of pages.

Wireframes are the foundation of good web design, similar to a blueprint for a house. They help teams align on requirements and communicate design concepts to clients, management, and other stakeholders. Wireframes typically include loose page layouts, the header with navigation bars, elements of UX and UI design, and a storyboard of videos or the interactive elements.

User experiences and User Interface

Image 14-12

Web designers need to be UI and UX heroes.

AI Practicum} Firefly use landscape aspect ratio with art content and format with art four prompts with same format: cartoon of a woman/man in business attire wearing glasses and cartoon of a woman/man muscular and serious. In Photoshop blend images together and clean up with spot healing brush. Used Photoshop AI two prompts create a photo/painting of a busy city at night with wet streets reflecting lights.

User experience (UX) pertains to functionality, whereas user interface (UI) concerns aesthetics. They enhance one another to produce a product that is both aesthetically pleasing and practical, providing satisfaction to users.

UX design improves the user experience with products and systems. This requires knowing the user's needs, behaviors, and motivations and designing an intuitive, frictionless, and enjoyable trip. UX designers attempt to make products useful, user-friendly, and accessible. Graphic designers rarely desire to learn user experience.

Research begins with interviews, questionnaires, and usability testing to identify user needs and problem spots. Identifying typical users and tracking their product journeys is next. Web designers are active in prototyping and wireframing, product structure and flow design. Web designers often experience frustration when attempting to enhance their designs through user testing. It's easier to let developers and UX professionals handle that aspect. However, site designers should prioritize user experience.

Conversely, UI design emphasizes the aesthetic and sensory aspects of the product. It involves crafting the visual components that enhance a product's appeal and engagement, guaranteeing a pleasurable user experience. User interface pertains directly to online design and necessitates skills in color selection, typography, and imagery that correspond with the brand and establish an appealing look.

Graphic designers are adept at maintaining a consistent style across all web pages and elements. The UI process entails graphic designers organizing components on the screen to guide users and establish a unified, balanced design. Designers create interactive elements such as buttons, sliders, forms, and other features that engage users.

The user interface

Users typically expect a specific arrangement of elements on a webpage. Graphic artists should comply with these standards to enhance the user experience. For both desktop and mobile platforms, browsers can use a device-agnostic site, but this may compromise the user experience. Users may have a poor experience if they need to scroll multiple times to locate the desired information, and the arrangement of the information may change. The limited display of a mobile site should not possess the complexity or content volume characteristic of a bigger, higher-resolution desktop monitor.

The majority of consumers quickly decide whether a web page contains the information they seek and continue reading or it does not and leave. Unless they easily discover the information, they will return to the search results. The design's objective should be to engage a visitor for a length of two to three minutes. The user experience must be positive.

If the contact information is not readily available, the user may get frustrated and move on. When a visitor clicks on a linked button, but it takes them to an error page without a way to get back to the home page, they will leave the site.

The website must implement a responsive design methodology. The site must be compatible with various devices, including computer displays and tablets. Instead of relying on tools like WordPress, we must manually optimize the photos for expedited downloading.

Image 14-13
Example of flat design for buttons with recognizable icons.

Flat design is favored in web design due to its emphasis on simplicity, small file sizes and usability. The fast download speeds are consistent with successful digital experiences. It emphasizes two-dimensional components stripped of superfluous adornments, resulting in a minimalist aesthetics. It consists of simple icons, with the basic three level color palettes, and large and accommodating white space, making it easy for users to navigate and locate information quickly.

The website should fill the browser screen with color and graphics but on some screens that could be 1920 pixels wide and others 800 pixels wide. The common width for is 1024 pixels which is approximately 12.5 inches wide. The widths have changed from 800 pixels in the early 2000s to many websites being built at 1280 pixels. Some designers start with a width of 1920 pixels for viewing on all devices and a TV screen. They feel that with the faster download speeds available, the web page can contain more content. Videos are interesting to visitors and the designer will need to decide between better image quality or faster download speed. These designers do not realize that many DSL services are still set at a 25 Mbps download speed.

The top of the desktop website has a banner, called a header. This area contains the company branding and marketing message.

- The logo should be linked to the homepage to allow visitors to easily start over.
- A company tagline or slogan placed here will tell the potential customer what the company offers in the way of services.
- The telephone number should be prominent. Do not risk a potential customer giving up and going to another website
- The navigation menu needs to be readable and not too wordy.
- A navigation menu can have dropdowns, but more than two levels can be confusing to the user.
- Make sure the dropdown reads when it goes outside of the header onto the body.
- Have the page label being visited in a different color than the other pages for the user to know where they are in the website..
- Keep the header clean with visual space but it may need a call to action button.

A site user may be attracted to a large image situated within the body content area. This "hero" image can be presented in multiple formats, including a still image, a slideshow, an animated GIF, or a movie. If the hero image occupies the full page, the file size will be larger, leading to extended download durations. The visitor must scroll down to access the content located below the fold.

Extend the background color or texture to its full width. Determine the suitable quantity of rows for the arrangement. An image or content will not extend beyond a single column, unlike a grid arrangement used for printing or publishing. The layout may comprise multiple rows that extend horizontally and vertically across the page.

Image 14-14

Example of the up arrow, dot navigation and shortcut links that keep the visitor flowing from one point of information to another.

How users navigate and interact with a website is UI design. For instance, users can bypass scrolling up the page by incorporating arrows that quickly ascend to the top. An additional convenience is the dot navigation bar, which directs the visitor to specific sections of the page. Selecting a labeled dot in a sidebar can direct a user to a specific content area on the page.

Under the hero shortcuts to important information on the page or website can be listed with a button that will take the user to the information. This accomplished through linking a button or just the shortcut subhead.

Image 14-15

Select the Web Developer Tools to open a code view of the page. Selecting the Page Source option will open the entire code for the web page in another tab.

Brief explanation of website code

A website is made up of coding such as HTML, JavaScript, and CSS that when strung together are converted by a rendering engine into a visual appearance for viewers. The text, images, links, and formatting elements make up the structure and content of that page through html code. While researching sites, graphic designers will find typefaces, leading, and pixel size in a Page Source tool to use for reference.

When browsing websites, if a designer sees a pleasing color, the web designer can discover that color callout in the code. Use the command F shortcut to find the code. The code is usually the word color with a # sign followed by letters such as color #ffffff for white and #000000 for black. These are known as hex color codes which can be looked up a color in Photoshop, see the hex color number and use it in the design.

To save time, start a file using Excel, Numbers, or Google Sheets, to list web fonts, show what they look like, with their Hex color # set up color samples that are appealing and divide into palettes for different industries and impressions.

Basic website elements

A website must include a Home page, an About Us page, a Services or Products page, and a Contact Us page. The site will quickly locate desired content while adhering to Google and Bing searchability rules, thereby enhancing discoverability in search results. Searches get results due to automated programs traversing the websites. An error page must inform the user that the requested page is nonexistent and should provide a link to the homepage. Assigning titles, establishing a site structure for search engine submission, and incorporating alt descriptions for images are essential non-creative activities.

Include a headline that will captivate visitors. While website design programs may use points for type, pixels are more precise and maintain the ratio in accordance with the screen's resolution.

Rather than employing point sizes to denote the height of type, website design employs pixels.

Graphic designers will establish their own sizes according to the resolution of their computers. However, given that not all terminals are identical, there are several alternatives to consider when initiating a design.

The average paragraph text size is 16px to 18px, but it may be larger for minors and the baby boomer generation. Set all legalese, including copyrights and a link to the webmaster, to 12px.

Headlines, subheads type that needs to be emphasized are referred to as headings. The largest and most important line of text should be labeled as Heading 1. There should only be one on a page and should be set at 42px to 48px with a line height of 1.5em. Subheads and type that is not Paragraph oriented can be labeled Heading 2 – 6 with 2 being the largest and 6 usually the smallest. Heading 2 can be set from 34px to 40px with a line height of 1.7em. Heading 3 should be 28px-32px with a line height of 1.7em. There can be more than one line of type that is labeled Heading 2, or 3, etc.

Home Page   **Scroll 1**   **Scroll 2**

Image 14-16

Home page with two scrolls down. Note the "UP" button on the left to zip the user back to the top.

Web design software

While design software is limited to the Adobe Creative Suite and Canva (which recently acquired Affinity Designer), internet software programs are numerous and varied in capabilities

The introduction of website programs such as Adobe Dreamweaver and WordPress allowed graphic designers to design without writing code. They are visual editor programs that allow the graphic artist to see changes as they are made. There are many website design programs, but beginner website designers should check the advantages and disadvantages before spending time building and publishing a website. Many do not work well with certain search engines.

A couple of popular website visual editors are Divi and Eliminator. These programs are no-code solutions that allow beginners to use templates and advanced designers to start with a blank page. They are a design framework that utilizes WordPress for its content management system such as creating users with different levels of responsibilities, logging in page, and, adding plug-ins. These editors load as themes but the features function similar to print design programs. The internet has countless lesson videos.

Image 14-17

As in any job, web design can be frustrating but with the evolving technology, it will not be boring, and it will be rewarding. It just depends on the urge for exploration.

AI Practicum} Firefly prompt:mountain sunset and milky way.

Web design job outlook

Website design careers most likely are not going to get a person rich — except in being paid to be creative and color things. The U.S. Bureau of Labor Statistics compiles employment for different occupations yearly[4] The latest is 2023 for Website designers which does not include graphic designers. In 2023 there were approximately 111,060 employed web designers across the United States which was a 3% over 2022.

The profile of a web designer may or may not include these responsibilities:

- Develop, test layouts, interfaces, functionality, and navigation menus for compatibility and usability across browsers and devices.
- Assess web design and optimize websites for marketability and search engine rankings.
- Design and test interfaces with a focus on aesthetics and design.
- May produce visuals for websites and manage website content and links.

If a website designer is thinking of moving to a different state, in addition to investigating the cost of living, they should look at the available opportunities. For instance, Alabama ranked # 43 with 150 employed web designers but paid the lowest of any state and ranked #50 with a median wage of $26.10 per hour. Surprisingly, South Dakota employs 90 web designers (#44) with a median hourly wage of $52.36 (#7).

The top two states to employ web designers were #1 California had 25370 with a median wage of $65.95 per hour and #2 New York had 15180 at $60.15 p/h. While Texas was #3 in employment with 8460, they dropped to #8 at $50.64 p/h. Other states in the employed list of web designers: Oregon was #17 employing 1620 but #6 at $53.11 p/h; Nebraska was #27 with 840 employed and #44 at $32.07 p/h; and Alaska #46 had 60 employed and #42 at $34.14.

These figures will give you an idea what the salaries are for web design. Self-employed web designers are not included in these statistics.

Portfolio Building Assignment – Use AI to create A Flyer

1. Make up a name for a Top 40 Pop Music band with five tour dates and cities. Produce a call to action on where to buy tickets. Research pop bands and their album covers (such as iTunes, Spotify, eMusic), as well as advertising and flyers. Pop music is characterized by repeated choruses and hooks, short to medium-length songs are written in a basic format (often the verse–chorus structure), and rhythms or tempos that can be used for dancing.

2. Adobe Firefly | Using prompts, create an image for a Pop band on tour flyer. The flyer is vertical and should show 5 different band members on stage with stage lights, audience, and fog. Check the band members for complete faces, fingers, and ears. Allow room for type. Using InDesign, on one letter sized page show both artworks at 17 picas X 22 picas each. Try at least 2 options and list your "Prompt" verbiage below your image to show in an interview.

3. Chat GPT | Using prompts, create a short headline and content from the information in #1. Try at least 2 options and list your prompt verbiage below your image. In the same InDesign file as #2, add one letter sized page and show both text solutions with your prompts.

4. Adobe Express | Using prompts, design a text effects headline for the on-tour flyer. Think about the colors and how the type will look on the image from #2. Try at least 2 options and in the same InDesign file as #2, add one letter sized page and show your generated graphic headlines and list your prompt verbiage below each solution.

5. Adobe Photoshop | Combine your image and text in layers. Using generative fill, add image area for the content. Retouched the headline area to make it readable. Do not use outlines and drop shadows to make it the type readable—that is a sign of a defeated designer. Use your skill to make the background work for readability. Use saturation and color adjustments to make the image jump off the page. Using the same InDesign page created in #2, show the retouched artwork at 17 picas X 22 picas next to the original Firefly generated image.

6. Adobe Illustrator | Using Text to Vector create an icon for the Pop Band. Then add type and stylize the font with the icon into an eye-catching logo. In the same InDesign file as #2, add one letter sized page and show your generated icon with your font solution and list your prompt verbiage.

7. Export the InDesign file by creating a print quality pdf.

References

1| (2022, December 16). 75% of Website Credibility is Dependent on its Design. CXL: User Experience & Persuasive Design. https://cxl.com/blog/first-impressions-matter-the-importance-of-great-visual-design

2| (2023, April 26). 75% of consumers judge a company's credibility by its site design. Medium. https://medium.com/@leefuhr/75-of-consumer-judge-a-companys-credibility-by-its-site-design-8a78118e1560

3| (2006, November 15). How to Make Your Web Site Sing for You. The New York Times.

4| (2024, April 3). Occupational Employment and Wage Statistics. U.S. Bureau of Labor Statistics. https://www.bls.gov/oes/2023/may/oes151255.htm

The future of graphic design

Learning objectives

By the end of this chapter, the reader will be able to manage a modern style to apply to a restaurant menu. They will be able to judge the graphic design being created around the world. The student will be able to compose a design critique.

Image 15-1
Colors are approximations and may not be exact.

Graphic designers should stay informed about trends in the United States and around the world. Certain business operations spend time and money on researching the developments and changes making them ideal for graphic designers to follow. Automobile design may be curved but slowly in four years change to angular. Fashion designers are famous for setting styles. Retailers will market trying to establish a fad. The company WGSN issues reports on consumer and design trends that are available to graphic artists as downloadable pdfs. Their reports are based on data and forecasting experience.

Commercial artists should record as much as they discover by keeping notebooks or digital libraries. They learn about the latest photography techniques, discover new typography families, record color trends, take samples of the latest textures, and find out about the current approaches to layouts.

Graphic designers are integrating conventional 2D elements with 3D components. The dynamic and layered appearance of these styles is achieved by integrating flat design with 3D shapes, animations, and texturing techniques.

Color trends

Color shades and tints change continuously because so many industries want to be on the edge of the latest trends to appeal to their target markets. Graphic designers examine and research the latest use of color in multiple industries.

Color is such a personal choice that it may be the most difficult element of a layout to select. The graphic artist must remain detached and decide what the target market would be interested in seeing. The best way to accomplish the attractive color palette is studying fashion and interior color trends.

Pantone has been publishing the Pantone Fashion Color Trend Report for 30 years, which serves the fashion audience by emphasizing the season's most significant color trends. The increasing importance of color's emotional impact is transforming the industry's approach to color and design. Pantone has re-imagined the Pantone Fashion Color Trend Report to align with this transformation, incorporating the key color drivers that inform the seasonal edit and supporting inspirational visual imagery for each of the top colors and seasonless hues.

Recognized for decades as the authority on colors, Pantone® predicts the trends they feel will be popular in the coming year. There are multiple lists for color trends in industries such as interior design, clothing, architecture, and manufacturing. They create numbers to correspond to ink mixtures and also names to bring a sense of passion to the colors. For 2025, Pantone® has chosen their top ten fashion color trends as well as five of the shades and tints they feel will be seasonless.

For instance, the color Pantone® 16-3115 is entitled Crocus which they define as "An enchanting harmony of pink and purple, Crocus emanates joy, love, and health. A captivating botanical hue, Crocus draws you in with its beguiling charm." For Pantone® 19-3810 TCX Eclipse they describe as "A shadowed blue, Eclipse displays an air of credible importance. Trusted and recognizable, Eclipse is a pillar of substance." Graphic artists who looked up these trend reports can use the names and descriptions when presenting to their clients.

According to a spokesperson of the Pantone Color Institute, Gen Z is particularly fond of vibrant colors such as neon green, electric blue, and brilliant pink. These colors are indicative of their aspiration for self-expression and individuality.

Coloro is an innovative color system that aids the design industries with color management. They were introduced in 2017 as an alternative to Pantone by WGSN. They prognosticate that "Future Dusk," a hue situated between dark blue and purple, will gain popularity in the coming year. The Coloro system bears watching for future color methods.

Many companies in a wide range of industries have also selected their colors of the year for 2025. Miniwax is leaning toward a violet for the stain tint. Graham & Brown is a British wallpaper company, and their color of the year is Elderton which is a rich brown. "Turbonite" is a gray hue with a tawny bronze undertone, that was recently introduced by the luxury automotive company Porsche. This color is explained as "underscoring the symbiotic connection between materials and color that are harvested from the earth."

Image 15-2
Colors are approximations and may not be exact.

Sherman Williams® annually predicts color trend for the upcoming years. The colors they chose are for painting interiors. They also describe their paint colors. One color is Malabar which is a "sandy beige neutral can turn any environment into a soft, inviting haven. It's ideal for layering with delicate, warm hues to create serenity in an abundance of design aesthetics."

Three-dimensional design

This relatively new graphic design style blends traditional 2D and 3D elements to create a layered, multidimensional impression. Three-dimensional design digitally produces 3D objects, textures, graphics, and photographs are combined to create depth and a sense of realism. This style makes a design come to life by combining 3D items with 2D backdrops and employing highlights and shadows.

3D modeling software as well as programs such as Illustrator and Photoshop can generate realistic and stylized objects. Designers employ them to enhance the visual appeal of planar compositions by incorporating texture, depth, and a sense of physical space. This may encompass 3D typographic elements, realistic models, or abstract shapes.

The three-dimensional design style is a contemporary and visually impactful method of conveying ideas, which is why it is so popular in industries such as advertising, web design, social media content, and branding.

Mixed media design

A style that integrates a variety of visual styles and techniques is the use of mixed media collage. This technique evolved from Maximalism and involves the addition of textures and gradients to create a tactile effect, the layering of 3D models over photographs, and the incorporation of hand-drawn illustrations. The combination of these styles enables greater creative license and can distinguish designs by establishing a tactile, "crafted" appearance.

Mixed media design shares common techniques with Maximalism, since both methodologies incorporate layered components, striking graphics, and a variety of styles. Maximalism is characterized by its "more is more" concept, wherein designers amalgamate many textures, colors, patterns, and styles inside a single item to produce a visually opulent and expressive outcome. Mixed media has elements of maximalism but focuses on the integration of diverse media types, such as 3D components with photographs or illustrations, rather than merely increasing visual density.

Maximalism emphasizes the creation of a lavish, opulent aesthetic with numerous elements, whereas mixed media concentrates on the amalgamation of several media forms. Mixed media design offers greater flexibility, capable of being either minimalist or maximalist based on the combination of elements. In order to produce distinctive, aesthetically pleasing designs, this method combines several media.

Image 15-3

Motion graphic design

The process of using animation and visual effects to transform static drawings into moving visuals is known as motion graphic design. To produce realistic motions and scenes for various media, such as television, movies, and the internet, motion designers employ a range of approaches. Short interactive animations are gaining popularity in web design and social media, invigorating user interfaces and social content while augmenting user engagement.

Motion graphic artists build visual storytelling with software such as Adobe After Effects. They use a range of design components, such as: Selecting tunes that complement the visuals; Using font sizes, styles, and timing to draw in readers; and expressing emotions, effects, and moods using color theory.

They are frequently instructed in conventional graphic design, but motion graphic designers also acquire the ability to integrate sound, space, and time into their work. They must comprehend how to bring design elements to life without a natural reference, as is the case in traditional cell animation.

Motion graphics are employed in a variety of projects, such as:

- Film and television credits
- Advertising and digital marketing
- Website design
- Social media channels
- Trailers and movie sequences
- Commercials
- Promotional videos
- Screen transitions

Bright colors, geometric patterns, and dynamic gestures are frequently employed in motion graphics, which are information-based. Mixed media is also frequently employed in motion design, as animated 3D elements and textures introduce a new level of interactivity. Subtle animations of 3D elements can enhance the engagement and lifelikeness of a design on websites and social media.

Motion design involves integrating with typography, producing moving text that reacts to human interaction or synchronizes with scrolling. This transforms text from a mere static visual element into an interactive component of the user experience. Anticipate enhanced dynamic typographic effects in websites, applications, and advertising, where typography reacts to motions, hover states, or auditory stimuli.

This demand for this area of design is growing faster than the training. NBC has an academy to train called NBCU and it has a free, innovative, multi-platform journalism training and development initiative aimed at equipping college students for careers in the media sector.

Students at affiliated universities and colleges obtain instruction and practical experience, along with access to distinguished journalists and industry experts from NBC News, MSNBC, CNBC, and Telemundo News. NBCU Academy provides engaging learning opportunities and educational resources to assist both emerging professionals and experienced journalists in acquiring new skills and advancing in the rapidly evolving news industry.

View the YouTube video that discusses how viewers of broadcast news rely on the on-air graphics to put the day's events into perspective. Two creative directors at Artworks—the top in-house graphics department at NBC—Sarah Schultz and Ventura Castro discuss their process for making graphics magic. Find out more at www. youtube.com/watch?app=desktop&v=gkhItWZMCbI and discover the skills necessary.

Image 15-4

AI-generated design

As AI technologies become increasingly accessible, numerous designers are investigating AI-assisted or entirely AI-generated images. This style introduces a distinctive, occasionally erratic element to digital work. It is a design style being used now but will advance in many directions.

Many graphic designers feel that the artificial intelligence generation of images and type will open up solutions to different approaches and expand the creative opportunities. It is also unpredictable since what the program designs is up to the AI software.

Another problem or at least a frustration point is that entering the same prompt will not generate the same image. This book has the prompts used to attain images, but the words had to be finessed to achieve the images shown. If the reader enters the same prompts with the same specs, they will not get the same results.

Rarely, are the images used right from the AI generator. Photoshop and Illustrator are used to revise and adjust the images to create a workable attractive communication. The possibilities of AI are exciting and will save time.

Image 15-5

The future of typography

To develop AI generated type, it requires creative and knowledgeable prompts. Understanding the need for space is not an AI quality. Even when prompted to leave space for type and content, the solutions are packed with color, texture, and forms.

AI tools are helping designers build adaptive font that changes styles, tones, and weights per context. AI-enhanced typography may adapt to certain visual impairments or design sensibilities. Type is accessible and individualized. The primary visual element is now abstract, large-scale AI generated typefaces that may convey feelings and business identification just as well as images.

In the imminent future, variable fonts will enable designers to modify font weight, width, and slant instantaneously, allowing typography to adapt dynamically to varying screen sizes or user activities. This adaptability enhances the versatility of typography, which is crucial for facilitating seamless user experiences across various devices.

Fonts that appear hand-drawn or imprecise are also becoming increasingly popular as design becomes more digital and AI-driven. Designers illustrate fonts to convey authenticity and add a human touch. Custom, hand-drawn, or brushstroke types will remain in demand, particularly among brands that wish to convey a personal meaning.

Designers are persistently challenging norms with avant-garde typography that is exceptionally expressive and unconventional. Anticipate an increase in distinctive, tailored fonts that embody brand identity, frequently presented in deformed, fragmented, or abstract forms. Brands, particularly in creative sectors, are increasingly adopting fonts that are more characterful and whimsical.

Typography may become simpler and legible when the audience is being overwhelmed with messages. Minimalist typefaces that emphasize simplicity and encourages classic, legible fonts that work across platforms may become the popular style again.

Typography is rapidly exceeding the flat screen, as three-dimensional effects provide depth, realism, and a tactile quality. Integrating text with 3D rendering or incorporating it into mixed-media designs enhances its visual prominence, transitioning from conventional 2D formats to multidimensional and interactive environments.

As a medium for both practical and artistic expression, typography will continue to develop and shape the future of immersive and interactive storytelling, brand identity, and user experience design.

Graphic design job outlook

To choose a career in graphic design, a person must find satisfaction in creating marketing solutions that will be changed by their clients. It is not a money making venture like being a financier and it is not respected like scientist. Graphic design is a fun and a changing industry. Many careers become boring because they lack new challenges — but not graphic design. Just look at how artificial intelligence is changing the creative process.

In 2023 there were approximately 212,720 employed graphic designers across the United States which was a rise of 7% over 2022.[3] The U.S. Bureau of Labor Statistics compiles employment for different occupations yearly. The latest is 2023 for graphic designers which does not include website designers or freelance graphic designers.

The U.S. Bureau of Labor's profile of a graphic designer is defined as "Design or create graphics to meet specific commercial or promotional needs, such as packaging, displays, or logos. May use a variety of mediums to achieve artistic or decorative effects."

The top five states with the highest percentage of employment out of the workforce are California, New York, Texas, Florida, and Illinois. The top ten cities with graphic design jobs are the metro areas of NYC, LA, Chicago, DC, Dallas, San Francisco, Miami, Boston, Atlanta, and Seattle. The hourly mean wages for those cities start at the highest in San Francisco at $45.87 with the lowest being Dallas at $29.91.

The top five non-metropolitan areas for a graphic designer for hourly mean wages are NW Colorado at $34.54, non-metro areas of Massachusetts $30.60, North regions of California at $30.57, East Central New York at $ 30.18, and North Vermont at $ 30.12. These areas are located near large metropolitan cities and perhaps utilize remote employment.

The final portfolio pieces will be showcasing your ability to create brand identified marketing for a restaurant. The content is after the instructions. The final mechanicals will be printed in 4 colors (CMYK). Use AI to create images

Menu Design

1. Research menu designs to learn how they flow and for inspiration.

2. Analyze the supplied content provided. There are many formatting and spelling errors which you will need to fix. All the type is the same size, which does not convey a visual hierarchy of importance. The information is scattered and in an illogical order. Determine what items need to have a relationship and express that visually through your design. Eliminate items that are not relevant to the project.

a. Establish a color strategy that can also be used with the business card design. Create a two sided, four color menu. The menu design will be on letter sized paper with a front and a back 4/4 (2 sides) which is shorthand for the four colors, CMYK, for printing on two sides.

b. Before starting the design, thumbnail 6 different ideas. Do not use a computer to create the thumbnails. Make the layouts completely different. Try to make your largest font look like a font and not handwriting.

c. Have a focus so if the focus is type, spell out that part or if it's an image, sketch it. Indicate the body copy the by using thin lines and indicate which words are larger by making some of the lines bigger and bolder. Try adding loosely sketched graphics and use lines, shapes, and textures. Review the 4 design principles and 7 rules of engaging design.

3. Based on your thumbnails, choose one and create a comp of the menu. For this part, use a computer with the InDesign program.

a. Decide what the most important parts of the menu are and make sure they are readable and easy to find. Then decide the next item of importance and treat it accordingly.

b. Pay attention to scale, size of type, and keep the design easy to read and not too colorful. Most companies do not want to use up their ink supply printing out menus needs to be in CYMK - not RGB or PMS.

(Assignment continued on next page)

Business card design.

1. For inspiration, collect examples of well-designed business cards (i.e. search the internet for examples and take screen grabs).

2. Sketch 4 different thumbnails at ½ size.

3. Analyze the supplied text below. Then on the computer recreate two of the thumbnails in either InDesign, Photoshop, or Illustrator as presentation comps.

4. Use the company logo from Chapter 7.

5. Decide what needs to be on the business card and how many sides it needs to have printed.

   Design the cards with vital information such as the logo, president info, tel# address, and possible a call to action or copy to sell the product. The business card has the option of bleed or non-bleed, printed 4/0 (1 side) or 4/4 (2 sides), vertical or horizontal orientation.

6. Provide a printer quality PDF of each business card for your records.

Business Name: Au Bonheur Grand Restaurant | Business type/industry: Restaurant

Age of Business: New | Impression: Fashionable cuisine | Owner: Phillipe Gunter

Target Market: 33 - 55 year old male and females

Address: 101 Argus Blvd, Timbuktu, OK 73111 | Telephone: 615/555-1212

Email: P.Gunter@ABGrand.com | Website: ABGrand.com

Sales hook: Our cuisine takes you from hungry to satisfaction.

Content for Business card:

Info: website: https://www. ABGrand.com (615) 555.1212

Tagline: The sustenance that takes you from hungry to satisfaction.

Content for Menu:

Appetizers: Ask for the daily specials

Satisfying Salads:

Hawaiian Tuti-Fruiti Salad $16 : A large colander of greens with fruity bits of delight to whet your appetite

Maine Organic Pasta Salad $24 : Free range chicken, raised in private farms adorn this farm fresh made spinach pasta

Entrees

Under the rock Mushroom Burger $16 : Farm fed beef grilled on hickory wood served under a silky mushroom sauce on yeast bread.

Out of the field Onion Talapia $20 : Vidalia onions adorn this light whitefish on a bed of Onion, carrots, peas and Colby cheese rice.

California Style Vegetarian $21 : Organic garden vegetables and sweet cornmeal create a sensation for the taste buds.

Oklahoma style BBQ Beef $22 : Marinated in a sharp barbecue sauce, the pulled pork immersed in feta cheese, is topped with roasted garlic and includes a hill of shoestring potatoes.

New York Style Pizza Pie $24 : 3 large slices of sour dough pizza covered with zesty Italian sauce; Kobe beef combined with Brazilian llama.

Philadelphia Twice Baked Pasta $26 : Lean pulled chicken sautéed in a creamy mozzarella and Italian tomato basil sauce over angel hair pasta.

Colón Cheez Pork Kabob $28 : Imagine your pork fused with thyme kernels, provolone cheese, and farm fresh vegetables prepared on a mesquite wood grill

.

Delightful Desserts

Nogales Fried Ice Cream $8 : Breaded & fried golden brown, then smothered rich sauce of your choice: chocolate, strawberry, boysenberry

Montreal Boiled Peanut Meringue $9 : Citrus tangy bread coated with a light mixture of stiffly beaten egg whites and sugar, baked until crisp.

Fountain Creations $8 each

Bing Cherry Coca Cola

Spearmint Sprite

Guava Ginger beer

Peachy Dr. Pepper

See our Wine List for the best California Wines

See our beer list for the best American and European beers on tap

Additional content: Family Food that hits that hunger spot—not the pocketbook!

Final Progress Measurement

Questions from Chapters 1–15

1. What design style focuses on decluttering the layout by using limited elements and restrained color palettes to communicates a simple message? (11)

    a. Maximalism

    b. Modernism

    c. Minimalism

    d. Monetarism

2. In directing AI to create and image, we use words. What is the technical term for that action? (4)

    a. Describe

    b. Prompt

    c. Write

    d. Adversative

3. When designing a brochure, who should the message be directed at? (13)

    a. Target Market

    b. User Interests

    c. Consumer

    d. Representative

4. To a graphic designer, why was Art Nouveau significant? (10)

    a. Commercial artists were recognized for being more than an arts-and-crafts occupation which utilized the same elements in design as art used.

    b. Created a new modern look with its sleek contours and stylized geometric patterns, characterized by symmetry, and repetition of the elements.

    c. Color palettes became popular for logos, ads, motion graphics, websites, posters, and app design for that time.

    d. Inspired Constructivism and Swiss design styles due to the limited use of color and angular images mixed with typeset headlines.

5. On the color wheel what is the tertiary color between orange and Yellow? (8)

    a. Orange Yellow

    b. Blood Orange

    c. Yellow Orange

    d. Hex #FF5349

6. How is the Closure Principle used by designers? (9)

    a. Used by designers to get past client rejected concepts.

    b. Humans visually fill in the missing gaps of incomplete objects to form a whole shape.

    c. Humans perceive objects or shapes as distinct from their backgrounds.

    d. How colors interact with each other and how they are perceived by humans and the psychological effects of colors.

7. In the 1920s, which of these theories was not a developed by a group of psychologists in Germany on visual perception? (9)

    a. Proximity

    b. Similarity

    c. Constance

    d. Symmetry

8. What are we trying to achieve when we set up color palettes? (8)

    a. Create a more cohesive solution that works with all the elements.

    b. Provide contrast in monochromatic solutions.

    c. Achieve contrast by using five analogous tones.

    d. Use four primaries as the main colors and a one as the accent

9. Which answer best explains what a 'line' can be used for in visual communications? (3)

    a. Amounts of time.

    b. Direction.

    c. The horizon.

    d. All of the answers are correct.

10. What is one of the least expensive USPS options to bulk mail? (13)

    a. Postcard second class mail.

    b. Food supplement inserts.

    c. Metered Stamped Mail MSM®.

    d. Every Door Direct Mail® (EDDM).

11. What does this code #82c0c7 refer to? (8)

    a. Pantone Color.

    b. Hex color that is blue grey.

    c. The coating on matte stock.

    d. 82% Cyan minus 7%.

12. True or False: Andy Warhol was a great designer between 1940 – 1948. (10)

13. True or False: Adding black or white to the hue creates tints. (8)

14. What is a good way to push yourself in the creative process? (1)

    a. Get out of your comfort circle.

    b. Start on the computer

    c. Copy the fine art masters.

    d. Make everything the same size, color, and tone,

15. What is a good reason to crop an image? (1)

    a. Create a visual impact and visual interest.

    b. Remove an interesting part of the image.

    c. Focus the viewer on the lack of contents.

    d. To change the image.

16. All 2-D shapes are essentially derived from three basic delineations. (3)

    a. The square, the triangle, and the circle.

    b. The cube, the pyramid, and the sphere.

    c. The square, the sphere, and the circle.

    d. The square, the triangle, and the cone.

17. True or False: A flyer can have three or 5 sides. (13)

18. What is the size of a two sided business card? (12)

    a. 2 inches by 3 inches.

    b. 3 inches by 2 inches.

    c. 2.5 inches by 3 inches.

    d. 2 inches by 3.5inches.

19. What does the color scheme convey? (8)

    a. A sensation about the product or attract attention

    b. The organization of the product.

    c. A smaller font size.

    d. Motivate the reader.

20. How many inches is 18 picas? (13)

    a. 5 inches.

    b. 3 inches.

    c. 3.5 inches.

    d. 6 inches.

21. True or False: Art deco was no longer popular after 1899. (10)

22. What artist influenced Art Nouveau? (10)

    a. El Lissitzky.

    b. Le Corbusier.

    c. Henri de Toulouse-Lautrec.

    d. Adrian Frutiger.

23. Why does a website need a domain? (14)

    a. The server needs it to be secure.

    b. It is the address.

    c. It is where the elements are hosted.

    d. It is the SSL.

24. What is the shortcut to look at the code of a website? (14)

    a. On a PC use the function left key.

    b. On a Mac use command F.

    c. Command NE.

    d. Alt NE.

25. True or False: In 2023 there were more people employed in graphic design jobs than in web design jobs?

References

1| Pressman, L. (2024, September 4). Pantone® Fashion Color Trend Report For New York Fashion Week. Pantone USA. www.pantone.com/articles/fashion-color-trend-report/new-york-fashion-week-spring-summer-2025

2| Wadden, S. (n.d.). 2025 - Color Capsule of the Year. Sherman Williams®. www.sherwin-williams.com/en-us/color/color-of-the-year

3| (2024 April 3). Occupational Employment and Wage Statistics. U.S. Bureau of Labor Statistics. www.bls.gov/oes/current/oes271024.htm

Professional Terminology Index

www.ingramcontent.com/pod-product-compliance
Lightning Source LLC
LaVergne TN
LVHW011802070326
832902LV00025B/4602